D0216440

Canada at the Polls, 1984

Canada at the Polls, 1984

A Study of the Federal General Elections

EDITED BY HOWARD PENNIMAN

An American Enterprise Institute Book

Published by Duke University Press

1988

© 1988 AEI (American Enterprise Institute
for Public Policy Research)
All rights reserved
Printed in the United States of America
on acid free paper ∞
Library of Congress Cataloging in Publication Data
appear at the end of this book.

Contents

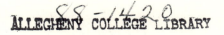

Tables and Figures

FIGURES

Preface

HOWARD PENNIMAN

———— *Canada at the Polls, 1984: A Study of the Federal General Elections* is another in the series of national elections studies in selected democratic countries published by the American Enterprise Institute for Public Policy Research (AEI). The series was undertaken in the belief that policymakers and scholars can profit from a knowledge of political parties and elections in a wide variety of democracies. The greater their understanding of the political consequences of elections in many societies, the deeper will be their insights into the impact of the electoral rules and practices at home.

As of mid-1987 the At the Polls series included more than two dozen books describing national elections in Australia, Canada, France, West Germany, Greece, India, Ireland, Israel, Italy, Japan, New Zealand, three of the four continental Scandinavian democracies, Spain, the United Kingdom, the United States, and Venezuela. Also in the series is *Democracy at the Polls: A Comparative Study of Competitive National Elections*, which discusses the similarities and differences in the conduct of democratic elections in twenty-eight countries. More recently, AEI has added *Competitive Elections in Developing Countries*, edited by Myron Weiner and Ergun Özbudun, which describes efforts to establish democratic institutions in nine developing countries.

Federal General Elections

Canadians, like most democratic political descendents of Great Britain, elect members of the lower house of the national legislature from single-member districts by plurality vote.[1] The number of legislative seats that a party wins depends not on the party's share of the total national vote, but on the number of districts in which nominees of the party win pluralities. It is not unusual for a party to win control of the national legislature even as it fails to win a majority or even a plurality of the national vote. The party that wins the most votes may finish second or even third in the number of seats it has carried.

Small parties participating in provincial campaigns may affect the national election results. John Meisel argues that the Liberal party and the Conservative party (later renamed the Progressive Conservative party) have dominated Canadian politics. He points out, however, that "at least four parties have played active and sometimes critical roles on the national scene since the thirties, [so] Canada must be recognized as having a multiparty system. . . . But Canada's multiparty system is obviously quite different from that of a country like Israel or Italy, where there are so many contestants that every government is a coalition. There are only two ministerial parties at the national level in Canada, and of the two, the Liberals are so much the stronger that their position is unique."

Meisel also makes the important point that "there are regions where the party battle is not a contest between the Liberals and Conservatives, but between one of these" and one of the lesser parties.[2] The pattern of Canadian politics has changed significantly over the nation's history. The Conservative party won a majority of the popular vote and a majority of the seats in the House of Commons in six of the ten elections between 1878 and 1917. The Liberal party won legislative majorities in the remaining four elections, but on one occasion it failed to win a majority of the popular vote. In 1896, although the Liberals finished behind the Conservatives in the national vote, their popular support was distributed in such a manner that they carried thirty more legislative districts—and therefore thirty more seats—than the Conservatives. Complicating the election results that year were two small parties and an independent, who together won 8.9 percent of the popular vote and seven seats in Parliament. Such are the vagaries of the electoral system that the small parties and a handful of supporters may have determined which major party would control the House of Commons for the next term.[3]

In the twenty national elections since 1917 the Liberals have won a majority of the seats in Parliament on nine occasions and the Conservatives on three. In the eight remaining elections, neither party won a majority of the seats, but each party won a plurality on four occasions and therefore led the government until defeated on a major issue. The first parliament that lacked a single-party majority was elected in 1921 when the Liberals won 116 of 235 seats. The Liberal government survived nearly four years. Of the other parliaments without single-party control, four lasted less than a year, while the rest survived more than a year, but less than three.

In the same twenty elections a party won a majority of the national popular vote only three times. In 1940 the Liberals were supported by 51.5 percent of the voters. They fell just short of 50 percent on several other occasions. The Progressive Conservatives (PC) twice won a majority of the popular vote and enormous majorities in the House of Commons. In 1958, under the leadership of John Diefenbaker, the PC won 53.6 percent of the national vote—the second-largest share of the popular vote in Canadian history. Only in the wartime election of 1917 did a coalition government receive a larger share of the ballots. The Conservatives in 1958 won 208 of a possible 265 seats, or 78.5 percent of the membership of the House of Commons. Howard A. Scarrow said of that result, "The Progressive Conservative victory was of proportions unequaled in the history of Canadian politics."[4] It remains a record three decades later.

In 1984 the Conservatives won a bare 50.04 percent of the national vote. Nonetheless, as both John C. Courtney and George C. Perlin have noted in this volume, this election marked the first time in Canadian history that a party has won a majority of the seats in every province and territory. The share of the seats won by the Conservatives was the second largest in Canadian history—211 seats of a possible 282, or 74.8 percent of the total vote.

Both in 1958 and in 1984 PC candidates managed to win a large majority of the Quebec seats in the House of Commons. In 1958 the Conservatives won fifty of the seventy-five Quebec seats and in 1984 their success was more impressive as they won fifty-eight of the possible seventy-five seats. These were the only two occasions since 1887 when the Conservatives came close to winning a majority of the Quebec seats in the national Parliament.

Prior to that time the Conservatives had won considerably more seats than the Liberals in the House of Commons. Beginning in 1885, however, a series of events alienated many of the citizens of Quebec from the Conservatives, and led to a sharp decline of French Canadian electoral support for the party.

In 1885 a French Canadian, Louis Riel, who had led two rebellions against the Dominion government, was captured, tried, and convicted of treason. After some hesitation, the prime minister refused to stop the execution. George C. Perlin has pointed out elsewhere that in the next election French Canadian support for the Conservatives resulted in a decline in seats from fifty-three to thirty-three.[5] Four years later only sixteen Conservative M.P.s were elected in Quebec.

Quebec support continued to decline for most elections over the next seventy years. In 1917 the French Canadians were angered by the decision to pass a conscription law to increase Canada's contribution of manpower to the Allies in World War I. Unlike the Canadians of British ancestry, who maintained very close ties to English relatives and to Great Britain, the French Canadians had few ties to France or Europe. They were slow to enlist. To some degree, therefore, the draft law was directed against them. In the 1917 election the Conservatives won only three seats from Quebec—all candidates with British backgrounds. In 1921 the Conservatives won no seats from Quebec.

Except for their victory in 1930, the Conservatives showed little improvement. In nine of the ten elections from 1917 to 1953 the PC won no more than five of Quebec's sixty-five (seventy-five by 1953) seats in Parliament.

Since 1867, Quebec has been allotted somewhat more than one-fourth of the seats in the House of Commons. In the early years of the Dominion of Canada the Conservative party won a large percentage of the seats from Quebec. That province's votes, if heavily for one party, as was often the case, provided the victorious party 40 or even 50 percent of the seats needed to control Parliament for the next four years. This made Quebec a very attractive target for the major parties that had a chance of gaining a majority in Parliament. As we have seen, the PC have won so few Quebec seats in most elections during the past eighty-five years that the Liberals have been able to look forward to a national campaign with the reasonable expectation that in four of every five elections Quebec voters will give the party a major boost toward a majority in the House of Commons. When the PC have won one-third or more of the Quebec seats—a very rare occurrence—the Liberals have found it difficult to win a majority of the seats in Parliament, or even enough to lead a minority government.

If the Conservatives are to compete consistently on even terms with the Liberals, they must increase their share of the Quebec seats in Parliament. For roughly a century, however, the PC have never been able to put together a string of successful Quebec elections. The massive victory of 1958 (fifty seats for the PC and twenty-five for the Liberals) was bounded by an election in 1957 in which the party won only nine seats and an election in 1962 when it won fourteen. Each of these elections gave the Conservatives a plurality in Parliament, but not a working majority. Both governments lasted less than a year in office.

If the Conservatives can win a consistently high support level in Quebec, they can expect to play a more important role in the governance of Canada. No contributor to this volume, however, seems prepared to suggest that the Conservatives have a particularly good chance to win another national election soon.

Lawrence LeDuc's research leads him to say, "The true longer-term meaning in the 1984 election may not be known for some time. However, it should not be assumed that this election result, however dramatic, necessarily signals the beginning of a major political realignment in the Canadian polity."

John C. Courtney found that among "Mulroney's closest advisers there is unanimity on this point: the future success of the Conservative party depends more on Quebec than anything else."

Contributors

All the essays in this volume have been contributed by Canadian political scientists. John Meisel, of Queen's University, writes the introductory chapter, which deals with the last four and one-half years of Pierre Elliot Trudeau's career as prime minister and leader of the Liberal party. Lawrence LeDuc, of the University of Windsor, examines the changes in the electorate's attitudes before and during the campaign. R. Kenneth Carty, of the University of British Columbia, discusses the nature of Canadian political conventions that choose party leaders and the impact of the system on the parties. George C. Perlin, of Queen's University, describes the road to the Progressive Conservative victory in 1984. Stephen Clarkson, of the University of Toronto, provides the story of developments within the Liberal party leading to the change of leadership that preceded the party's defeat in the 1984 election. J. Terence Morley, of the University of Victoria, discusses the background of the New Democratic party and the problems of national third parties in a system with single-member districts. Khayyam Z. Paltiel, of Carleton University, analyzes developments in the laws and practices for the financing of party campaigns for Parliament. Frederick J. Fletcher, of York University, argues that the media's coverage of the campaign may influence the election results. John C. Courtney, of the University of Saskatchewan, analyzes factors that were important in the outcome of the elections and some that may affect parties in the near future. As has been the custom in all books in the *At the Polls* series, Richard M. Scammon, director of the Elections Research Center, compiled the electoral data for the appendix. Finally, I am grateful to Randa H. Murphy for her help throughout the preparation of this volume.

Notes

1. Initially there were a few districts that elected two members of Parliament. The number of such districts declined over the years. The last two were abolished in 1966.
2. John Meisel, "The Party System and the 1974 Elections," in Howard R. Penniman, ed., *Canada at the Polls: The General Election of 1974* (Washington, D.C.: American Enterprise Institute, 1975), p. 18.
3. Thomas T. Mackie and Richard Rose, *The International Almanac of Electoral History*, 2d ed. (New York: Facts on File, 1982), pp. 72–75.
4. Howard A. Scarrow, *Canada Votes* (New Orleans: Hauser, 1962), p. 175.
5. George C. Perlin, *The Tory Syndrome: Leadership Politics in the Progressive Conservative Party* (Montreal: McGill-Queen's University Press, 1980). See chapter 3 of that volume for a brief account of the Louis Riel case and the impact of the French Canadian opposition to conscription of military personnel during both world wars.

1 Introduction

JOHN MEISEL

──── The causes of electoral outcomes can be likened to factors affecting the surfaces of oceans. Fluctuations in the sea level are determined by very long-term and imperceptible developments relating to the subsidence of the earth's crust and the shrinking of glaciers; in the shorter term it is the tides that set the water level and in an even more fleeting perspective, waves cause choppy seas or smooth sailing. In the ebb and flow of elections, long-term historical and environmental conditions resemble the sea level by providing the basic framework for the whole political process. Events occurring for the most part since the previous election can be likened to the tides; and the equivalent of waves is provided by the parties' activities during the campaign proper. This book, being the work of political scientists, notes the tides but focuses particularly on the waves. We will accept the sea level largely as given and leave its analysis to the historians.

This introductory chapter deals in the main with the four and one-half years ending with the election of September 4, 1984, in which the born-again Trudeau government held office after its fleeting sojourn in the wilderness in 1979 and 1980.[1] Despite the major focus on the era between the two elections, however, some sorties into the more distant past will also be undertaken, since the character and style of parties, and the issues they confront, are longer in the making than the span separating any two successive polling days. We shall first survey the general conditions and circumstances prevailing in Canada during the period under review; then examine the major actions of the Trudeau government elected in 1980, and the responses to them. We will conclude with a brief look at developments more closely related to the fortunes of the political parties during the period preceding the calling of the election.

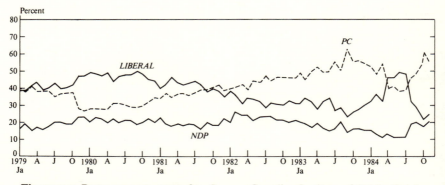

Figure 1.1 Party support, 1979–84. *Source:* Canadian Institute of Public Opinion, *Gallup Report*, January 1979–December 1984. *Note:* Ja = January; A = April; J = July; O = October.

General Political Conditions and Circumstances

The Basic Political Context   By far the most important difference between the 1979 and 1980 elections on the one hand, and that of 1984 on the other, is that two of the three major parties were headed by different leaders. After the fall of the Clark government in December 1979, Trudeau reversed his earlier decision to retire from politics and led his party to a modest victory in the subsequent February election.[2] But although the Liberals won a majority of seats in the House of Commons, the result could in no way be seen as a resounding public endorsement. Had it not been for the continuing massive allegiance of Québecers, Trudeau would very likely have had considerable difficulty in regaining power. But even this shaky level of support soon dissipated. As Figure 1.1 shows, the Liberals' lead over the Conservatives narrowed steadily until it vanished completely by the middle of 1981. The usual postconvention spurt in the polls produced a short-lived Liberal lead early in 1984 which, however, was the precursor of a disastrous drop that sealed the party's fate in the election.

Because the Liberal party has been in office for so much of the twentieth century, and particularly since World War II, it is often assumed that it has enjoyed the overwhelming support of Canadians. It has certainly been seen, and has increasingly acted, as the "government party"—one naturally and fittingly occupying the government benches.[3] The exuberant early enthusiasm for Lester Pearson's successor, aptly described as Trudeaumania, as well as the fact that the new leader headed the government continuously from 1968 until his resignation in 1984, with a hiatus of only nine months, have made many think that Canadians perpetually bestowed warm and sustained approbation on the Liberal party and the Trudeau government. Electoral and poll data belie this impression.

Table 1.1 General Election Results, 1968–84.

Year	Total seats	Liberal			Progressive Conservative		
		Percent vote	Seats	Percent seats	Percent vote	Seats	Percent seats
1968	264	45	155	59	31	72	27
1972	264	38	109	41	35	107	41
1974	264	43	141	53	35	95	36
1979	282	40	114	40	36	136	48
1980	282	44	147	52	33	103	37
1984	282	28	40	14	50	211	75

Year	New Democratic Party			Other		
	Percent vote	Seats	Percent seats	Percent vote	Seats	Percent seats
1968	17	21	8	7	16	6
1972	18	31	12	9	17	6
1974	15	16	6	7	12	5
1979	18	26	9	6	6	3
1980	20	32	11	3	0	0
1984	19	30	11	3	1	—*

*Less than 0.5 percent.
Sources: Hugh G. Thorburn, *Party Politics in Canada* (Scarborough, Ont.: Prentice-Hall, 1979); and *Canadian News Facts*.

Table 1.1 shows that even at the time of his government's first election, when the country appeared to be in the throes of a frenzied love affair with Trudeau, only 45 percent of the electorate voted Liberal. Four years later the "government party" managed to attract only 38 percent of the voters and was forced into a minority position in the House of Commons. As the table indicates, every Trudeau majority was followed by an electoral rejection depriving it either of its majority or, as in 1979, of power altogether. The illusion of Liberal popularity was caused by the party's capacity to cling to power and its holding office for so long—factors created by the vagaries of the electoral system, the division of the opposition into two or more parties, the fortuitous geographical distribution of the votes, and also by its inspired capacity to survive.

During the Trudeau years at least one other element favored the Liberals. Their leader was a television natural who consistently outperformed his rivals on that powerful medium. But even this advantage was to little avail as the tumultuous Thirty-second Parliament lumbered toward its inevitable end. The discontent with the performance of the federal government grew steadily, particularly insofar as its ability to deal with the major problems confronting the country was concerned. The short-run disaffection recorded in figure 1.1 was, however, only the most recent manifestation of a long-term trend associated with the one-party dominant nature of the federal party system.[4] Among the most troubling features of the Liberal party was its growing inability to maintain a national base and thus to contribute effectively to national unity. It had taken creative and successful initiatives with respect to the potentially disastrous tensions between English and French Canada but had failed miserably in responding to the concerns of the west. This is reflected dramatically in the popular vote received there by the Trudeau party during its years in office. Table 1.2 presents the deviation from the national vote, in percentage points, of Liberal support in the Prairies, British Columbia, and Quebec from 1968 to 1980. Mounting alienation of the west on the one hand, and acceptance by Quebec on the other, offer eloquent testimony to the Liberals' problems in offering a genuinely national government.

The regional lopsidedness and vulnerability, more than any other party weakness, were blamed on the prime minister. His preoccupation with language questions, constitutional reform, and a nationalist economic policy were perceived as ignoring the serious concerns and dominant interests of Canadians in the west. Despite his success with the Quebec electorate, the view kept gaining ascendancy that the party needed a new leader. This sentiment was strengthened by the widely held opinion that in John Turner, a former Liberal minister waiting in the wings, the party had a winning successor to Trudeau. The latter decided in February 1984, after considerable delays and wavering, to leave office, and a leadership convention was called for the following June. Turner won. The Conservatives and the New Democratic Party (NDP) thus confronted a new Liberal government under a prime minister who repudiated many of the positions and practices of the Trudeau government.

The Conservatives, for their part, had already replaced Joe Clark with the much more telegenic Québecer, Brian Mulroney. The ousting of Clark, who was blamed, among other things, for the party's failure to win a majority in 1979 and for its defeat nine months after coming to office, was achieved only at the cost of seriously exacerbating deep divisions within party ranks. Mulroney, despite the bitter convention fight against Clark, succeeded in healing the wounds quickly and in leading an unprecedentedly harmonious party into battle.[5]

With only the New Democratic party's Ed Broadbent representing the former leading dramatis personae on the electoral stage, the 1984 contest promised to be a vastly different experience from its immediate predecessors. While this was certainly the case with respect to the key personalities involved, the underlying sociopolitical and economic conditions remained unchanged. Long-term factors, some of which were noted above, clearly contributed to

Table 1.2 Liberal Vote: Regional Deviation from National Vote, 1968–80.

	1968	1972	1974	1979	1980
National popular vote (percent)	45	38	43	40	44
Deviation:[a]					
Prairie provinces	−10	−11	−16	−18	−20
British Columbia	−3	−9	−10	−17	−22
Quebec	+9	+11	+11	+22	+26

[a] Difference in percentage points between percentage regional vote and percentage national vote.
Source: Adapted from Barry J. Kay, Steven D. Brown, James E. Curtis, Ronald D. Lambert, and John M. Wilson, "The Character of Electoral Change: A Preliminary Report from the 1984 National Election Study," paper presented at the annual meeting of the Canadian Political Science Association, Montreal, 1985, p. 15.

the attrition of the Liberal party's ability to hold office. In this context the 1980 election was something of an aberration, a momentary reversal of secular trends. In commenting on the contest held only nine months before, I noted that it might "in the long run be seen as a systems-altering election in the sense that the Canadian polity would develop quite differently after a Liberal than after a Conservative victory."[6] This judgment was premature because of the ephemeral character of the Clark government, but in essence it was correct. History simply stuttered a bit in 1979 and 1980 before pronouncing its final verdict in 1984.

The Referendum   After the change of leaders and government, the most significant event of the interelection period was probably the Quebec referendum. The independentist Parti Québécois (PQ) government, elected in 1976 under the magnetic leadership of René Lévesque, had committed itself to a policy of *étapisme*—proceeding toward independence in stages—and accordingly planned to hold a referendum on the matter on May 19, 1980. Electors were asked to vote "Yes" or "No" on the question of whether they wished to grant a mandate to the Quebec government with respect to negotiating a new agreement with the rest of Canada. This agreement would have given Quebec complete sovereignty while maintaining a common currency and some form of economic association with Canada. The question further stated that no political change would be imposed as the result of the negotiations without the holding of another referendum of the newly negotiated terms. The campaigns for and against were to be managed by two umbrella committees, respectively embracing all interested parties. Ceilings on the permitted expenditures were placed on the coordinating organizations.

The Parti Québécois and the Quebec provincial Liberal party were obviously the central actors, but the rest of the country, including the federal government, clearly had a vital interest in the Quebec referendum. Claude Ryan, the provincial Liberal leader, was elected chairman of the "No" committee, but Jean Chrétien, one of the senior federal cabinet ministers from Quebec, played a pivotal role as well. Joe Clark campaigned vigorously on the federalist side, and Ontario's premier, William Davis, and the western premiers became involved. Trudeau announced that all the federal cabinet would actively oppose the "Yes" vote and, indeed, the Quebec ministers did campaign unceasingly for the federal cause.

The prime minister, himself a Québecer, also played a major part, despite the delicate situation posed by the fact that Claude Ryan, with whom Trudeau had serious constitutional disagreements and with whom relations were shaky, was the "No" chairman. In a major address to an estimated audience of ten thousand, Trudeau vowed that a "No" vote would be followed by immediate moves for constitutional change in Canada, which would respond to the aspirations of the Québecers. He also stated later that the people of Canada understood Quebec's discontents and that they were ready for change.

Over 85 percent of the eligible voters cast their ballots and, with 59.56 percent voting "No," the PQ proposal was decisively rejected. It is probable that the number of francophones denying the Quebec government its proposed mandate was small, but all other ethnic groups likely rejected Premier Lévesque's initiative, as did 95 out of the 110 ridings whose boundaries were used in the organization of the balloting.

Ottawa, under Trudeau's leadership, thus won a major and critical victory. It did not, however, escape accusations of having adopted unfair and improper practices. During the campaign it spent $2–$3 million on advertising beamed at the referendum voters, outside the framework of the umbrella committee and therefore outside the spending restrictions imposed on both camps. A billboard campaign, allegedly directed at excessive alcohol consumption, loudly urged all to say "No,"[7] and every federal family allowance check in May contained a leaflet that was seen, by the "Yes" supporters, as an unwarranted intrusion into the referendum campaign.

Trudeau's reaction to the referendum outcome was both firm and conciliatory. He took the vote to be a call for renewed efforts to bring about constitutional change and was willing to negotiate on all issues except two: the continuation of Canada as a true federation (that is, no sovereignty-association was tolerable) and he insisted on a charter of rights and freedoms in the constitution that would protect, among other items, language rights of Canadians. We shall see below how he managed to translate these resolves into a new constitutional order.[8]

Western Separatism   While the referendum appeared to defuse at least temporarily the crisis posed by Quebec separatism, and to provide a breathing space, troubling clouds were gathering in the west. The February 1980 defeat of the Clark government was seen there as yet another example of the inability of Canada to respond positively to western interests and was followed by the revival of various movements intended to protect the west against what appeared as intolerable exploitation and slighting by eastern Canada. Two organizations, the Western Canada Concept (wcc) party and the Western Federation Association (West-Fed) were the foci of this anti-eastern and of much western separatist sentiment. Although many of the early members of these and similar organizations were perceived as constituting a right-wing fringe group composed of alienated and marginal individuals, the various memberships grew and managed to attract some respectable individuals, including a prominent Calgary oilman and former member of Parliament. By the end of 1980, however, a certain lack of direction and considerable disunity combined to weaken the western separatist movement and to appear to make it ineffectual.

A new impetus was provided by the Alberta provincial by-election held in Olds-Didsbury on February 17, 1982. The constituency had been held by the Social Credit leader and it was assumed that a close contest would take place between the Social Credit and Conservative candidates. Gordon Kessler, an oil scout and rodeo rider, was nominated by the wcc and, to the immense surprise of everyone, won with 42 percent of the vote. The wcc slogan was "Send Them a Message"; "them" clearly referred to the east and Ottawa.

In the 1982 Alberta provincial general election the wcc nominated candidates in all but one of the seventy-nine constituencies. Its campaign was, however, thoroughly disorganized. In addition to espousing a strongly provincialist position, its candidates also attacked bilingualism, metrification and the exclusion of property rights from the entrenched clauses of the new constitution.

Twelve percent of the voters supported the wcc but the party failed to win a single seat. Even its one sitting member, Kessler, who had switched ridings, was defeated. This phase of the western separatist movement was therefore unable to reach an effective takeoff stage. But western separatism during the period under review had a way of reemerging in different places and under different guises. The Confederation of Regions Western party (crwp) contested ten of Manitoba's fourteen ridings in the 1984 federal election and came second in three of them. Although it only won a little less than 7 percent of the vote, the number of ballots it managed to amass was almost one-third of that cast for the Liberals.

The virulence and extent of western separatism was never as menacing to Canada's integrity as that existing in Quebec, but there can be no doubt that the persistent and widespread hostility to the east and to the Canadian state was troubling and gave cause for concern.

Language Rights in Manitoba   A matter closely related to western attitudes toward the fabric of Canadian society erupted into a major crisis in 1983 and subsequently engulfed both the new Liberal and Conservative leaders in awkward controversies. Manitoba's NDP government introduced legislation intended to enshrine French and English as official languages in the province and to provide a modest number of services to Franco-Manitobans in their mother tongue. The intention of the legislation was to correct the repudiation by the government of 1890 of constitutional guarantees of French language rights. A Supreme Court of Canada decision in 1970 had found the 1890 action unconstitutional, thereby probably depriving every piece of legislation passed by the Manitoba legislature since 1890 of its legality.

Despite the obvious moral imperative behind this constitutional initiative of Premier Howard Pawley's government and its wisdom in the light of Canada's accommodation with Quebec, and despite the extremely modest nature of the services to be made available in French, there was a frenzied outcry against it. Numerous citizen groups, some municipalities, and the Manitoba Conservative party conducted a bitter campaign against the measure involving referenda and the virtual closing of the Manitoba legislature.

In the end the government capitulated, but not before the national Liberal and Conservative parties became involved. A resolution was introduced in Parliament urging Manitoba to proceed with the measure—a resolution that threatened to divide seriously the federal Tory party. Mulroney, very early in his new role as party leader, strongly supported the French cause in the face of implacable opposition from some of his western colleagues. He stood his ground, however, and ensured that the Conservative party was seen, like the Liberals, as a vigorous defender of fair language practices in Canada.

John Turner referred to the Manitoba language crisis when he opened his campaign for the Liberal leadership. Flying against the position taken by the Trudeau cabinet (and the Conservatives and the NDP), he asserted that the protection of minorities was a provincial responsibility. There was a considerable outcry against this statement, which was seen by some as blatantly opportunistic. Turner subsequently issued a "clarification" of his earlier pronouncements: Ottawa, he acknowledged, has an obligation to intervene, if necessary, when minority language rights are in peril. Turner's behavior with respect to the Manitoba situation likely did him no good in the west and certainly not in Quebec.

But whatever the effects of the most recent manifestation of Canada's language crisis on the new federal leaders, the whole situation indicated that French-English relations, despite many strides at the federal and some at provincial levels, were still a subject of intense political delicacy, capable of provoking extremely vigorous and impassioned responses from Canadians.[9]

Table 1.3 Federal By-election Results, 1980–84.

Date	Constituency	Party (percent)				Summary of results
		Liberal	PC	NDP	Other	
September 18, 1980	Hamilton West (Ont.)	41	32[a]	7	—	PC → L
April 13, 1981	London West (Ont.)	47[a]	45	8	—	L → L
	Cardigan (N.S.)	49[a]	47	4	—	L → L
May 4, 1981	Levis (Que.)	46[a]	30	15	9	L → L
August 17, 1981	Joliette (Que.)	30	65[a]	1	3	PC → PC
	Spadina (Ont.)	33[a]	30	34	3	L → NDP
October 12, 1982	Timiskaming (Ont.)	33[a]	36	30	1	L → PC
	Toronto Broadview-Greenwood (Ont.)	10	18	39[a]	33	NDP → NDP
	Leeds–Grenville (Ont.)	21	57[a]	9	14	PC → PC
May 24, 1983	Brandon Souris (Man.)	17	62[a]	21	—	PC → PC
August 29, 1983	Central Nova (N.S.)	25	60[a]	13	1	PC → PC
	Mission–Port Moody (B.C.)	5	51	43[a]	1	NDP → PC

Note: Percentages may not add to 100 due to rounding.

[a] Party of incumbent.

Sources: Pierre G. Normandin, ed., *Canadian Parliamentary Guide*; and *Canadian Newsfacts*.

By-elections By-elections are usually seen as useful weather vanes indicating which way the wind is blowing between national contests. The outcomes of the twelve local confrontations held between the 1980 and the 1984 elections were, however, of little help to political prognosticators. The Liberals, as shown in Table 1.3, retained three seats and lost two, one each to the NDP and the Conservatives; the latter party held on to four of their ridings, lost one to the Liberals (in 1980) and gained one each from the government party and from the NDP. The social democrats retained one seat, lost one to the Tories and gained one from the Liberals.

The contest leading to the defeat of the Liberals in the riding of Spadina attracted the most interest among all the by-elections. Spadina, a heavily ethnic and reliably Liberal seat in downtown Toronto, was opened up when its young Liberal occupant, Peter Stollery, was elevated to the Senate in 1981. The move was seen as a blatant effort by the prime minister's closest political cronies to propel Jim Coutts, Trudeau's principal secretary, into the national consciousness and to give him a base from which to contest the Liberal leadership when it became vacant. Coutts, a westerner, was deemed by his promoters to be a more promising successor to Trudeau than the front-running Turner. The episode was seen by many as a cynical use of patronage and as an example of the unprincipled manipulative politics resulting from the Liberal party's long years in power. The other main parties both nominated strong candidates in Spadina and, in a very tight race, the NDP standard-bearer, a local alderman, carried the day.

Three other by-elections were of special interest. In another Toronto riding, Broadview-Greenwood, the right-wing editor of the *Toronto Sun*, Peter Worthington, unsuccessfully contested the Conservative nomination, against what was seen as an "ethnic" candidate, William Fatsis. Central Nova in Nova Scotia was vacated by the sitting Tory after the Conservative leadership convention so that the newly elected leader could contest a House of Commons seat; Mulroney won handily. In British Columbia, the seat vacated in Mission-Port Moody by Mark Rose, a stalwart NDP member, was lost by the NDP. The Conservative win in this constituency suggested to close observers that the NDP might be in difficulties in British Columbia—a development that strengthened some critical rumblings within the party about the leadership of Ed Broadbent.

Provincial Elections   By the time of the 1979 and 1980 elections the Liberals had been banished from office in all the provincial capitals. Nothing occurred in the period preceding the 1984 contest to alter this situation. If anything, the plight of the Liberal parties throughout the country grew. As table 1.4 reveals, the party gained votes and seats only in Quebec, more or less held its own in Ontario, but failed to elect a single seat west of that province. While it was not wiped out in Atlantic Canada, it lost support in each of those four provinces.

The New Democratic party wrested Manitoba from the Conservatives in November of 1981 but lost Saskatchewan to them the following year in a surprise upset.

Overall, as the 1984 election approached, seven provinces were in Conservative hands, and one each was in those of the Social Credit party (British Columbia) and the NDP (Manitoba). The Liberal party was greatly weakened everywhere except in Quebec and perhaps in Ontario.

Economic Conditions   Economic conditions in Canada are rarely, if ever, completely susceptible to indigenous control. Worldwide trends, and particularly developments in the United States are "fixed" items, largely out of reach of Canadian decisionmakers. Still, Ottawa and the provinces can shape events to some extent. Since the federal government has substantially greater powers over the economic system than the provinces, it is normally held responsible for the economic state of affairs, particularly when things go badly. And they did go very badly indeed in the interval between the 1980 and the 1984 elections.

Interest rates and inflation both rose to unprecedented heights during Trudeau's last term in office. The former, as can be seen in figure 1.2, nudged 20 percent in the late summer of 1981, whereas the latter exceeded 15 percent in January of that year. Both rates declined subsequently, following changes in the United States, but the Canadian improvements were considerably less marked than those registered by its neighbor. The inflation rate dropped substantially by 1983, and again in 1984, and never exceeded 8 percent during the last two years of the Trudeau government. At one point it was as low as 2 percent.

But whatever benefits may have accrued in this sector of the economy, other indicators were disastrous. Bankruptcies, loan defaults, and farm foreclosures indicated that Canada was in a deep depression, resembling that of the late twenties and early thirties. Unemployment figures, reproduced in figure 1.2, almost reached 13 percent (representing one and one-half million Canadians) late in 1982 and then hovered around the 11 percent point until the election. As if these gloomy conditions were not enough, the value of the Canadian compared to the American dollar declined substantially in the period under discussion. During most of 1979 and a good part of 1980 the Canadian dollar fluctuated around the eighty-five-cent level in relation to the American dollar, but there then was a gradual drop, leaving the value near seventy-five cents at the time of the election. While this helped exporters and the tourist industry, it had negative consequences on other sectors of the economy; in addition, its symbolic significance harmed the prestige of the government.

A major economic change originating outside Canada seriously undermined the government's calculations and negatively affected its energy and fiscal policies. In 1980, when Trudeau returned to power, it was assumed by the government that oil would continue to be in short supply and that its world

Table 1.4 Provincial Election Results, 1980–84.

Province and date of election	Seats in legis- lature	Government party		Perce of vo
		Party	Seats	
Newfoundland April 6, 1982	52	PC (PC)	44 (+11)	61 (+1
Prince Edward Island September 27, 1982	32	PC (PC)	21 (0)	52 (–
Nova Scotia October 6, 1981	52	PC (PC)	37 (+6)	48 (+
New Brunswick October 12, 1982	58	PC (PC)	39 (+9)	47 (+
Quebec April 13, 1981	122	PQ[b] (PQ)	80 (+1)	49 (+
Ontario March 19, 1981	125	PC (PC)	70 (+12)	44 (+
Manitoba November 17, 1981	57	NDP (PC)	34 (+11)	47 (+
Saskatchewan April 26, 1982	64	PC (NDP)	57 (+40)	54 (+1
Alberta November 2, 1982	79	PC (PC)	75 (+1)	68 (+1
British Columbia May 5, 1983	57	SC (SC)	35 (+4)	50 (+

Note: Party names in parentheses indicate government or opposition party before election; numbers parentheses indicate change (in seats or percent of vote) from previous election.
[a] Receiving more than 5 percent of the popular vote.
[b] Parti Québécois.

price would continue to rise. The early 1980s, however, witnessed an oil glut and continually falling prices. This put almost intolerable strains on Canada's National Energy Program (NEP), on the relations between Ottawa and the oil-producing provinces, and also on the revenues accruing to the Canadian government. The extraordinarily huge annual deficit of $32 billion (along with the high unemployment rate and the federal government's confrontational style) was probably the most serious political liability of the Trudeau administration, and was in part caused by a substantial shortfall in the revenues expected from oil sales.

It is never easy to distinguish clearly between circumstances imposed on a polity from the outside and those it has itself had some role in creating. Still, it is clear that most of the general political and economic events and

	Opposition party		Other parties[a]			Independent seats
arty	Seats	Percent of vote	Party	Seats	Percent of vote	
(LIB)	8 (−11)	35 (−6)	—	—	—	—
(LIB)	11 (0)	45 (+1)	—	—	—	—
(LIB)	13 (−4)	33 (−6)	NDP	1 (−3)	18 (+4)	1
(LIB)	18 (−10)	41 (−4)	NDP	1 (+1)	10 (+4)	—
(LIB)	42 (+15)	46 (+12)	—	—	—	—
(LIB)	34 (0)	32 (+1)	NDP	21 (−12)	18 (−10)	—
(NDP)	23 (−10)	44 (−5)	LIB	0 (−1)	8 (−4)	—
P (PC)	7 (−37)	36 (−12)	LIB	0 (0)	5 (−10)	—
P (SC)[c]	2 (+1)	19 (+3)	WCC[d]	0 (na)	12 (na)	2
P (NDP)	22 (−4)	45 (−1)	—	—	—	—

ial Credit party.
stern Canada Concept party.
ces: Pierre G. Normandin, ed., *Canadian Parliamentary Guide*; and *Canadian Newsfacts*.

developments adumbrated above were imposed on the federal government and on federal political parties by factors largely independent of their own making. Nevertheless, they were an important element in the political game, providing an appreciable level of external constraints on federal political action. In the next section we shall see how the government and opposition parties responded to them and to other challenges confronting them between 1980 and 1984.

Governmental Actions and Responses

Constitutional Reform The most far-reaching action of the last Trudeau government was its successful effort to bring about constitutional reform—a feat that had eluded his predecessor and was considered by some to be unattain-

Figure 1.2 Economic Indicators 1979–84. [a]Seasonally adjusted. [b]Bank of Canada rate. [c]Federal Reserve Bank of New York discount rate. [d]Average noon spot rate. [e]Quarterly changes in real domestic product (in 1971 dollars), seasonally adjusted. *Sources:* Statistics Canada, Labor Force Survey Division, *The Labour Force*, 1979–84; Statistics Canada, Prices Division, *Consumer Prices and Price Indexes*, 1979–84; Bank of Canada, *Bank of Canada Review*, 1979–84; Statistics Canada, *Current Economic Analysis*, 1979–84; U.S. Department of Commerce, Bureau of Economic Analysis, *Survey of Current Business*, 1979–84; Board of Governors of the Federal Reserve System, *Federal Reserve Bulletin*, 1979–84.

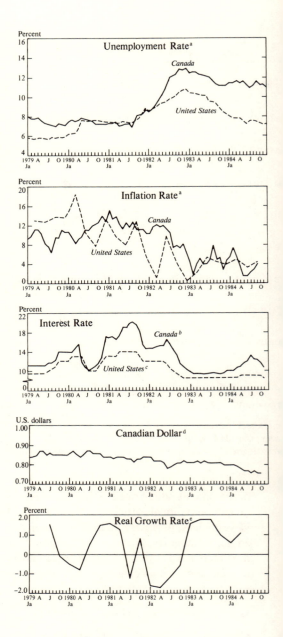

able. Efforts in this direction had been going on since the 1960s [10] but received particular emphasis, as we noted earlier, as an aftermath to the Quebec referendum. The details of the process and substance of revising the constitution are extremely complex and cannot be reviewed here. [11] What is important in the present context is how the roles of the principal actors in the constitutional debates affected the government party and its competitors.

Only a few weeks after the referendum, Jean Chrétien, the minister—other than Trudeau—most directly concerned with the constitutional dossier, visited the provincial premiers to lay the ground for an Ottawa meeting of first ministers and to prepare an agenda for further discussions. The federal position reflected a distinction Trudeau had made earlier between "people's issues" and "government issues." The former embraced patriation (the British North America Act, the written cornerstone of Canada's Constitution, was still an act of the British Parliament), an amendment formula, an entrenched Charter of Rights, and provisions for economic equalization. The latter related to the respective jurisdictions of the federal and provincial governments. Ottawa sought a quick agreement on the former, followed by a request to Westminster for the implementation of the changes. The allocation of government powers, a matter of the most intense interest to the provinces, was to be left for further study and negotiation. The provinces, many of which were greatly concerned about the control of their natural resources, found this splitting of the agenda unacceptable.

Intensive negotiations by officials and ministers in different parts of the country representing all parties were followed by a five-day meeting of first ministers in Ottawa in September 1980. It ended in failure, a result some observers and participants thought was what Ottawa had wanted all along. Two leaked memoranda by the most senior federal officials involved in the negotiations had envisaged the federal government taking a unilateral initiative in constitutional revision. [12]

The federal government did in fact claim the power to ask Westminster for desired constitutional changes without the consent of the provinces and introduced the needed legislation in October. The provinces were outraged but the NDP leader agreed to support the government's resolution provided Ottawa would confirm and enhance provincial jurisdiction over natural resources. Broadbent made this decision without consulting his caucus and despite vigorous opposition to the government's stand in the west—one of the areas of greatest NDP strength. The constitutional issue therefore caused considerable tension within NDP ranks. Discord was also evident among the Conservatives. The party's federal caucus was united enough in its opposition to the government's approach, but the Ontario and New Brunswick Conservative governments condoned Ottawa's unilateralism. Under Joe Clark's impressive leadership, the Tory M.P.s launched a ferocious attack on the government's resolution. One of the results was the establishment of a joint parliamentary committee to examine the proposal, which held a large number of public hearings. Clark's onslaught was so effective that the government was compelled to invoke closure, and even this extreme measure failed in the face of the official opposition's procedural ingenuity.

In the meantime the opposing provinces launched a major lobbying campaign in London, intended to persuade British parliamentarians not to accede to a unilateral request from Ottawa. The provinces also took the issue to the courts. When the Newfoundland Court of Appeals declared that Westminster could not accede to a unilateral request, the parliamentary debate in Ottawa was suspended pending the final resolution of the matter by the Supreme Court of Canada. Its decision was truly worthy of King Solomon. The majority of the justices found that it was technically legal for Parliament to petition Britain without provincial consent but that constitutional conventions in Canada required substantial consent from the provinces. In the aftermath of this decision a return to the bargaining table was inevitable.

Since the Supreme Court decision gave conditional support to both views, the incentives toward reaching a compromise were powerful. At yet another first ministers' conference in November, nine of the provinces and the federal government found an acceptable formula. But Quebec was unable to agree to the newfound compromise and was, in fact, excluded from the last-minute informal negotiations among the provinces that led to a break in the constitutional logjam. Although some changes proposed by the federal government, intended to meet at least some of Quebec's interests, were subsequently agreed to, and the door was left open for eventual modifications acceptable to Quebec, the Quebec government thought it had been betrayed. One of the main objectives of the recasting of Canada's constitutional framework was therefore left unfulfilled.

It took Parliament only two weeks to pass the resolution embodying the new federal-provincial compromise. An outcry from some women's and native peoples' groups led to last-minute modifications, but the battle for a made-in-Canada constitution and for a Charter of Rights and Freedoms was won. Trudeau achieved his wish. Although it was not quite all he wanted, in essence, his political agenda had been completed. The Liberal government had often been provocative and arbitrary in its dealings with the provinces, reinforcing its long-standing unfavorable image on this score. On the other hand, it had won and it had on occasion been conciliatory; it gave as much as it gained. The basic quid pro quo between Ottawa and all the provinces except Quebec was that the federal government agreed to the amending formula favored by the provinces, while the provinces accepted the Charter of Rights. Many Canadians gave a sigh of relief in expectation that the ceaseless bickering between the two senior levels of government would now come to an end.

In partisan terms the Liberals and Conservatives both benefited from their role in the constitutional issue, although obviously for quite different reasons. The NDP likely suffered, since the position taken by the federal leader clearly sapped party unity.

The National Energy Policy   Most observers agree that the two major policy initiatives of the post-1980 Liberal government were constitutional reform and the National Energy Policy. Both absorbed a prodigious amount of time and effort; both aroused intense political controversy; and both had far-reaching implications for federal-provincial relations. Both also reveal a great deal about the approaches of the two largest parties to the character of Canada. The relevance of the fundamental charter to federalism is obvious, but that of the energy policy, while perhaps less apparent, is equally telling in Canada. The reason is that the British North America Act gave the provinces jurisdiction over the development of natural resources and direct taxation of resource production within their territory, while it gave the federal government jurisdiction over prices of resources moving across provincial or international boundaries and the ability to tax directly and indirectly.[13] In the 1980s Ottawa was locked into ferocious fights with several of the provinces, not all of which shared a common problem. According to E. A. Carmichael and J. K. Stewart, "in specific terms, the two levels of government had to reach agreement on constitutional issues of resource ownership and control, the distribution of windfall gains (economic rents) from oil and gas production, the appropriate fiscal regime for the petroleum industry, and the process of formulating energy policy in Canada."[14]

On the east coast, questions of who can claim offshore oil caused serious strains between the federal and the Newfoundland and Nova Scotia governments, but the most serious controversies affected Alberta and, to a lesser extent, British Columbia and Saskatchewan. The Clark government experienced great difficulty in finding an appropriate accommodation with Alberta despite its sympathetic attitude to provincial interests. Toward the end of 1979 an agreement was reached between Ottawa and Edmonton that would have increased the price of oil, given Ottawa a larger share of energy revenues, and accelerated the development of some Alberta energy-producing megaprojects. It was never implemented, however, because of the defeat of the Clark government.

When the Liberals returned to power they intended to implement a pricing policy based on a blending of the high world cost and the low domestic cost of oil. In general the new government's approach was congenial to eastern consumers and anathema to the producing provinces, notably Alberta. Intensive bargaining between Ottawa and Alberta during a good part of 1980 was accompanied by each party's taking various measures to enhance its own position. Among other things, the Alberta government passed legislation empowering it to limit oil production; Ottawa threatened to impose an export tax on natural gas.[15] Finally, in its October budget, the federal government played its trump card: it introduced a comprehensive, long-term energy policy.

Three objectives were central to the new program: fairness in energy pricing and revenue sharing between the two levels of government and the producers; security of supply, including Canada's independence, by 1990, of the world oil market; and Canadian ownership of at least half of the country's petroleum industry, including the opportunity to share in the benefits of future expansion. Alberta reacted by announcing a planned reduction of 15 percent over nine months of oil production, launching a legal challenge to the federal excise tax on natural gas, and by continuing to withhold permits for the construction of megaprojects aimed at gaining access to energy derived from heavy oil and oil sands.

Reactions to the government's announcement ranged from jubilation among Canadian nationalists and proponents of a genuinely mixed economy to dismay on the part of most of the industry, the western provinces, and ultimately the United States. There was a good deal of uncertainty about the likely impact of the new policy, particularly since the promised legislation was slow in materializing. Alberta and Ottawa continued their cold war, although they never abandoned efforts to reach a mutually acceptable accord. The one area in which Ottawa's goals were being realized was the Canadianization of the country's oil industry.

Petro-Canada, the publicly owned oil company, bought over 70 percent of the shares of Petrofina from its Belgian owners and thus acquired a refinery in Montreal and 1,100 retail outlets in eastern Canada to match its extensive holdings in the west. The federal government imposed a special tax on crude oil to finance this transaction. Other major acquisitions by Canadian companies followed, not only Canadianizing much of the hitherto almost exclusively foreign-controlled oil sector, but also acquiring interests in some American enterprises. Many of the takeovers were financed by Canadian banks which, in turn, raised substantial sums abroad. These activities were in part held responsible for the very steep decline in the value of the Canadian dollar and the related unprecedentedly high interest rates. The latter had devastating effects on the economy and therefore on the rising unemployment. By the summer of 1981 the minister of finance had to ask the banks to reduce their financing of takeovers. Their compliance and extraordinarily high interest rates substantially slowed down the Canadian takeover of foreign-owned assets. Still, while the American presence in the oil and gas industry remained substantial, impressive gains were made with respect to the third goal of the NEP, reducing foreign domination.

The other two goals, freeing Canada of dependence on world markets and ensuring fairness in pricing and revenue sharing, remained elusive. Indeed, early in 1981 an astute observer noted that the new policy was "producing more lawsuits than energy." [16] Mounting pressure from the industry and the media helped create an atmosphere in which continued dogfights between Ottawa and Edmonton became intolerable. Intensive negotiations continued, and just as Alberta was about to implement the third stage of its cutbacks, on September 1, 1981, an energy pricing and taxing agreement was signed between the federal and Alberta governments, intended to last until 1986. Differences between the national government and Saskatchewan and British Columbia were ironed out shortly afterward. With respect to offshore resources, Nova Scotia and Ottawa reached an agreement in February 1982 which, however, left the ownership issue unresolved and postponed settling the question of pricing. But Newfoundland and Ottawa were unable to reach an accord. Their bitter struggles involved repeated intensive negotiations, recourse to the courts, and a premature provincial election, but to no avail.

Even the agreements with the western provinces failed to resolve the energy issues adequately. The principal reason was that the NEP and the subsequent agreements were predicated on certain assumptions that proved incorrect. Oil prices, contrary to expectations, did not continue to rise; a world glut occurred with the inevitable concomitant drop in price. Among the consequences was the collapse of the delicate compromise between the producing provinces, who had wanted to eliminate the gap between Canadian and world monetary worth, and the consuming provinces and Ottawa, who wished to maintain a differential favoring indigenous users. The ceiling on Canadian oil, expressed as a percentage of the world standard, became impracticable when the latter fell. In 1982 it was estimated that the energy-producing provinces and Ottawa faced a shortfall of $47 billion in revenue from what had originally been anticipated under the earlier agreements.[17] In the face of these unexpected developments Alberta rolled back its royalties so as to increase the industry profits, and Ottawa tabled an update to the NEP, making it more flexible and abandoning or lowering some federal energy taxes. But none of these adjustments or earlier agreements was able to save the two megaprojects: the consortia created to develop the tar sands (Alsands) and heavy oil extraction (Cold Lake) were abandoned. The result of governmental policies (and also, of course, of world conditions) was, therefore, that the Canadian oil industry had been opened to Canadian producers but that the overall health of the oil sector had deteriorated. Exploration crews and equipment left Canada for greener pastures and the industry failed to act, as had been expected by the government, as a key guarantor of the country's prosperity.

In addition to the economic difficulties, political storms exacerbated the situation. We have already noted some of the deep conflicts straining the relations between the federal and provincial governments. At the level of exclusively national politics horrendous confrontations were associated with various phases of the energy policy. The most serious concerned the somewhat belated effort of the federal government to introduce the legislation needed to implement its program. No fewer than eight fairly substantial pieces of legislation were required, in addition to the agreements with the provinces and the Canada Oil and Gas Act of 1981. Some of the eight consisted of revisions to existing acts of Parliament. Marc Lalonde, the minister of energy, presented all these statutory proposals in February 1982 as an omnibus bill, C-94.

Quite apart from some of its provisions, the format of the bill enraged the opposition. It is the usual custom in the House to separate legislation affecting tax changes from other kinds of legislation. The main reason is that regular legislation is considered in committee, whereas tax items are debated by the entire House. Hybrid bills are normally split on the insistence of the Speaker if the government does not do so itself. In this instance the Speaker, Jeanne Sauvé, refused opposition requests to force the normal division. This refusal brought Parliament to a standstill. Unable to change the mind of the Speaker or that of the government, the Conservatives precipitated what has come to be known as the "bell-ringing episode." The Tory M.P.s simply refused to return to the House when division bells were ringing, thereby bringing business to a halt. They succeeded in tying up the legislature for two weeks until the government agreed to split the proposed Energy Security Act into eight parts. The opposition, for its part, agreed to pass all bills by the end of June. While the bell-ringing caper no doubt did not add to the prestige of Parliament in the eyes of most Canadians, it did focus public attention on what was interpreted by many as yet another instance of Liberal arrogance, intransigence, and casualness with respect to the niceties of the democratic process.

Economic Initiatives   The central policy instrument available to a government in its management of economic issues is the budget. Confronted by a recession related to the triple curse of rising unemployment, strong inflationary pressures, and a high deficit, Allan MacEachen, Trudeau's minister of finance, was put on his mettle when preparing his financial blueprint. The previous government, it will be recalled, fell because the budget it had introduced in December 1979 was voted down by the Liberals and the NDP—a parliamentary upset in which MacEachen had played a central role. The Conservative budget attempted to reduce the government deficit and appeared to distribute the burden reasonably evenly throughout society. The new government delayed introducing a new economic map for Canada, in part, it claimed, because it had encountered difficulties in negotiating oil pricing and taxation schedules. A mini-budget was presented to Parliament in May, but the centerpiece of the new government's economic policy was not to see the light of day until the end of October 1980. It was awaited with great expectations, both because of the importance of its substantive provisions and because it would give a clear indication of the economic and social outlook of the Trudeau government. Even the autumn budget succeeded only partially in revealing the direction in which the government intended to steer Canada's economy in the 1980s. Its main innovation was to launch the NEP. For a more fundamental indication of which way the wind was blowing among the government's top economic planners, Canada had to wait for the budget introduced in November 1981.

This document revealed that inflation was still seen by the government to be a greater priority than either unemployment or the deficit, despite the alarming increase in both. Although a good deal of lip service and some modest provisions attempted to deal with the last two problems, no evidence was provided that the government had any concrete and immediate plans to return substantial numbers of people to work or to curb its own spending. In fact, a growth in government spending was foreseen. Such reductions in the deficit as were expected were to be derived from increased tax revenues, to accrue in large part from the energy sector. A noteworthy reform of the tax system was included, in an attempt to plug the many loopholes and eliminate the perquisites heretofore available primarily to earners of high incomes.

Unfortunately for the government, many of the provisions were ill conceived and threatened to reduce economic activity and hence slow down or prevent economic recovery. They engendered a paralyzing aura of uncertainty. It was a central assumption of the finance minister that the most serious economic ills of the country would be remedied if inflation were contained and the conditions for economic growth ensured. But the budget provided a wide range of provisions that actually stood in the way of the realization of these assumptions.

MacEachen's long-awaited tax and expenditure plan was met with howls of disapprobation by the vast majority of interested individuals and organizations, and not only by those whose special advantages were being abolished. It became increasingly evident that in many instances the budget would have the opposite of the hoped-for effect. The document also made it clear that the government had no fully coherent set of policies designed to cope with Canada's major economic challenges. Many of the provisions of the budget had to be amended because they turned out to be an acute embarrassment to the government. Not only business, labor, and consumer groups found it wanting, but also Liberal M.P.s and even ministers, some of whom were so provoked as to commit one of the most unpardonable offenses in the parliamentary system: they made their displeasure public.

It was widely assumed that the minister of finance would sooner or later have to be replaced, but the pivotal position and respect he enjoyed within the party prevented an immediate relocation. He was given an opportunity to present another budget in June 1982. Apart from eliminating many of the reforms introduced in 1981 and providing some new loopholes for the well-to-do, the government used this occasion to introduce an anti-inflationary program that came to be known as the "Six and Five World." It suspended contracts with half a million public servants and employees of Crown corporations, outlawed public-service strikes, and imposed ceilings of 6 and 5 percent on their salary increases in the first and second years, respectively. Those under federal contract, recipients of subsidies or grants, or those regulated by regulatory agencies were eventually also expected to abide by these rules.

These measures, which evoked sympathetic and cooperative responses from many sections of the business community and from several provinces, revealed the government's belief that high wages were in large part to blame for high inflation. This contention, however, was hotly contested by labor groups, among others. Jean-Claude Parrot, the leader of the Canadian Union of Postal Workers, argued that since the mid-1970s government spending had risen by 120 percent, whereas weekly earnings had increased by only 65 percent, seven percentage points below the augmentation in the cost-of-living index.[18]

Nevertheless, the "Six and Five" initiative proved to be one of the few acts of the government that gave the impression that it was seriously attempting to cope with the economic crisis confronting the country. It had received considerable support from most groups other than labor and clearly went some way toward mollifying the business community. The latter, however, was stunned by MacEachen's revelation that the forecast he had made in November about the deficit had been hopelessly wrong: the estimated shortfall of a whopping $10.2 billion had now actually reached a sum close to $20 billion.

Under these circumstances the "Six and Five" program was intensified and touted as a signal success. On the anniversary of its introduction, Trudeau stated in a national broadcast that economic recovery was under way and noted that inflation had been driven down to 5.4 percent. Although this low mark was not to last, as figure 1.2 shows, the days of double-digit inflation were over and the rise in the cost of living, while still worrisome, became manageable. Many economists argued, however, that the drop in the cost of living would have happened even without the "Six and Five" program; the depression and the lower rates in the United States were more potent factors. Others suggested that only the government's policies of restraint led to the slowdown of salary increases among public servants. But the belt-tightening was never as effective as the "Six and Five" rhetoric led everyone to believe. Data released later revealed that because of the reclassification of categories and other such tricks, the increase in civil servant salaries during the first year of the program was actually about 10 percent rather than 6 percent.[19]

Another indication that the government had failed to develop and apply an effective industrial strategy—a goal it had established for itself—was seen in its haphazard practice of bailing out faltering economic enterprises. Instead of channeling resources toward likely international winners, Ottawa seemed to be propping up losers. Massey-Ferguson, Chrysler, Maislin—all were rescued by the government, either because of the large number of jobs at risk or perhaps in some instances because of the personal relations prevailing between the management of some of these companies and members of the government. A somewhat different but related matter concerned the massive losses of some Crown corporations, which had to be backed by the government. Canadair, for instance, the manufacturers of the Challenger jet, lost $1.4 billion in 1982 and appeared before a parliamentary committee to justify another infusion of $240 million. The government had little choice but to accede to the request.

The opposition parties naturally tried to capitalize on the economic woes of the government and on its great difficulty in coping with them. Pierre Trudeau's earlier preoccupation with Quebec and francophone rights and his more recent commitment to constitutional reform were often cited as reasons why economic problems appeared to be mismanaged. The prime minister did not seem to be interested in economics. His patience with and seeming un-willingness to move MacEachen from Finance after his budget fiasco only confirmed this view. In 1982 Mr. Trudeau did in fact replace MacEachen with Marc Lalonde, perhaps the ablest of his ministers. MacEachen was reappointed minister of external affairs—a post he had found very congenial earlier—and Lalonde was shifted from the Department of Energy to that of Finance.

Although this move was first met with dismay by the business community (for Lalonde was identified with the nationalist and dirigiste NEP), he managed, after *his* first budget, which bore no resemblance to MacEachen's earlier missteps, to win the respect of and some support from important elements of the public. Many of his proposals were designed to tackle unemployment and foster economic growth. His performance was much more competent than that of his predecessor, although he too did not escape unscathed. Lalonde unwittingly leaked an item in his budget when a television camera, during the traditional prebudget photo opportunity, focused on a page of the highly confidential document he was holding. To silence opposition cries for his resig-nation, he subsequently added $200 million to his budget's special recovery program, thus ensuring that the sum revealed on television had not been that included in the budget.[20] No one was fooled by this strategem, least of all opposition parliamentarians. Still, with Lalonde at the Department of Finance, the opposition confronted a less vulnerable target than previously, particularly because there were signs that the economy was picking up, although both unemployment and the deficit continued to be at quite intolerably high levels. As the election approached, the former was hovering around 11 percent and the latter was well over $30 billion.

Both opposition parties agreed that the government's economic policies were inadequate and incompetently applied, but they differed fundamentally in their criticism. The NDP, not surprisingly, placed enormous emphasis on unemployment, maintaining that if it were substantially diminished most other economic difficulties would also attenuate. They claimed that greater purchasing power among the population would restore the economy and decrease the deficit because of lower welfare payments and higher tax revenues. The party, which had welcomed the nationalist features of the New Energy Program, was also strongly opposed to the government's retreat from its original resolve to diminish American economic penetration of Canada, as expressed, for instance, in the weakening of the Foreign Investment Review Agency (FIRA).

At the heart of the Tories' response to Liberal economic initiatives was their greater confidence in the private sector. They favored less government intervention and the creation of a climate in which private enterprise could flourish. They also strongly objected to what they saw as the centralizing and autocratic ways of the cabinet. Their position was encapsulated in a dramatic gesture: in the wake of MacEachen's disastrous first budget they conducted fifteen hearings across Canada at which citizens were invited to discuss their reactions to the government's plans.

In addition to their ideological disagreements with the government, the opposition parties were critical of what they took to be a lack of general direction in government policies. They decried the absence of a clearly articulated industrial strategy and accused the government of *responding* to crises as they arose, rather than pursuing a coherent economic strategy that would *prevent* them from surfacing in the first place.

When, in the autumn of 1982, the government finally launched a thorough probe designed to help it arrive at comprehensive policies to tackle Canada's fundamental problems, it was nevertheless roundly criticized. The inquiry was undertaken by the Royal Commission on the Economic Union and Developmental Prospects for Canada under its chairman, Donald S. Macdonald, a former Liberal finance minister. The commission's terms of reference were sweeping, but as its title suggested, the economy was paramount. The reception of the inquiry was greeted almost universally with hostility. It appears that the matter had not been discussed widely even within the cabinet; there were some who believed that the whole scheme was an effort to give Donald Macdonald extensive media exposure. He was expected to seek the Liberal leadership, and opponents of the candidacy of John Turner hoped that he would carry the day. The commission was seen as a useful launching pad for his eventual campaign. The expected high costs of the probe were also attacked, particularly when it became known that the chairman's stipend would be $800 per day. The reaction of the opposition parties was perhaps best expressed by the NDP House leader, Ian Deans, who observed that "If the government needs a Royal Commission to find out what is wrong with the country, what should be done about it, it's time they got the hell out of here." [21]

Transportation Issues   Few matters are as sensitive and as likely to elicit violent reactions in Canada as those touching on communications and transportation. This is hardly surprising, given the size of the country and the wide dispersal of its relatively small population. From the very beginning governments have had to contend with the often extraordinarily difficult problem of effectively bridging space in a politically acceptable manner. The Trudeau administration was no exception. It attempted to meet three major challenges in this area during the early 1980s, at considerable political cost, as it turned out. They were proposals to reduce passenger train services, to eliminate the historic Crowsnest Pass freight rate, and to foster greater competition in air traffic.

The minister of transport, Jean-Luc Pépin, announced in 1981 that the government would eliminate almost one-fifth of the services operated by VIA Rail—the Crown corporation responsible for passenger train transport. The Atlantic eastern link between Montreal and Halifax and one of the two transcontinental routes between Winnipeg and Vancouver were seen by many as particularly important casualties of this policy, and caused the loudest outcries. The government had been confronted by mounting deficits and declining traffic on many lines, along with the need to upgrade service in the lucrative Quebec City to Windsor corridor, encompassing the two great eastern metropolises of Montreal and Toronto. It therefore resolved to bite the bullet and institute what it saw as an inevitable reform, no matter how unpopular.

The vigorous public protests were directed not only at the substance of the decision but also at the method by which it was reached and announced. Pépin chose to reveal his plans only after Parliament had adjourned for the summer and without consulting anyone outside his ministry, not even the Canadian Transport Commission (CTC), which would presumably have held hearings on the question. Although he was under no legal obligation to involve the CTC or to bring his decision before Parliament, his failure to do either appeared unjustifiably high-handed. It was interpreted by many as showing that the post-1980 Trudeau party had not learned as much as might have been expected from its electoral defeat in 1979: its authoritarianism and central Canadian perspective had not been diminished by being out of office for a while.

Opposition to the cutbacks and to the approach the government adopted toward VIA Rail was widespread, vigorous, and well organized. One of the chief opponents of the railway policy, an organization called Transport 2000, collected 55,000 signatures on a protrain petition, and when Parliament reconvened the first no-confidence motion the government confronted grew out of its stance toward VIA.

Both opposition parties launched scathing attacks and the Tories went so far as to create a Task Force on Rail Passenger Service, which held hearings in thirteen cities and produced a report that managed to weaken many of the arguments invoked on behalf of the cutbacks. Among other things, it cast considerable doubt on the accuracy of the data the government had used when defending their approach to VIA. The Department of Transport's credibility was not enhanced by the fact that its most senior official on railway policy had been vice president of one of the country's largest bus lines and a director of the bus lobby's Motor Coach Association.[22]

Any possible economic merit of the VIA policy aside, its political consequences were probably quite serious. "Mr. Pépin and the cabinet," as one commentator noted,

> overlooked several important factors. For many Canadians the Liberal cabinet did not truly represent the national interests of the country. With only one elected member from the west of Ontario in cabinet, many Westerners believed their views were inadequately represented. . . . Secondly, and of greater importance, the Eastern-dominated cabinet did not sufficiently take into account the negative psychological impact of cutting out transportation rail services. For many Canadians, though they might prefer other means of transportation, the railway was an essential historical link in the development and evolution of Canada as a national entity. To destroy and weaken such links was to contribute to the further fragmentation of an already weakened federal system.[23]

A crisis fraught with symbolic significance erupted as the result of Ottawa's desire to rationalize yet another transportation arrangement. The Crowsnest Pass freight rate for grain had been established in 1897. It was an agreement between the Canadian Pacific Railway (CPR) and the government of Canada, giving the railway title to pass into British Columbia and a subsidy in exchange for reducing, in perpetuity, certain tariffs. It had last been revised in the 1920s and by then applied also to the Canadian National Railway (CNR). The railways had been claiming for a long time that they were losing substantial sums under the agreed rate and that under those conditions they could no longer maintain the equipment essential for satisfactory service. By the 1980s the rate covered only about one-fifth of the cost. Attempts at revision were politically beset with peril because the rates were considered part of the arrangements under which some western provinces became part of confederation. The Crow was seen as the Magna Carta of the Prairies. Although the need to make changes was becoming accepted, there was no agreement, even in the Prairies, on what should be done. Early in 1982, Jean-Luc Pépin announced that changes would be made and that the government would act after it received a report on the matter from Professor Clay Gilson, a University of Manitoba agricultural economist who was charged with reconciling the diverse interests in a set of practicable recommendations.

After extensive study and wide consultation, Gilson produced his eagerly awaited report in July 1982. While it received considerable support from many quarters, some formidable interests including the feisty National Farmers' Union and the government of Saskatchewan, were opposed to its recommendations. After several months of continued widespread discussion, Jean-Luc Pépin introduced bill C-155, the legislative expression of what the government called its "Western Transportation Initiative." The measure was not to have an easy passage, despite the minister's claim that it was "the greatest exercise in compromise since God created Adam and Eve." [24] The hearings of the Commons' Transportation Committee, held at several sites in the west, received a veritable avalanche of contradictory evidence and advice. Over two hundred groups conveyed their views to the government and shared their hopes and anxieties with it. If the government hoped to see an inevitable policy emerge from this process, it was to be disappointed. Even Conservative M.P.s were not unanimous until the new leader managed to fashion some order within their ranks. The governments of Alberta and Saskatchewan differed between themselves, with the latter becoming something of a leader of those opposed to the new arrangements. The Quebec Federation of Agriculture was also a vigorous foe—a development that led to opposition crystallizing within the Liberal caucus itself.

As the controversy and debate continued, the positions of the three political parties solidified and allowed for little compromise. The government insisted, as it had all along, that *something* had to be done: existing rates were so low that adequate equipment and services could no longer be maintained. It asserted that even in the late 1970s more than a billion dollars worth of grain trade was lost because of the inefficient transportation system. A substantially higher rate was inevitable, as was the need to enable the railways to upgrade their equipment. Action now was therefore inescapable. The Tories agreed with the need for change but wanted to delay matters for three years, during which further consultations and study could occur. The NDP, on the other hand, opposed any change in the freight rate and sought to separate that aspect of the issue from that of the improvement of services. The original 1897 agreement remained sacrosanct to them. If the railways were to be given a new deal, then they should return the millions of dollars' worth of benefits they had received in land transfers, including highly lucrative oil and mineral rights.

In the middle of the acrimonious discussions of the Crowsnest bill, the prime minister reshuffled his cabinet. Lloyd Axworthy, the Liberals' only western M.P., was moved from the Department of Immigration and Labour to become minister of transport. He espoused the Western Transportation Initiative with zest, claiming that the proposed changes would create new jobs everywhere in Canada (because of the heavy investment by the railways), that it would lead to new trading opportunities, and that it would create an expanded base for economic growth.

Parliamentary opposition continued unabated, however, and led to the imposition of closure, another bell-ringing episode, in which the NDP brought the House to a standstill, and the temporary ejection by the Speaker of two NDP members for challenging her decisions.

Under these pressures, the government made some concessions to the opposition by agreeing, for example, to tie the new freight rates to grain prices. The new act provided for a fivefold increase in rates by 1991, at which point farmers would be paying 60 percent of the actual cost instead of 20 percent. An annual payment of $651 million would be made to the railways for ten years to compensate them for grain-handling losses. During this period the railways would spend $16.5 billion on improved facilities and the provision of higher carriage capacity to handle not only grain but also coal, potash, and other natural resources.[25]

The protracted process of finding a solution to the Crowsnest Pass issue fanned and revived animosities that had been dormant or nearly forgotten in the country's collective memory. Once again it looked as if eastern interests were pitted against those of the west, and the railways against the western farmers. There can be no doubt that the former were generally happy about the government's initiative, which filled the latter with anguish. The electoral consequences were therefore clear: the west's already strong disinclination to identify with the Trudeau party was strengthened considerably by the government's position on the Crowsnest Pass rates, and the image of the opposition parties was enhanced by their resistance to it.

International Affairs and Defense   Foreign policy issues normally affect electoral outcomes in Canada less than economic and social matters. They nevertheless deserve brief notice in the present context because, in the period just preceding the election, the prime minister launched a major foreign policy campaign which, whatever its other merits, was hoped would reflect well on the Liberal party.

Of all its international concerns, Canada's relations with the United States are inevitably the most important. They affect virtually every aspect of the country in some way and are absolutely critical to its economy and its cultural life. In the early 1980s two factors played a particularly important role in shaping how the two neighbors got along, at least formally. They were the somewhat nationalistic stance adopted by the Trudeau government after its return to power in 1980, and the presence in Washington of the Reagan administration. The New Energy Program, designed, as we saw, to control the country's petroleum industry, and the attempts of FIRA to reduce the takeover of Canadian enterprises by foreign owners were deeply resented in the United States. Canada, on the other hand, had little sympathy for what were often seen as selfish, jingoist, and socially callous positions of the new Republican administration in Washington.

In addition to these issues of economic nationalism, the question of environmental protection also constituted an irritant in the relations between the two countries. While Canada was particularly concerned about the spreading threat of acid rain, the American position that further studies were needed before any controls might be considered was viewed in both Ottawa and the provincial capitals as a mere excuse for inaction.

There was, however, one area where the two countries managed to proceed with reasonable harmony. This was in the field of defense collaboration. Here the professionals carried out their business without too much interference from either the politicians or the media. The major issue at this time was posed by American efforts to test the Cruise missile. Canada provided a highly suitable terrain for the experimental deployment of this weapon and Ottawa agreed to the necessary field trials.

From the perspective of party competition, the Conservatives were less enthusiastic than the Liberals and the NDP about nationalistic economic policies and were, in fact, bitterly critical of both the Trudeau energy policy and of FIRA. Not surprisingly, the party alignment differed in relation to the issue of the Cruise missile. Here, the Conservatives were in general on the government's side, but the NDP presented implacable opposition to the presence on Canadian soil of U.S. nuclear weapons.

Pierre Trudeau's peace initiative, launched in the autumn of 1983, was by far the most striking and visible of the Liberal party's foreign policy ventures in the period under review. Its purpose was to defuse the intensifying conflict between the Soviet Union and the United States by a campaign of personal diplomacy. The prime minister traveled to numerous NATO and Warsaw Pact countries, where he sought to persuade leading politicians of the need to work intensively for an easing of East-West tensions.

Although his plan was at first rather vague, it evolved into a proposal for the convocation of a conference of the five nuclear states, the strengthening of the 1970 Nuclear Nonproliferation Treaty, cuts in the numbers of conventional forces in Europe, and the abolition of research on the creation of antisatellite ("Star Wars") weapons. Trudeau's reception was warm in several countries, most notably Romania and East Germany, but Washington was lukewarm and

Moscow was immobilized by the illness and ultimate death of Yuri Andropov.

Despite the fact that in many quarters in Canada there was a certain suspicion that Mr. Trudeau's motives were at least in part tainted by partisan electoral considerations, support for what looked like his last hurrah was widespread and warm. Who could possibly object to so praiseworthy an effort by the indisputably distinguished and able prime minister? The Conservative reaction was at first wary but ultimately turned into strong support. The NDP, while obviously wishing Trudeau well, nevertheless argued that a more concrete and effective measure would have been to dissociate Canada from the tests of the Cruise missile and from other involvements in the Western nuclear buildup.

In the end, the Liberal leader's efforts had virtually no effect on world tensions and, while no doubt somewhat enhancing his image abroad, their political effects in Canada were insignificant. It is even possible, although no convincing data exist supporting this view, that the suspicion that the whole campaign was in part motivated by self-serving considerations diminished Trudeau's stature in the eyes of some Canadians.

Party Developments and the Political Game

The manner in which Trudeau's peace initiative was viewed, at least in some quarters, shows how difficult it is to separate the electoral impact of policy issues from more narrowly partisan developments in the political arena. Still, the activities of the Trudeau administration and the reactions to them described earlier were *primarily* involved with substantive policies rather than strategic partisan advantage. We now turn briefly to those aspects of the interelection period which arose directly from the warfare among the major contenders for political power. Since many are intimately related to the election proper, and so are discussed in some of the chapters that follow, they are only touched upon here.

Insofar as the general political mood of the country was concerned, one factor towered over all others: the atmosphere within which political battles were waged was not only tense but dangerously laden with distrust, extreme hostility, and lack of tolerance among the principal actors. The give-and-take so essential to the effective functioning of the parliamentary system was absent. In the eyes of the public this squabbling gave rise not only to a general impatience with politicians, but also to the perception that it was responsible for their inability to cope effectively with the country's serious economic difficulties.

The reasons for the low state of political civility were related to long-standing factors such as the one-party dominant political system and the personalities of the principal actors.[26] However, short-run developments (for instance, the virtual certainty that the next election would feature at least two new party leaders) also contributed to the acrimony. This suggested that the long-standing party alignment in Canada might undergo a major change, as foreshadowed by the 1980 election.

The Liberal Party   Two concerns almost obsessed the Liberal party: how to remain in power and what was to happen to its leadership. The two preoccupations were of course so closely related that they virtually became one. The prime minister, once back in office, had become deeply committed to certain objectives: "winning" the Quebec plebiscite, patriating the constitution, enshrining a charter of human rights, and pursuing certain nationalistic goals. Once these were either completed or shown to have been unrealizable, he seemed to remove himself somewhat from the center of the fray but without in any way indicating when he was going to make way for a successor. The period after 1982 therefore became increasingly marked by intense uncertainty and ambivalence.

A number of mutually reinforcing factors contributed to the widespread unease about the Liberals which, as is shown in figure 1.1, was clearly reflected in public opinion polls. Apart from the disquieting economic conditions and the perpetual bickering between Ottawa and the provinces, some particular characteristics and activities of the Liberal party caused disquiet. One of these concerned the status of the party itself in the decisionmaking process. It often happens in Canada that the government party comes to be dominated by its leader and his intimates, with the consequence that the party machinery as such is allowed to deteriorate. This is precisely what occurred during the Trudeau years.

While the meetings and conventions prescribed by the party constitution were duly held, the key decisions about anything of importance were made by the prime minister and his entourage. This did not sit well with all party members and a minor challenge to the status quo was mounted at the party's policy convention in the autumn of 1982. A motion was adopted at a previous gathering of the Young Liberals condemning "manipulative electoral shams," "polls, propaganda and patronage orchestrated by a small elite," and the trend that "non-accountable, non-legitimate, non-elected members of the party should have a direct informal role in advising the government." The national convention accordingly dealt with the issue and supported the position taken by the youth wing.[27] Ultimately, a reform commission was established that in 1984 produced a report proposing wide-ranging changes. The criticism sparked by the Young Liberals was aimed primarily at Senator Keith Davey, the party's chief electoral strategist, Jim Coutts, the prime minister's principal secretary, and a small group of other advisers who were seen by many to exercise undue influence within the party.

We noted earlier that the appointment of a young Liberal M.P. to the Senate, allowing Jim Coutts to contest a by-election in Toronto, had created a good deal of hostility. At the very end of the Trudeau era, wholesale patronage appointments created a scandal that became an important element in the electoral campaign. But other maneuvers dimmed the Liberal appeal even earlier. Thus, former ministers were accused of violating conflict of interest guidelines and of receiving substantial sums, presumably for influence-peddling.[28] Some ministers, particularly Lloyd Axworthy from Winnipeg and Allan MacEachen from Cape Breton, were severely criticized for causing extraordinarily large sums of public money to be spent in their constituencies.[29] A more widespread use of the taxpayers' money for narrowly partisan purposes became known when it was revealed that Liberal M.P.s had been invited to submit proposals under the Employment Creation Grants and Contributions Program that enabled each of them to spend half a million dollars for job creation programs in their ridings. Although the existence of the scheme had been known, the M.P.s of the other parties were not only denied special opportunities to apply, but encountered difficulties in finding out how to use these funds. The result was that sums spent in constituencies in which Liberal incumbents would contest the impending election were disproportionately higher than those directed toward Conservative or NDP seats.

These and similar attempts by the government to use its position in office for partisan advantage did not, however, succeed in creating a well-organized national party machine. Events ultimately revealed that, compared with the Conservatives and even the smaller NDP, the Liberal party organization was shaky. It lagged badly behind in its use of modern information and communications facilities—a weakness that resulted in a comparatively ineffective procedure for raising funds, particularly from individual contributors. Both of its major opponents were able to collect larger sums from personal, as compared to corporate donors, than was the government party.

The uncertainty about the party leadership was terminated at least in one sense on February 29, 1984, when Trudeau announced that he would be stepping down. A leadership convention was called for June 14, at which John Turner was chosen as the new leader in a process that had a strong impact on the election and which is therefore analyzed in a subsequent chapter.[30]

The Progressive Conservative Party   Unlike the Liberals, the Conservatives, under Robert Stanfield and Joe Clark, had built up a highly efficient party machine and a lively and active extraparliamentary party. Their primary difficulties arose out of a seemingly irremediable lack of unity and a related tendency to challenge the authority of the party leader. Joe Clark, despite heroic efforts to overcome these impediments, was plagued with disloyalty and systematic efforts to unseat him, to which he ultimately succumbed.[31]

It is highly significant that Brian Mulroney, the new leader, was able to break the dominant pattern of disunity so characteristic of the party. He managed to do this despite having originally waged a covert but nevertheless ferocious campaign against Clark, and despite his relatively close margin of victory over Clark on the fourth convention ballot.[32] Mulroney's conciliatory style and political skills were unquestionably important reasons for the party's newfound unity, but Joe Clark's superb behavior in defeat was also very important. He scotched all attempts by his followers to weaken the new leader and was unfailingly loyal to and supportive of his successor.

Developments within the two major parties in the period between the 1980 and 1984 elections thus created an unprecedented situation in modern Canadian political history. The Conservatives were united behind their new leader, whereas the Liberals were still affected by the legacy of the recent bitter and divisive struggle for the leadership.

The New Democratic Party   The New Democrats had teamed up with the Liberals to defeat the Clark government in 1979. They had also, as we saw, strongly supported many of the main points of Trudeau's constitutional proposal. This identification with the government party, which was of course only partial and was outweighed by many profound differences, nevertheless affected the manner in which the NDP was perceived by the Canadian public. It is likely that the decline in its popularity, evident in the polls (see figure 1.1), was in part caused by a loss of distinctiveness in the eyes of some of the electorate. Ed Broadbent also antagonized some of the party by strongly identifying with Trudeau on the constitution, and by the way in which the decision to do so was reached.

Another factor that affected the NDP negatively in the preelection period was the strong resurgence of the Conservative party. The probability of a Conservative win endowed the party with an attractive aura and, furthermore, invited those who wished to defeat the unpopular Liberal government to back the likely winner rather than scatter the antigovernment vote.

As the election approached, therefore, the NDP appeared to be less well placed than it had been in most previous recent contests. The question confronting the party was whether it could hold on to its former reasonably well-entrenched position in the west and in parts of Ontario. None of its competitors was as likely to be affected by the quality of its electoral campaign and the performance of its leader. These developments and their antecedents are described and analyzed below in the chapter by Terence Morley.

Conclusion

As the preelection period drew to a close, a number of related questions of particular interest both to the country and to students of Canadian parties and elections emerged: Would the slow decline in the popularity of the Liberal party, foreshadowed in 1979 and even earlier, continue? In other words, would the "new" party of John Turner succeed in arresting what seemed to be a long-term slide in Liberal popularity? A key element in the future of the Liberals (and therefore also, of course, that of the Conservatives) was the political orientation of Quebec. Would it continue its almost Pavlovian preference for the Liberals or would it find some attraction in a Conservative party led by one of its own sons? And finally, there was the question of the NDP. Would it manage to overcome its almost disastrous drop in support, as indicated in the polls, or would it benefit from what was generally expected to be a substantial Liberal loss?

One overarching question, subsuming all others, is related to the political sea level as defined in the metaphor at the beginning of this chapter: would this election confirm a long-standing realignment in the Canadian party system, presaged by the 1979 outcome, or would it continue the tendencies of one-party dominance that have been so characteristic of Canadian politics since the 1920s?

Although most of the polls gave an inkling to what might happen, they were by no means safe guideposts to the future. Quite apart from the normal fickleness of opinion, manifested, for instance, in the Liberal resurgence after the party's leadership convention, the number of undecided voters continued to be very high. The outcome was therefore by no means certain and would, perhaps more than usually, depend on the character of the campaigns and particularly on the performance of the Liberal and Conservative leaders, who had yet to be tried by the electoral fire. The events of the campaign, detailed in the following chapters, would therefore be of unusual importance to the outcome.

Notes

1. William P. Irvine, "Epilogue: the 1980 Election," in Howard R. Penniman, ed., *Canada at the Polls 1979 and 1980* (Washington, D.C.: American Enterprise Institute, 1981), pp. 337–55.

2. Ibid., pp. 355–88.

3. Reginald Whitaker significantly entitled his excellent study of the organization and financing of the Liberal party from 1930 to 1958 *The Government Party* (Toronto: University of Toronto Press, 1977). For some consequences of the "government party psychology" see John Meisel, "Howe, Hubris and '72: A Study in Elitism," in John Meisel, *Working Papers on Canadian Politics*, 2d enl. ed. (Montreal: McGill-Queen's University Press, 1975), pp. 217–52.

4. John Meisel, "The Larger Context: The Period Preceding the 1979 Election," in Howard R. Penniman, ed., *Canada at the Polls 1979 and 1980* (Washington, D.C.: American Enterprise Institute, 1981), pp. 24–54; idem, "The Decline of Party in Canada," in Hugh G. Thorburn,

ed., *Party Politics in Canada*, 5th ed. (Scarborough, Ont.: Prentice-Hall, 1985), pp. 98–114; idem, "The Boob-tube Election," in John C. Courtney, ed., *The House of Commons: Essays in Honour of Norman Ward* (Calgary: University of Calgary Press, 1985), pp. 173–94.

5. For a full discussion of the leadership conventions of the Liberal and Conservative parties, see chapter 3 in this volume.

6. Meisel, "The Larger Context," p. 54.

7. The text read, "Non merci . . . ça se dit bien" (No thanks . . . it's easily said).

8. Most of the material in this section is derived from R. B. Beyers, ed., *The Canadian Annual Review 1980–83* (Toronto: University of Toronto Press, 1982–85), pp. 38–58.

9. The above discussion of the crisis grossly oversimplifies an exceedingly complex situation. The Manitoba government finally left the question to be determined by the Supreme Court of Canada which, on June 13, 1985, ruled that almost all laws in Manitoba were invalid and would have to be translated into French.

10. For a brief discussion of four cycles in the negotiations during the last two decades, see Keith Banting and Richard Simeon, "Federalism, Democracy and the Constitution," in K. Banting and R. Simeon, eds., *And No One Cheered* (Toronto: Methuen, 1983), p. 4.

11. Some of the best sources are Banting and Simeon, *And No One Cheered*; Ronald James Zukowsky, "Struggle over the Constitution: From the Quebec Referendum to the Supreme Court" (Kingston: Institute of Intergovernmental Relations, Queen's University, 1981); Sheilagh M. Dunn, "The Constitution," in Sheilagh M. Dunn, *The Year in Review 1982* (Kingston: Institute of Intergovernmental Relations, Queen's University, 1982), pp. 36–50; David Milne, *The New Canadian Constitution* (Toronto: James Lorimer, 1982); Roy Romanow, John Whyte, and Howard Leeson, *Canada . . . Notwithstanding* (Toronto: Carswell-Methuen, 1984); and Robert Sheppard and Michael Valpy, *The National Deal* (Toronto: Fleet Books, 1982).

12. For details of the Pitfield and Kirby memoranda, see Milne, *The New Constitution*, pp. 219–37 and passim; and Romanov, Whyte, and Leeson, *Canada . . .*, pp. 90–95.

13. Ronald J. Zukowsky, *Intergovernmental Relations in Canada: The Year in Review 1980*, vol. 1 (Kingston: Institute of Intergovernmental Relations, Queen's University, 1981), p. 62.

14. Edward A. Carmichael and James K. Stewart, *Lessons from the National Energy Program* (Toronto: C. D. Howe Institute, 1983), p. 9.

15. For details of these and other measures, see Zukowski, *Intergovernmental Relations*, pp. 63–66.

16. Don McGillivray, *Edmonton Journal*, January 3, 1981, cited in Donald C. Wallace, "Ottawa and the Provinces," in R. B. Beyers, ed., *Canadian Annual Review 1981* (Toronto: University of Toronto Press, 1984), p. 157.

17. Donald C. Wallace, "Ottawa and the Provinces," in R. B. Beyers, ed., *Canadian Annual Review 1982* (Toronto: University of Toronto Press, 1984), p. 67.

18. Ian Anderson, "New Fear and Anger in a 'Six-per-cent Society'," *Maclean's*, July 12, 1982, p. 18.

19. Eric Beauchesne, "Government Ignored Own Guidelines," The *Whig Standard*, July 4, 1984.

20. *Canadian News Facts*, 17, no. 8 (May 4, 1983), p. 2870.

21. *Canadian Annual Review 1982*, p. 26.

22. *Maclean's*, November 9, 1981, pp. 41–42.

23. R. B. Beyers, "Parliament," in Beyers, *Canadian Annual Review 1981*, pp. 117–18.

24. Dale Eisler, "Bidding Farewell to the Old Crow," *Maclean's*, February 14, 1983, p. 18.

25. *Canadian News Facts*, 17, no. 20 (November 19, 1983), p. 2967.

26. See Meisel, "The Larger Context," and idem, "The Decline of Party."

27. Mary Janigan and Carol Goar, "Disrespecting Their Elders," *Maclean's*, November 15, 1982, p. 25. See also Carol Goar, "The Liberals Divided," *Maclean's*, November 28, 1983, p. 35.

28. See Mary Janigan, "Deal over Energy Generates Heat," *Maclean's*, February 28, 1983, p. 11; and idem, "Uncommon Scent of Scandal," *Maclean's*, March 7, 1983, pp. 14–15.

29. "Axworthy Delivers," *Maclean's*, January 16, 1984, p. 16.

30. A quick and ready treatment of the Liberal leadership race can also be found in Charles Lynch, *Race for the Rose* (Toronto: Methuen, 1984), chs. 1–13. See also Norman Snider, *The Changing of the Guard* (Toronto: Lester and Orpen Dennys, 1985).

31. Patrick Martin, Allan Gregg, and George Perlin, *Contenders: The Tory Quest for Power* (Scarborough Ont.: Prentice-Hall, 1983); and Snider, *The Changing of the Guard*.

32. The vote was 1,584 to 1,325.

2 The Flexible Canadian Electorate

LAWRENCE LEDUC

The dramatic Conservative victory in the 1984 federal election seemed to many observers to signal fundamental changes at work in the Canadian political system. An electorate that had returned the Liberal party to power in six of the preceding seven elections (see table 2.1) appeared suddenly to change its collective mind, not only turning the Liberals out but in the process handing the party its worst electoral defeat since the Diefenbaker sweep of 1958. Indeed, the Liberal showing of forty seats and 28 percent of the total vote compared unfavorably with even the forty-nine seats and 34 percent of that landslide election. So thorough was the Liberal defeat that even traditional areas of Liberal strength such as Quebec were overwhelmed by the Conservative tide.

The true longer-term meaning of the 1984 election may not be known for some time. However, it should not be assumed that this election result, however dramatic, necessarily signals the beginning of a major political realignment in the Canadian polity. For many years the Canadian electorate has been a much more volatile and unpredictable entity than is suggested by aggregate election results alone.[1] Liberal election victories in Canada have resulted neither from any ability of that party to overwhelm its opponents, nor from the unwavering support of large numbers of committed partisans. Nor have Conservative victories, such as those of 1958, 1962, or 1979, produced significant or lasting changes in the makeup of Canadian party politics. Rather, nearly every Canadian election for which survey data exist has shown an electorate with sufficient instability and short-term movement at the individual level to produce at least the potential for significant disruption of seemingly well-established electoral patterns.[2] That large-scale electoral upsets do not occur more frequently in Canada is due largely to the difficulty that any party finds in effectively harnessing the many short-term forces at work in a large and diverse country with many distinctive regional and subregional trends operat-

Table 2.1 Distribution of Vote and Seats in Canadian Federal Elections since 1963.

Party	Year							
	1963	1965	1968	1972	1974	1979	1980	1984
Liberal	41%	40%	46%	39%	43%	40%	44%	28%
	(129)	(131)	(155)	(109)	(141)	(114)	(146)	(40)
Progressive	33%	32%	31%	35%	35%	36%	33%	50%
Conservative	(95)	(97)	(72)	(107)	(95)	(136)	(103)	(211)
New Democratic	14%	18%	17%	18%	15%	18%	20%	19%
	(17)	(21)	(22)	(31)	(16)	(26)	(32)	(30)
Other	12%	10%	6%	9%	6%	6%	3%	3%
	(24)	(16)	(15)	(17)	(12)	(6)	(—)	(1)
Percent turnout	79	75	76	77	71	76	69	75

Note: Number of seats shown in parentheses.
Source: Chief Electoral Officer, "Reports of the Chief Electoral Officer," Ministry of Supply and Services, Ottawa, for individual elections.

ing simultaneously in its politics. However, on the relatively rare occasions, such as 1958 or 1984, when all short-term factors appear to move more or less in one direction across the country, the extent of change that can occur is striking indeed.

The Canadian Electoral System

As is common in British-style, single-member-district electoral systems, electoral majorities are often distorted in one or more ways merely by the mechanics of the system. This is especially true in Canada, where national trends do not always coincide with regional, provincial, or local ones.[3] Thus, the Conservative landslide of 1984 (211 out of a total of 282 seats, or 75 percent of the seats) was achieved on a total popular vote of just under 50 percent. The forty seats won by the Liberals (14 percent of the total) represented a much poorer showing than even their record low 28 percent of the vote might suggest. A similar pattern occurred in the 1958 landslide, when the Conservatives took 208 out of a possible 265 seats (78 percent) on 53 percent of the popular vote. In that election, as in 1984, the Liberal total of forty-nine seats (18 percent) painted a more dismal picture of that party's showing than did its 34 percent of the popular vote. Thus, the Conservative victory of 1984, however impressive in parliamentary terms, should not be misread. As many Canadians voted for other parties in 1984 as voted for the Conservatives. And the Liberals, while reduced to a small parliamentary rump for the next several years, almost certainly possess enough residual electoral strength to fight again.

The existence of minor parties further complicates Canada's electoral picture. While single-member parliamentary systems frequently make life difficult for minor parties, one well-established "third" party—the New Democratic party—has fared well in recent elections, partly because of the strength the party possesses in the west, where the Liberals have been weak in recent years. The New Democrats thus salvaged a respectable thirty seats (11 percent) on their total of 19 percent of the popular vote. Although nearly always "underrepresented" in Parliament by this measure, the NDP came through this landslide election in much better shape than has generally been the fate of minor parties in such elections in the past. Generally, the minor parties have done better in elections where the votes for the two major parties were more evenly divided. Other minor parties in 1984 did not fare as well as the NDP. The Social Credit party, which is gradually fading from the Canadian electoral scene, did not elect a single member in 1984. An attempt by some members of the Parti Québécois in Quebec to mount an entry into the federal political arena by running candidates under the banner "Parti Nationaliste" failed to make any significant impact.

While the Canadian electoral system often distorts electoral majorities and underrepresents minor parties, landslide elections of the type that took place in 1984 are nevertheless relatively rare in Canada. More common have been elections such as those of 1965, 1972, or 1979, when the system failed to deliver a clear parliamentary majority to any party. In 1979, the Conservatives managed to win a plurality of parliamentary seats even while finishing more than four percentage points behind the Liberals in total votes, in part because of the sharply skewed regional distribution of seats and votes which characterized that election and the one that took place less than a year later (see table 2.1). But in 1984 a volatile and somewhat more unpredictable Canadian electorate handed the Liberal government of John Turner a devastating electoral defeat. Brian Mulroney led a new Canadian federal government which, for the first time in a decade, had both a decisive parliamentary majority and representation from all parts of the country.

The Canadian Party System

As noted above, Canada's party system in recent years has not conformed to a classic two-party model. The Liberal party, which has been the dominant party in federal politics in recent years, suffers from persistent weakness in western Canada and has been unable to compete effectively at the provincial level in most provinces. Historically, the Liberals have been able to put together federal election victories by combining solid support in Quebec with pockets of strength in urban Ontario and in the Atlantic provinces. The party has generally done well among French-speaking Canadians, Roman Catholics, women, and younger voters. The Conservatives, in contrast, have enjoyed success in provincial elections, controlling the provincial governments of seven of the ten provinces, but until 1984 had been unable to make a clear breakthrough in the federal arena, in part because of their persistent electoral weakness in Quebec. Since the time of Diefenbaker they have been particularly strong in western Canada, and have also traditionally won support in the rural areas and small towns of Ontario and the Atlantic provinces. Both major parties in Canada have historically been broadly based centrist parties competing in elections for wide and shifting coalitions of support. The more left-wing New Democratic party, in contrast, has emphasized its ties with organized labor in national campaigns in recent years, and indeed does well in certain urban constituencies in industrial Ontario. Nevertheless, Canada's principal "third" party continues to win most of its seats in areas of historic socialist strength in the west, although it has also enjoyed success in recent years as a type of "protest" party, picking up support from diverse groups of voters expressing dissatisfaction with one or both of the older parties. Social and demographic variables have generally been poor predictors of individual party support in Canada, and traditional factors such as occupation and social class are particularly weak, as may be seen in the regression analysis of the Liberal vote in the 1980 federal election shown in table 2.2.[4] Twenty years ago Robert Alford characterized Canada as having "pure, non-class politics," a description which, with minor exceptions, is still largely valid today.[5] Religion continues to exist as a minor factor in Canadian partisanship, but it is often confounded with linguistic and regional patterns.[6]

In spite of the relative weakness of traditional long-term sociodemographic factors in Canadian politics, most Canadians do identify with one of the federal political parties. While party identification in Canada has not been highly stable across time, relatively few Canadians think of themselves as political independents, in contrast to recent trends in the United States. As is seen in table 2.3, only about 11 percent of national samples taken at three widely separated points in time failed to report a federal party identification. More than two-thirds of those sampled in all three of these studies reported an identification that was at least "fairly strong."

There is evidence, however, to suggest that for a substantial number of Canadians, party identification does not constitute a highly stable, long-term, psychological tie. Many hold differing party ties in federal and provincial politics, particularly in provinces with distinctive provincial party systems, such as Quebec and British Columbia. Over one-third of the 1980 national sample reported different federal and provincial partisan leanings (see table 2.3). Such "split partisanship" contributes to changes at either level of the system through the absence of mutually reinforcing federal and provincial attitudes.[7] In addition, party identification in Canada exhibits patterns of movement across time

Table 2.2 Multiple Regression Analysis of the
Liberal Vote in Canada, 1980 Federal Election.

	r	Beta
Region		
Atlantic provinces	.01	−.04
Ontario	−.02	−.12*
Western provinces	−.24*	−.26*
Religion		
Catholic	.27*	.17*
Other non-Protestant	−.05	.02
None	−.07*	.00
Social Class		
Subjective: working class	.01	.02
Objective: Blishen SES	−.03	.00
Union member	.00	−.01
Language/Ethnicity		
French	.24*	.01
Non-French Non-English	−.01	.03
Age (years)	−.03	.00
Sex (F)	.06*	.05*
Community size	.02	.01
$R^2 = .11$		

* Significant at .01.

that are considerably higher than those found in many other countries with long-standing party systems.[8] More than a third of the respondents in Canadian national samples reported past changes in party identification, and panel data suggest that this estimate may be a very conservative one. Over a three-wave panel study conducted from 1974 to 1980, 41 percent of a national sample were found to have changed their party identification, while 59 percent maintained identification with the same federal political party. Party changers divided about evenly between those who moved directly to a new party and those who moved to or from nonidentification with any party. Although a majority of the sample did *not* change their party identification over this period, the level of change found in the panel is nevertheless substantial.

We might therefore consider the Canadian electorate in the aggregate as holding partisan ties that diverge in varying degrees from a model of strong, stable, consistent partisanship. Slightly more than one-third of the electorate are "durable" partisans, who hold at least "fairly strong" identification with a political party and who identify with the same party at both federal and provin-

Table 2.3 Attributes of Party Identification in Canada,
as Measured by Three National Election Studies.

	Year		
	1965	1974	1980
Direction			
Liberal	42%	50%	45%
Progressive Conservative	28	24	28
New Democratic party	12	11	15
Social Credit	6	3	2
Independent-None	12	12	10
Intensity			
Very strong	23%	28%	31%
Fairly strong	42	40	42
Weak	23	20	17
Independent/No party identification	12	12	10
Stability			
Percentage who recall "ever" having identified with another party	38%	36%	37%
Percentage of 1974–80 panel reporting a change of party identification	—	—	41%
Consistency			
Percentage reporting directionally consistent federal and provincial party identification	75%	70%	66%
Percentage reporting different federal and provincial identification	25	30	34
Summary			
Number of deviations from strong,* stable, consistent partisanship			
0	34%	37%	36%
1	44	35	37
2	18	21	21
3	4	7	6
N	2,692	2,343	1,747

*From at least "fairly strong" partisanship.
Source: Author.

cial levels. Such partisans are unlikely to change their partisanship readily, and indeed do not report such change in either panel or cross-section surveys. The balance of the electorate, however, might be characterized as "flexible" partisans who deviate on one or more dimensions from a position of strong, stable, consistent partisanship.[9] Some of these are political independents or hold only weak ties to any party. Others hold different allegiances in federal and provincial politics. They are also more "changeable" in their partisan attitudes, being likely to report a change of partisanship at some time in their lives, or to be observed to have changed in a cross-time study. The fact that such a large proportion of the electorate exhibits this flexibility in partisan attachment helps to create the climate of electoral volatility that characterizes Canadian politics and of which the sudden and dramatic upheaval of 1984 constitutes solid empirical evidence.

The "Changeable" Canadian Voter

The relative volatility of the Canadian electorate is not a phenomenon to be associated only with the sharp swing to the Conservatives in the 1984 election. Indeed, the fluidity of the Canadian voter is well documented in the wide swings in the monthly Gallup poll, extending back through the last several elections. A tracking of the Gallup surveys over a ten-year period discloses a see-saw pattern, with a lead of as much as fifteen to twenty percentage points of one party over the other sometimes turning into a deficit of equal magnitude in a period as short as eight to twelve months.[10]

Such volatility was especially in evidence in the six months leading up to the 1984 election, in part because of the resignation of Pierre Trudeau and the assumption by John Turner of the office of prime minister following his election as leader of the Liberal party. During most of the period from mid-1982 through February 1984, the Conservatives held a wide lead over the Liberals in the polls, both before and after Brian Mulroney's election as Conservative leader in June 1983. However, the announcement by Prime Minister Trudeau of his intention to resign his office appeared to precipitate a sudden revival in Liberal fortunes, as measured by polls taken in March and April of 1984 (see figure 2.1). Within a month of Trudeau's announcement the Conservative lead had evaporated, and a Gallup poll taken at the end of March placed the Liberals six percentage points ahead. This swift Liberal recovery held up through the summer, and did not begin to disappear until the early stages of the election campaign. Following the televised debates between the party leaders on July 24–25, the standing of the Liberals in the polls dropped precipitously, and the spread between the two major parties continued to widen right up until the election (see figure 2.1).

The extent of movement at the individual level that lies beneath these patterns was measured by a two-wave panel study undertaken by the Centre de Recherche sur l'Opinion Publique of Montreal (CROP) for the *Toronto Globe and Mail* immediately following the close of the Liberal leadership convention.[11] Over a period of approximately six weeks, from late June following the convention to mid-August in the midst of the election campaign, 31 per-

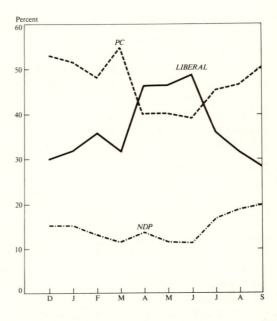

Figure 2.1 Trends in Public Support of Political Parties, as Shown by the Monthly Gallup Poll, December 1983 to September 1984. *Source:* Canadian Institute of Public Opinion, *The Gallup Report*.

cent of a national sample of 1,398 respondents interviewed by CROP were found to have changed their voting preferences. While significant movement was detected among supporters of all parties, the erosion of Liberal strength was most pronounced, with 44 percent of all previously declared Liberal supporters indicating a change of voting intention over this period.[12]

Such a rapid change in the standing of the parties in the public opinion polls is not without precedent in Canadian politics. Following the victory of the Parti Québécois in the 1976 Quebec provincial election, the standing of the federal Liberal party improved sharply, as the issue of Quebec sovereignty became a pressing national concern. Similarly, the short-lived Clark government suffered a steep decline in the polls following the introduction of its ill-fated budget in Parliament in the fall of 1979.[13] Because such a large number of Canadian voters do not have strong, stable, consistent, long-term attachments to political parties rooted in ideological or group loyalties, the electorate often responds swiftly to short-term changes in the political landscape. Such responses are more readily reflected in monthly polls than in periodic events such as elections.

Substantial changes in voting intention over the course of an election campaign are also commonplace in Canadian politics. Previous studies indicate that as much as 40 percent of the electorate makes its decision during the course of the campaign, and preelection polls normally turn up large numbers of "undecided" voters.[14] Nearly one-fifth of all voters may not decide how to

Figure 2.2 Stability and Change in Party Identification and Federal Vote, 1974, 1979, and 1980. [a]1974–80 panel. $N = 822$. [b]Includes 2 percent who report nonidentification at all three points. [c]1979–80 panel. $N = 1,565$. Excludes those not voting in at least one of the three elections. Percentages do not total to 100 as categories are not mutually exclusive.

A. Party Identification[a]

59%	22%	23%
Maintaining the same federal party identification at all three points	Moving to or from non-identification[b]	Changing party identification at least once

B. Federal Vote[c]

44%	32%	21%	13%
Voting for the same party in all three elections	Voting for a different party in at least one election	Not voting in one or more elections	New voters (1979-80)

vote until the final week of the campaign.[15] It is not surprising, then, that the weaknesses apparent in Turner's campaign in 1984 were quickly reflected in the Liberals' standing in public opinion polls taken during the course of the campaign.

Other evidence obtained from longer-term studies likewise supports this interpretation of the Canadian electorate as one containing large numbers of "flexible" voters, highly sensitive in their attitudes and behavior to a variety of short-term forces. In a national panel study covering the period 1974 to 1980, a relatively high level of change was detected in the identification of individuals with political parties.[16] Between the 1974 and 1979 elections 31 percent of the panel were found to have changed their party identification, while 22 percent did so over the much shorter (nine-month) period between the 1979 and 1980 elections. Over the entire six-year period (1974–80), 41 percent of the national sample were found to have changed their identification with a political party (see figure 2.2a). This change divides about evenly between those moving from one party to another and those abandoning or taking on an identification with a party during the period.

Similarly high levels of change in the panels were found with respect to vote-switching between elections. Between the 1974 and 1979 federal elections, 40 percent of the panel either supported a different party or moved to or from nonvoting. In the 1980 federal election, 32 percent similarly failed to support the same party as in the 1979 contest.[17] When the three time points are taken into account together, it may be seen that a majority of a national sample of the electorate did not support the same party consecutively in three federal elections. Nearly a third changed their vote in at least one of the elections, while others moved into or out of the active electorate over the six-year period (see figure 2.2b). Of course, new voters entering the electorate for the first time in 1979 or 1980, as well as those exhibiting more than one type of change (such as a switch in one election and nonvoting in another), must also be taken into account in these calculations.

Levels of partisan and voting change between elections are generally found to be somewhat higher in Canada than are shown in comparable analyses of cross-time data in the United States or Britain.[18] This is partly due to a tendency in Canada for party identification to travel with the vote for many individuals. Only 11 percent of the total 1974–80 national sample consisted of persons who changed their vote one or more times across the three elections without any disruption of party identification.[19] Both partisanship and vote show evidence of responsiveness to short-term forces for many Canadians.

This is not to argue, however, that party identification in Canada is eroding or weakening over time. There was no net increase between 1974 and 1980 in the proportion of Canadians reporting weak or inconsistent partisanship or abandoning a party identification altogether. Rather, a party identification that was weak, unstable, or inconsistent for a large number of voters essentially remained so throughout this period. Although the net shift of both voting choice and changes in party identification operated heavily in favor of the Conservatives in 1979, the Tories were able to retain very little of this support in the subsequent 1980 federal election, which took place only nine months later. Similarly, the argument sometimes made that the 1979 election was a short-term deviation while the 1980 Liberal victory represented a "return to normalcy" in the Canadian political system is clearly belied by the sharp swing of 1984. Survey data for this election, when it becomes available, will almost certainly show levels of change in both partisanship and vote at least as high as those documented in previous studies. The 1984 election, for all its drama, represents not a sharp break with the past but a continuation of a trend toward instability and change that has been evident in the Canadian political system for some time.

Issues and Images in Canadian Politics

The interpretation of volatility in the Canadian political process presented here rests heavily on a demonstration of the relative importance of short-term forces such as issues, leaders, and government style and performance in Canadian politics. This in turn should be viewed in the context of the weakness of longer-term correlates of voting choice such as religion, ethnicity, or social class, and the particular characteristics of partisan attachment of Canadian voters discussed above. Evidence regarding the weakness of long-term forces in Canadian elections is also found in the structure of political party images in Canada, as measured by a series of open-ended questions in three national surveys (see table 2.4).[20] Issue- and policy-related items (51 percent) made up the largest component of images that Canadians held of

Table 2.4 Content of Federal Party Images, 1974, 1979, and 1980 National Samples (percentage associating a party with one or more specific image dimensions[a]).

	1974	1979	1980
Policy/Issue	61%	51%	60%
Style/Performance	47	50	60
Leadership/Leader	38	37	51
General/Party	35	42	40
Area/Group	28	27	31
Ideology	14	15	18
N	2,445	2,670	928[b]

[a] Multiple response. Percentages do not total 100.
[b] Random half sample.
Source: Harold Clarke, Jane Jenson, Lawrence LeDuc, and Jon Pammett, *Political Choice in Canada* (Toronto: McGraw-Hill Ryerson, 1979).

the federal political parties in 1979, closely followed by those dealing with "performance" or "style" (50 percent). Similar patterns are shown in the data collected in the preceding (1974) or subsequent (1980) elections (see table 2.4). In general, the categories of images that recur with the greatest frequency are those which change most readily over relatively short periods of time in response to changes in party programs or leadership. Ideological or group-related images, an important psychological source of the stability of party systems in many countries, are distinctly weaker elements in the structure of political party images in Canada. Given the change in leadership of both major parties and the shift in emphasis from constitutional and federal-provincial issues to those involving the economy, it might be expected that the images of the parties would have been highly responsive to change in 1984. The passing of the leadership from Trudeau to Turner in the case of the Liberals, and from Clark to Mulroney for the Conservatives brought with it not only changes in personalities, but differences of style and emphasis that were bound to affect public perceptions of the parties themselves.

Issues in Canada have often tended to fluctuate sharply from one election to another. Over the three preceding federal elections there were substantial variations in the degree of importance ascribed by voters to economic issues such as inflation or unemployment, or to confederation issues such as "national unity" or the threat of Quebec independence.[21] More specific issues appeared and disappeared abruptly in each of the last several elections, as illustrated by the campaign emphasis placed on the issue of wage and price controls in 1974, the tax treatment of mortgage interest in 1979, or the concern with oil prices in 1980. Canadian elections, however, have rarely been single-issue affairs.

Rather, campaigns generally focus on a variety of concerns that can be loosely grouped into broad categorizations such as economic, social, confederation, and resource issues.[22] The particular mixture of these topics can vary widely across time and between regions of the country, and invariably there are also issues specific to a particular contest that attract the attention of voters. In 1984 issue concerns appeared to swing sharply away from the confederation and resource questions that characterized the late 1970s to a greater emphasis on general economic issues, particularly unemployment. Interspersed in the 1984 campaign rhetoric, however, were even more short-term matters such as the "patronage" issue, which arose as a result of a series of appointments made by Turner immediately following his assumption of the office of prime minister. This in turn was closely related to perceptions of the party leaders themselves, both of whom were new figures on the political scene.[23] Such movement of issue concerns and variations in leader images from one election to another is typical of electorates with relatively weak long-term issue or group loyalties and low levels of ideological commitment. These attributes certainly characterized the Canadian electorate of 1984. Canadian voters are highly responsive to the particular leaders, issues, and policies of the day, which themselves tend to exhibit considerable volatility from one election to another.

A Changing Electorate

Changes in issue perceptions or attitudes are, of course, not the only changes that electorates undergo from one election to another. Many measures of change more or less presume an electorate of fixed proportions, passing judgment retrospectively or otherwise on governments in each successive election. But the physical makeup of the electorate as it exists at a given point in time should also be considered. The voters who chose Brian Mulroney's Conservatives in 1984 were not the same voters who returned Pierre Trudeau to power in 1980. Changes in the physical composition of the electorate from one election to the next come primarily from two sources: the entry of new generations of voters into the electorate, and fluctuations in voting turnout. Over longer periods of time, the possible impacts of immigration/emigration and larger-scale generational changes would also have to be examined.

The size of the total eligible electorate in Canada rose to approximately 17.5 million in 1984, in part because of the addition of approximately 2.3 million new voters (about 13 percent of the total eligible electorate). While evidence suggests that younger voters in Canada in recent years have not been greatly different than the electorate as a whole in such things as partisan attachment, issue concerns, etc., new voters nevertheless represent an important potential source of volatility in elections.[24] Younger voters accounted at least

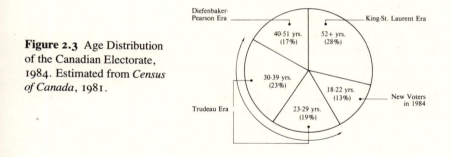

Figure 2.3 Age Distribution of the Canadian Electorate, 1984. Estimated from *Census of Canada*, 1981.

in part for the Liberal margin of victory in the 1974 federal election and, while many of these deserted the Liberals in 1979, many returned to that party in the 1980 election.[25] However, there is little evidence that the youngest cohort of voters holds the potential to effect permanent changes in the behavior of the Canadian electorate. Indeed, the partisan leanings of this cohort are as weak and unstable as those of the general electorate and it is unlikely that support from younger voters aided the Liberals appreciably in 1984. It is equally unlikely, however, that younger voters constitute a new "Mulroney generation" capable of sustaining a continued Conservative resurgence. In fact, the size and volatility of this component of the electorate would tend to suggest at least as much uncertainty in the electorates of the future as has existed in the recent past.

Viewed over a slightly longer period of time than two elections, the changes that have taken place in the composition of the Canadian electorate are nevertheless quite substantial. A majority of the Canadian electorate of 1984 had come of voting age in the "Trudeau era" or later (see figure 2.3). Only slightly over one-fourth of all those eligible to vote in 1984 might be said to belong to a "pre-Diefenbaker" generation of voters associated with the long and seemingly more stable King–St. Laurent era of Canadian politics. While such changes occur slowly over relatively longer periods of time, there is clearly no reason to believe that the Canadian electorate of 1984 was any more stable in its political alignments than those of the past. Indeed, the opposite may well prove to be the case.

Periodic nonvoters also represent a potentially important source of change from one election to another in Canada. The higher turnout of the 1984 election compared with that of 1980 brought back into the electorate a number of voters who had failed to vote in 1980. Some of these would also have contributed to the higher turnout of the 1979 election, although it would be a mistake to categorize them as "stay-at-home" Conservatives who returned to the active electorate only when their party's fortunes improved. While the

Conservatives were to some extent hurt by the lower turnout of 1980, non-voters in Canadian elections generally represent a diverse group, showing slight trends in one direction or another in certain elections, but almost never moving in large numbers toward a single party.[26] They are also voters with generally lower levels of political interest and partisan commitment, and as such represent a more unpredictable element from one election to another. Most Canadians vote at least occasionally in federal elections, and there is no long-term trend toward declining turnout in Canada, as has been observed in some other countries. Thus, in a relatively high turnout election such as that of 1984, the influx of a contingent of previous nonvoters, together with the entry of new voters, represented an additional source of potential volatility.

Beyond 1984

Political scientists often examine the outcomes of elections for evidence of lasting changes in political systems. The gradual erosion of the "New Deal" alignment in the United States, together with the increasing evidence of political independence among American voters, has led observers to characterize contemporary American politics as "dealigning." [27] Similarly, recent studies of British politics have found evidence of a decline in the traditional class alignment, with a consummate weakening of established party ties.[28] The result in both instances has been greater volatility in elections, as evidenced by an increase in the incidence of such phenomena as ticket splitting, switching of votes, support for third parties, and fluctuating turnout. While there may be a number of causes of volatility in elections, dealignment is often a condition under which various short-term influences can exhibit greater effects.

While evidence of dealignment of party systems has been well documented in several countries, corresponding evidence of the development of new alignments has been more uncertain. Although volatility in elections may be an intermediate step in an extended process of party realignment, one would expect that the development of new alignments would slowly result in the establishment of more stable, albeit new, electoral patterns. However, in spite of some evidence of the development of new electoral patterns in such countries as the United States, Britain, or Germany, there has as yet been no indication that such patterns will prove to be more stable over the long term than have those of the recent past.

In spite of the electoral shock of 1984 there is little indication in Canada at the present time of either genuine dealigning or realigning trends. Realignment would imply the replacement of one stable, long-term pattern of alignment by another. But, as has been argued here, long-term forces (at least at the individual level) are relatively weak in Canada, and there is no evidence to date that a new, stronger set of such forces is emerging. Indeed, Canadians continue to define much of their political world in terms of highly changeable short-term forces such as policy or issue factors, style and performance, or leadership. A realignment would require a solidification of at least some of the longer-term forces that affect voting in Canada, as well as a strengthening of individual party ties. Although there will undoubtedly be some temptation to interpret the 1984 Conservative victory in such terms because of its magnitude, no such strengthening of long-term trends appears probable in Canadian politics in the immediate future.

Neither is the pattern of dealignment that exists in Canada part of an ongoing, dynamic process that could lead to the abandonment or further weakening of party ties. Canadian federal politics is already quite substantially "dealigned," as evidenced by the relative weakness of individual party ties and the high levels of volatility in individual voting behavior. The proportion of flexible partisans remains more or less constant over time, but nevertheless accounts for nearly two-thirds of the total electorate. The interpretation of Canadian politics that best fits the data reported here is that of a political system that is already substantially dealigned, but nevertheless is undergoing relatively little fundamental change. This condition of dealignment is stable in the sense that it is not being significantly altered by electoral trends such as the Conservative victory of 1984 or by patterns of long-term replacement in the electorate. The Conservative landslide appears to differ from other recent elections only in the uniformity and size of the swing against the incumbent Liberal government. In this sense it bears similarities to the Diefenbaker landslide of 1958 or the less sweeping Conservative victory of 1979. Neither of these elections resulted in a permanent redrawing of the Canadian political landscape, although Diefenbaker did establish the new base of the Conservatives in the Canadian west. The short-term effects evident in virtually every Canadian election have generally left little lasting imprint on the partisan makeup of the electorate. Nor has generational change contributed to any longer-term process of dealignment or realignment, because the younger cohorts entering the electorate share many of the partisan attributes of older voters. Thus, although a majority of all those currently eligible to vote in Canada have attained voting age since the accession of Pierre Trudeau as prime minister in 1968, there is no evidence of fundamental changes that might be attributable to patterns of socialization of new voters or to the replacement of one generation by another. If the 1984 election in some way heralds the emergence of a new generation of Conservative voters, the forces that would lead to such a development almost certainly lie in the future rather than in the events of the recent past.

The Canadian electorate continues to be one with relatively weak long-term attachments to political parties, low ideological commitment, and high responsiveness to short-term forces such as leaders, issues, or political events. In such an environment, elections remain highly unpredictable, although the difficulty of harnessing all of these forces simultaneously in a large and diverse country will always present a formidable task to any party or leader. Events of the future may yet cause 1984 to be seen as the inauguration of a "Mulroney era" in Canadian politics. But it is more likely that the 1984 election, like that of 1958, will stand as compelling evidence of the underlying volatility of the Canadian electorate.

Notes

1. For a more detailed development of this argument, see Lawrence LeDuc, "Canada: the Politics of Stable Dealignment," in Russell Dalton, Scott Flanagan, and Paul Allen Beck, eds., *Electoral Change in Industrial Democracies* (Princeton: Princeton University Press, 1985), pp. 402–23. See also Harold Clarke, Jane Jenson, Lawrence LeDuc, and Jon Pammett, *Absent Mandate: the Politics of Discontent in Canada* (Toronto: Gage, 1984).

2. Studies have been conducted in every Canadian federal election since 1965. For a discussion of some of the findings of these studies with respect to individual voting behavior in Canada, see John Meisel, *Working Papers in Canadian Politics* (Montreal: McGill-Queen's University Press, 1975); Harold Clarke, Jane Jenson, Lawrence LeDuc, and Jon Pammett, *Political Choice in Canada* (Toronto: McGraw-Hill Ryerson, 1979); and Clarke et al., *Absent Mandate*.

3. For a discussion of some of these aspects of the Canadian electoral system and a review of various reform proposals, see William Irvine, *Does Canada Need a New Electoral System?* (Kingston: Institute of Intergovernmental Relations, Queen's University, 1979).

4. Sociodemographic variables have generally been able to explain no more than about 10 percent of the variation in individual partisanship and voting behavior in Canada. See Clarke et al., *Political Choice in Canada*, pp. 93–128. See also W. Irvine and H. Gold, "Do Frozen Cleavages Ever Go Stale?" *British Journal of Political Science*, 10 (1980), pp. 213–25; and Arend Lijphart, "Religious vs. Linguistic vs. Class Voting: The 'Crucial Experiment' of Comparing Belgium, Canada, South Africa, and Switzerland," *American Political Science Review*, 73 (1979), pp. 442–58.

5. Robert Alford, *Party and Society: The Anglo-American Democracies* (Chicago: Rand-McNally, 1963).

6. See W. Irvine, "Explaining the Religious Basis of Canadian Partisan Identity," *Canadian Journal of Political Science*, 7 (1974), pp. 560–65.

7. Federal-provincial inconsistency of party identification is correlated with instability over time in much the same way as is the more conventional modifier of partisanship—intensity. See Lawrence LeDuc, Harold Clarke, Jane Jenson, and Jon Pammett, "Partisan Instability in Canada: Evidence from a New Panel Study," *American Political Science Review*, 78 (1984), pp. 470–84.

8. Ibid., p. 477. See also Lawrence LeDuc, "The Dynamic Properties of Party Identification: a Four Nation Comparison," *European Journal of Political Research*, 9 (1981), pp. 257–68.

9. The terms "durable" and "flexible" partisanship, as applied to the Canadian electorate, are developed and explained in greater detail in Clarke et al., *Political Choice in Canada*, pp. 301–19; and in Clarke et al., *Absent Mandate*, pp. 55–75.

10. See Clarke et al., *Absent Mandate*, p. 186.

11. *Toronto Globe and Mail*, August 24, 1984, and August 25, 1984.

12. *Toronto Globe and Mail*, August 24, 1984, pp. 1, 4.

13. Clarke et al., *Absent Mandate*, p. 186.

14. In the July 5–7 Gallup Poll, for example, 398 out of a total of 1,049 respondents (38 percent) were classified as undecided. Gallup normally drops these in its computation of party percentages. *The Gallup Report*, July 15, 1984.

15. See Clarke et al., *Political Choice in Canada*, pp. 275–77.

16. These studies were directed by Harold Clarke, Jane Jenson, Lawrence LeDuc, and Jon Pammett, and funded by the Social Sciences and Humanities Research Council of Canada. Fieldwork was conducted by Canadian Facts, Ltd., of Toronto. The 1974 National Election Study was a single-wave postelection survey of the eligible Canadian electorate, consisting of extensive personal interviews with a national sample of 2,562 respondents. In 1979, 1,338 of these respondents were reinterviewed to create a 1974–79 panel, and two new cross-section samples of the electorate were also interviewed in a major postelection survey. Following the February 1980 federal election precipitated by the parliamentary defeat of the Clark government, all respondents to both the 1974–79 panel and the 1979 cross-section surveys were contacted by telephone. Successful reinterviews were obtained with 1,747 respondents, of whom 857 were also members of the 1974–79 panel. A fourth wave of interviewing was carried out in Quebec only following the May 1980 referendum. The findings of these studies with respect to partisan changes over time are discussed in greater detail in LeDuc et al., "Partisan Instability in Canada."

17. Excluding new voters and those not voting in at least one of the elections. Ibid., p. 474.

18. Although movement to and from nonvoting is greater in the United States because of the unique characteristics of the American electoral system. Ibid., p. 477.

19. Ibid.

20. These questions are similar to those employed in American election studies. "Is there anything in particular that you like about the federal Liberal party? Anything else? Is there anything in particular that you dislike about the Liberals? Anything else?", etc. The sequence was repeated for all parties (federal and provincial), and up to three like and dislike mentions for each party were coded for each respondent. Multiple responses to these questions were categorized according to type as shown in table 2.4. For a more detailed discussion of these data, see Clarke et al., *Political Choice in Canada*, pp. 171–205; and Clarke et al., *Absent Mandate*, pp. 10–16.

21. Some examples drawn from the 1974–79 data illustrate this point. While 57 percent of the national sample specifically mentioned inflation as one of the two most important issues in the 1974 election, only 18 percent of the 1979 sample took the same position. Similarly, 37 percent of the 1979 sample mentioned various confederation issues as most important, while only 5 percent of the 1974 sample had cited issues in this category. A more extensive discussion of the volatility of issues in Canada, with comparisons to similar phenomena in other countries, may be found in Kai Hildebrandt, Harold Clarke, Lawrence LeDuc, and Jon Pammett, "Issue Volatility and Partisan Linkages in a Period of Economic Decline in Canada, Great Britain, the United States, and the Federal Republic of Germany," paper presented to the annual meeting of the Canadian Political Science Association, Vancouver, 1983.

22. This categorization is employed in Hildebrandt et al., ibid. See also Clarke et al., *Absent Mandate*, pp. 77–84.

23. Turner was not really a new figure in that he had served in cabinet positions in both the Pearson and Trudeau governments and had been a candidate for the party leadership against Trudeau in 1968. However, his retirement from politics in 1975 began a nine-year absence from federal politics that effectively gave his 1984 comeback an appearance of freshness that it otherwise might not have had.

24. LeDuc, "Canada: the Politics of Stable Dealignment," pp. 411–14.

25. Ibid., p. 412.

26. Ibid., p. 414–16. See also Clarke et al., *Political Choice in Canada*, pp. 380–89.
27. See Norman Nie, Sidney Verba, and John Petrocik, *The Changing American Voter* (Cambridge: Harvard University Press, 1976), esp. chs. 3 and 4.
28. See Ivor Crewe, Bo Sarlvik, and James Alt, "Partisan Dealignment in Britain," *British Journal of Political Science*, 7 (1977), pp. 129–90. See also Bo Sarlvik and Ivor Crewe, *Decade of Dealignment* (Cambridge: Cambridge University Press, 1983).

3 Choosing New Party Leaders: The Progressive Conservatives in 1983, the Liberals in 1984

R. KENNETH CARTY

In 1979 and 1980 Joe Clark and Pierre Trudeau fought successive general elections in Canada. Clark's Progressive Conservatives won the first of these, and Trudeau's Liberals won the second. Four years later Canada's two major political parties were led by men who had refused to stand in those elections. Neither was a stranger to the Canadian public: Brian Mulroney had contested the Conservative leadership in 1976 and John Turner had run for the Liberal leadership in 1968. Yet when they captured control of their respective parties they did so from outside the parliamentary caucus—some might say *because* they were outside it. Such a development would be almost inconceivable in other Anglo-parliamentary systems. In Canada it was hardly an occasion for comment. Canadian parliamentarians had long ago lost the right to choose party leaders to mass conventions; and by the 1980s the convention process was orchestrating the development of elaborate, public campaigns for the parties' leadership.

Choosing Party Leaders

Parliamentary systems require that party leaders provide daily leadership in the intense and cloistered atmosphere of the House. Whatever other wider demands are put upon them by the political system, leaders must constantly provide direction to the caucus, set the pace, tactics, and mood for the parliamentary party, and be capable of rallying their troops when under attack. Little wonder, then, that elected politicians instinctively seek a leader from amongst themselves, wanting a colleague who can lead them in parliamentary battle, someone who has proved it by service in the ranks.

The norms and procedures for choosing, and deposing, leaders vary from party to party and country to country. Australian parties seem preoccupied with the electoral appeal of their leaders and have developed mechanisms that allow the leadership to be challenged on a moment's notice. Not surprisingly, this has a destabilizing effect on the parties, whether they are in government or opposition.[1] In Britain party leaders cannot be formally challenged so readily, and when contests occur those voting seem surprisingly unconcerned with electoral considerations.[2] What has traditionally been common to these systems, and to those of New Zealand and Ireland, which also inherited British parliamentary institutions, is an understanding that the party leader must be a member of the caucus, and that parliamentarians will decide who the party leader will be.[3] This has meant that few are eligible for their party's leadership and that the selection has been a closed, oligarchic process, "the kind that might occur in a medium-sized private club," in which votes are influenced by "personal likes and dislikes."[4]

Canadian Practice   Since confederation Canada's two leading parties have used three fairly distinct processes to choose their leaders, and each process has produced a characteristic type of leader.[5]

Before 1919. For the first half of the nineteenth century, Canadian party leaders were chosen by methods that would have been familiar to politicians anywhere in the British Empire. Extraparliamentary organization (beyond constituency associations) did not exist; the parliamentary caucus was the party and so chose its leader from within itself. Whether formal votes were taken or not, it was the opinions of the party's leading notables that counted most, and that small group normally determined who became leader. The process was one of soundings being taken, views being weighed, and then a new leader "emerging" to widespread party support. When the party was in office the choice of a new leader meant the choice of a new prime minister, so the governor general, exercising the still-important prerogative power of the Crown, was necessarily involved. During the 1890s this drew the governor general into the tangled leadership politics of the Conservatives as they sought to find a successor to Macdonald, who had led them for four decades.[6]

The men chosen as party leaders during this period took on the burden of organizing, directing, and personifying the party, both at election time and over the parliamentary year. As it involved significant personal sacrifice, considerable pressure was often required to get individuals to accept the leadership when their party was in opposition. Those chosen had typically served a parliamentary apprenticeship, most had ministerial experience, and they held office at the pleasure of their colleagues. This system, with much else in Canadian politics, passed away with World War I.

The coming of conventions. The conscription crisis and subsequent general election in 1917 tore the Liberal party apart, with many (English-speakers) deserting to enter the Conservative-led Unionist government. In the aftermath of the war Sir Wilfrid Laurier faced the task of finding a way to bring mutually disaffected Liberals back together. He settled on a plan for a large national convention charged with defining Liberal policy for the future. But Laurier died between the calling of the convention and its meeting in August 1919 which, willy-nilly, was transformed into a gathering to choose a new leader. The caucus itself chose a house leader in the customary way but no one assumed that this made him the party's national leader.[7]

The convention of 1919 marked a significant shift in the life of the party, for the politicians were handing over to partisan activists the power to choose their leader. This was all the more unusual because there really was no formal, mass extraparliamentary national party organization, or even regular party conventions—this was only the second such meeting in Canada since 1867! The 1917 election had reduced the Liberal caucus to little more than a Quebec rump, visibly unrepresentative of the country's diverse regions. The appeal of a convention was that it could overcome this deficiency and provide the party with a mechanism for incorporating all the regional interests in the selection of its leader. That similar conventions had already been used in many provinces, some influenced by neighboring Americans, no doubt helped to make the Liberals' 1919 national convention seem a natural development.

But however expedient, the Liberals' use of a convention to choose Mackenzie King as their leader was still seen as an exceptional device for coping with a special situation. Thus, the very next year, when the Conservatives came to replace Robert Borden they resorted to traditional practices in choosing Arthur Meighen. His electoral defeats at the hands of King made the Conservatives reconsider, and in 1927 they copied the Liberals by using a convention to select R. B. Bennett as their new leader. Bennett won the next election. His victory, like King's, legitimated the use of leadership conventions, which were soon being portrayed as the democratic face of Canadian parties.

In fact, the three Liberal and five Conservative conventions held prior to the 1960s were hardly models of party democracy. On the whole they were smallish (up to 1,500 delegates), not very competitive events. Between 40 and 50 percent of the delegates came in some ex officio capacity, while many of the constituency representatives owed their places to an M.P. and voted as he wanted. As Chubby Power (himself a candidate for the Liberal leadership in 1948) acknowledged, this "indirectly perpetuate[d] the old custom" of caucus selection.[8]

For all that, conventions did make a difference. Three times they chose men who were not members of the parliamentary party. (One of them, John Bracken, the Progressive premier of Manitoba, made the Conservatives change their name to Progressive Conservatives, to the subsequent delight of all who relish the idiosyncrasies of political language.) And on several occasions conventions downplayed parliamentary experience and opted for the more junior candidate. In both of these ways conventions opened up the party leadership to individuals who would not have been selected under the traditional rules.[9]

In both parties, national conventions stimulated the development of extraparliamentary organizations to direct their affairs between conventions. Eventually these organizations grew to compete with the caucuses as the decision-making heart of the party, with the issue of leadership at the center of the struggle. The problem was that while it was clear that the party-in-convention chose the leader, there was no agreement on who might depose him. Mackenzie King is alleged to have told his parliamentary colleagues that he was finally responsible only to the wider party that had chosen him. But it was in the Conservative party that the tension between extraparliamentary organization and caucus was to be fully fought out.

After defeats in the 1963 and 1965 general elections, many prominent Conservatives, led by the party's national president, decided that Mr. Diefenbaker had to be replaced as leader. Diefenbaker disagreed and, commanding the support of a majority of the Conservative caucus, refused to budge. Despite the position of the parliamentary party, after some prolonged maneuvering the party organization managed to call a leadership convention for 1967. Caucus members were forced to recognize it, and some, including Diefenbaker himself, became contestants. In the end Nova Scotia's premier, Robert Stanfield, won on the fifth ballot and it appeared that the convention had completely usurped the right to make and break party leaders. Not quite. Stanfield and his successor, Joe Clark, would both learn the hard way that authority had simply been divided. Neither ever completely commanded the caucus he had been imposed upon, and in a parliamentary system, that eventually proved fatal to their leadership.

The battle over the Conservative leadership in the mid-1960s marked the end of the tidy, controlled convention. The election of Stanfield, and then Pierre Trudeau by the Liberals in 1968, marked the beginning of a new leadership politics and the transformation of political organization from one end of the country to the other.

Modern Leadership Campaigns

Recent leadership contests have been sprawling, semipublic battles. As table 3.1 indicates, conventions have doubled in size to over 3,000 delegates. When another 2,000 alternates, and as many media representatives all crowd into a convention hall with them, the resulting crush of humanity becomes impossible to manage. Over three days simple communication degenerates into a welter of rumor and bravado and even the best-organized campaign verges on the incoherent.[10] And there are more campaigns, for there has also been

Table 3.1 Major Party Conventions: 1919–84.

Convention	Winner	No. of delegates	No. of candidates	No. of ballots
1919 Liberal	King	947	4	3
1927 Conservative	Bennett	1,564	6	2
1938 Conservative	Manion	1,565	5	2
1942 Conservative	Bracken	870	5	2
1948 Liberal	St. Laurent	1,227	3	1
1948 Conservative	Drew	1,242	3	1
1956 Conservative	Diefenbaker	1,284	3	1
1958 Liberal	Pearson	1,380	3	1
1967 Conservative	Stanfield	2,233	11	5
1968 Liberal	Trudeau	2,366	8	4
1976 Conservative	Clark	2,360	11	4
1983 Conservative	Mulroney	2,988	8	4
1984 Liberal	Turner	3,435	7	2

Source: Adapted from R. Krause and L. LeDuc, "Voting Behaviour and Electoral Strategies."

a growth in the number of serious candidates. This has meant that conventions have become genuinely competitive: they have required several ballots to determine a winner. At the last two Conservative conventions the first-ballot leader was defeated by a coalition that evolved on subsequent ballots; and in only one of the last five conventions (Turner in 1984) could the outcome have been safely predicted.

In these new, larger, competitive conventions the rules work against any ordered process of bargaining and coalition-building among candidates.[11] Delegates cast an individual secret vote, there is little time between successive ballots for candidates to assess the situation and respond appropriately, and those who are either eliminated automatically (the bottom candidate on each ballot) or choose to withdraw are given no opportunity to address their supporters. As a result, despite candidates' attempts to signal their preferences by moving to another's box on the convention floor, they cannot deliver their followers, who are driven to watching corridor television sets to find out what is going on. None of this facilitates brokerage; it fragments the process as candidates must appeal directly to individual delegates for first-ballot support, or their vote on subsequent ballots.

There has been a proliferation in the types of delegates eligible to vote at leadership conventions. So fragmented have the conventions become that there are at least eighteen different ways one can become a delegate. Delegates now comprise M.P.s, candidates nominated for the next election, members of provincial houses, a range of elected or appointed party organization officials, representatives of demographically identifiable groups such as students, youth, and women, as well as those elected from the local constituency associations. The number of local delegates (now six Conservatives and seven Liberals per constituency) has increased so that they remain a small majority of the convention, but the addition of other groups has tended to dilute the regional imperatives that led to the first conventions.[12] As we shall see, it also provides incentives for candidates to create fictitious organizations and flood existing ones with personal supporters in order to win delegates.

The individuals who attend leadership conventions are hardly typical Canadians. For one thing they have an unnatural appetite for politics and are willing to spend a good deal of their own time and money on it. About half of the delegates to the 1983 and 1984 conventions came from families with an annual income of over $50,000, and over 70 percent had postsecondary education and middle-class occupations. They reflect the country's roots inasmuch as half the delegates' families had been in Canada for four generations or more.[13] By any standard they constitute a socioeconomic elite. While those who become delegates tend to have more developed and coherent attitudes on public policy than average voters, they are far from being ideologues and, as one might expect, there is a wide divergence of views on most issues in both parties.[14]

The most dramatic change of all has been the development of a long, elaborate, and expensive preconvention campaign by leadership candidates. Chubby Power claims he asked no one to vote for him in 1948, and even twenty years later the most elaborate campaign reached only one-third of the delegates before the convention. By the 1980s, however, the candidates were attempting to win the leadership long before the convention actually met.[15] They developed highly personalized organizations to help them influence the delegate selection process and then to extract commitments of support from those chosen. Thus, by the time of the convention the vast majority of delegates have been subjected to an endless round of phone calls, mailings, and meetings with candidates, as well as the incessant probing of their preferences by the media.

Only two or three of the candidates are likely to be able to mount and finance a campaign stretching from one end of the country to the other over several months.[16] Other candidates must settle for more modest efforts and, while they can hope to influence the direction of the campaign, they cannot expect to capture the leadership. This means that there are two rather distinct types of campaigns going on simultaneously, and that the number and mix of candidates seeking delegate support varies across the country. Serious candidates can run from a base in the party organization or they can run as populists, claiming to represent ordinary party members and ordinary Canadians.

The 1983 Conservative and 1984 Liberal leadership contests had all this and more. Both were contested by a number of leading party figures, but in each case it was decided between the only two men able to build a national organization. Though Brian Mulroney and John Turner were both outsiders, their roads to the leadership were quite different. Mulroney was forced to run against most of the party's apparatchiks, who were huddled behind Joe Clark; Turner was embraced by the Liberal establishment and used it to defeat Jean Chrétien, M.P. and senior Trudeau minister, who was left to run as a nationalistic, populist tribune. It was this pair of outcomes that shifted the historic balance between the parties and set the stage for the electoral earthquake of September 1984.

The Tory Syndrome: 1983

Conservatives have fought over their leadership, and their leaders, for most of this century but the conflict has been particularly intense for the last twenty years. Many members of the parliamentary party never forgave Stanfield for replacing their beloved Diefenbaker, who continued to harrumph from the back benches.[17] After three electoral defeats Stanfield resigned and Joe Clark was chosen as his successor at a convention in 1976. Clark was a surprising choice—JOE WHO? screamed the headlines—for he was a young, unproven backbencher whose candidacy had not been taken seriously by many. He had finished third on the first ballot and gone on to win on the fourth, but he had virtually no support among his parliamentary colleagues.[18] Many were openly contemptuous of him, and his leadership of the caucus was never very secure. He brought the party to office in 1979 but it was a Pyrrhic victory, for the Tories were in a precarious minority situation and had in fact won a half-million fewer votes than the Liberals. Still, the defeat of his government, and the loss of the 1980 election to the much-vilified Trudeau, came as a shock and extraordinarily bitter pill to most Conservatives.[19] They fixed their disappointments and their blame on Clark. Many decided that he was really a wimp:[20] he had blown their first chance at power in sixteen years; he couldn't win another election; and he had to be replaced by a real leader.

Clark was determined to hang on, convinced that he could be prime minister again. His supporters prevailed at the 1981 Conservative general meeting, where there was a two to one vote against holding a leadership convention. But, with one-third signaling their discontent, Clark knew his position was precarious and that his opponents would do all they could to undermine his leadership. Despite the fact that the Tories led the Liberals in the Gallup polls from mid-1981 on, a hard core in the caucus was determined to unseat him.[21] Sometime in late 1982 a bargain was struck: if Clark had a better vote at the next general meeting there would be a truce; if not, a significant portion of the caucus would openly demand his resignation. Both sides went to work with a vengeance. By the time the 2,400 delegates gathered in Winnipeg for the party's biennial meeting in January 1983, Clark's leadership was the only topic on their minds. Two-thirds of the delegates again backed Clark—after two years of effort Clark had increased his support by less than 1 percent! Recognizing the writing on the wall he immediately called for a leadership convention to clear the air. To make sure all understood his intentions he also declared that he would be a candidate and that he intended to win.[22]

The Tories had come full circle. In 1966 the extraparliamentary party had effectively deposed a leader who had the support of a majority of the parliamentary party. In 1983 the caucus returned the favor by forcing a leadership convention against the express wish of a majority of the extraparliamentary party. Authority over the party leadership, divided and muddled by the events of the 1960s, is shared, and leaders must simultaneously ride two horses—the caucus and the extraparliamentary party convention.[23] The continuing dilemma of Progressive Conservative politics remained that of finding a leader who could keep both horses running together. Given that the party had now deposed the only two leaders who had led it to power since the Great Depression, its condition in the spring of 1983 was hardly encouraging. Yet, as the party prepared for another leadership campaign and convention, it soon became clear there would be no lack of candidates.

Candidates   Joe Clark was not going to roll over and play dead, and as the campaign started it was far from clear he would be defeated. He had, after all, just won the support of two-thirds of the party and many of those would stay loyal either for personal reasons or because they thought leadership squabbles were damaging the party's public appeal. As leader and former prime minister, Clark had the support of much of the party establishment, who owed their positions to him.[24] This gave him a solid base amongst many of those who would become ex officio delegates to the leadership convention, and a good deal of direct influence over the selection of many others. It also meant he had a campaign organization in place and could get a jump on any opponents. The problem he faced was gathering enough support to win quickly, for those who came out against him would obviously have a strong personal incentive to see to it that "anyone but Clark" (later known as the ABC factor) won.

There were two principal opponents: John Crosbie and Brian Mulroney. Crosbie was a leading figure in the parliamentary party. A jovial Newfoundlander who was very popular in the party, he had served in both Liberal and Conservative governments in his home province and had even run for the provincial Liberal leadership in 1969. After entering national politics he had articulated a moderately right-wing position and portrayed himself as a realist who would squarely face the country's economic difficulties. As Clark's minister of finance in 1979 he had convinced many that he had the ability to lead. Crosbie supporters had been secretly planning a leadership bid for two years and were ready. But in one important respect the candidate himself was not: John Crosbie had yet to learn French, the language of over a quarter of the electorate.

In contrast, Mulroney was an outsider who, despite running for the party leadership in 1976 and finishing second on the first ballot, had never stood for public office. But after two decades of service in the underpopulated back rooms of the Conservative party in Quebec, he was well known and well connected. Mulroney had been a successful Montreal labor lawyer and then jumped to the presidency of the American-owned Iron Ore Company of Canada, a major force in the Quebec economy. His first attempt at the leadership had been an expensive, flashy affair that had offended the party's Protestant sensibilities. The fiercely loyal personal organization he had gathered around him, in the style of the traditional Irish political machine boss, were determined not to repeat that mistake. This time they decided to run a low-key campaign that would emphasize his other persona: he would be Brian Mulroney, the working-class boy from the small Quebec town of Baie Comeau, who had been educated at Nova Scotia's Catholic St. Francis Xavier University and (in French) the Laval law school, and then made his way by ability and hard work. He would run as a Québecer who spoke the province's language and understood its impulses. He never tired of pointing out that of the 102 ridings with substantial francophone populations, only two returned Conservative M.P.s and it was this reality that kept the party in opposition. Mulroney promised the Tories he would win Quebec.

Three minor candidates joined the fray. Two of these, David Crombie and Michael Wilson, were M.P.s who had served in Clark's government, but decided to seek the top job once it was declared vacant. Crombie, a former mayor of Toronto and a self-proclaimed "Red Tory," was running to remind Conservatives of their party's progressive and collectivist traditions, and to try to halt the party's apparent drift to the right. Wilson, a former securities company executive in Toronto's financial community, portrayed himself as a pragmatic man of the center and hoped to emerge as a compromise candidate if the leading contenders did one another in. Both needed to establish a base in Ontario to be credible but found that impossible when many of the leading Conservatives refused to commit themselves until they knew whether Premier William Davis was going to become a candidate.[25] The third minor candidate was a complete outsider. Peter Pocklington, an Edmonton businessman, was best known across the country as the owner of the Edmonton Oilers hockey team. A rich, self-made entrepreneur, he represented the alienation of new western wealth from national decisionmaking. But he also disliked governments of any color and wanted to be prime minister so he could "restore" the free market and lead a return to traditional, conservative morality. His campaign organization of hired professionals and Amway distributors soon discovered that a Reaganite "New Right" appeal might be cheered but would win few delegate votes in the Canadian Conservative party.[26]

Two fringe candidates, John Gamble and Neil Fraser, rounded out the list. Gamble was an M.P. from Toronto who wanted Clark destroyed and his "leftish advisors" purged from the party. Gamble's own preference was for a sharp turn to the right, which was to be signaled by the restoration of the death penalty and the end to government handouts. Fraser was a rather eccentric case. His anti–metric system campaign had cost him his job in the federal public service and he was simply using the Conservative leadership race as an opportunity to continue his crusade. As his views often degenerated into an attack on things French, he was a considerable embarrassment to the party and ignored wherever possible. And, though all eight candidates persisted through to the first ballot of the convention, it soon became clear that it was a three-man race.

Selecting the Delegates   The leading candidates knew that the leadership could be won or lost in the struggles over delegate selection in the weeks before the convention even assembled. Clark's position as leader gave him an immediate advantage. He moved quickly to have as many of his declared supporters as possible named as ex officio delegates. This effort was a considerable success, and Clark ended up with the support of far more of these nonconstituency delegates (who constituted 47 percent of the total) than any one of his opponents. While many of these individuals were slow to commit themselves, it became clear in this early skirmishing that there were only three serious candidates: Clark had supporters in all provinces, but of his opponents only Crosbie and Mulroney could win support in at least half the provinces. To the surprise of many, especially in the Mulroney camp, Clark took over 60 percent of Quebec's nonconstituency delegates: to no one's surprise Newfoundland's native son, Crosbie, swept his home province.

Among the nonconstituency delegates one category seemed particularly elastic. Largely a consequence of the imaginative work of the three major candidates' organizations, the number of accredited PC student campus clubs mushroomed. Crosbie's team proved to be extraordinarily creative, ending up with twenty-one campus clubs in Newfoundland, a province with just one University. (Every driving school and beauty college suddenly seemed to sprout a Tory club, which was then quickly "recognized" by Crosbie's provincial allies.) In the end, the province's student delegates outnumbered its constituency representatives by 50 percent. But on the whole these, and many other organizational battles like them, took place behind the closed doors of party meetings. The selection of constituency delegates, on the other hand, generally occurred in the full glare of a public meeting.

Each of the 282 federal constituency organizations was entitled to send four senior and two youth delegates. In almost all cases they were elected by a meeting of all members of the local party association. Since membership is at best a loose concept in Canada's major parties, it could normally be purchased cheaply any time before the selection meeting. This made the process open to manipulation by the candidates' agents. The press was full of stories of how meetings were being packed, often by individuals with only the most dubious connection to the Conservative party; this was especially the case in Quebec, where a busload of derelicts from a Montreal inner-city mission who were brought to a local association meeting got headlines across the country. But this sort of activity took place only in a minority of constituencies, usually where there was no local organization of any strength. In about one-quarter of the cases delegates were selected as part of an identified slate; but well over half were chosen by their friends and neighbors without having made any commitment as to how they intended to vote at the convention. Clark again appeared to have done very well, capturing some 60 percent of the constituency delegates who had declared their preference. Of his opponents, only Mulroney had managed to win delegates from over half the provinces.[27]

The Campaign   Once the process of selecting the delegates was over, an intense campaign for their support, on the first or subsequent ballots began. Many, perhaps most of the delegates were publicly uncommitted at this stage. Clark was well ahead but he was still considerably short of the needed majority and there were widespread doubts that his support would grow. All the serious candidates spent April and May crisscrossing the country giving speeches and holding informal, personal meetings with as many delegates as possible. These campaigns were supported by mailings, position papers, and endorsements by party worthies, while elaborate computerized systems were used to track shifting support patterns. The media was reporting this campaign activity as assiduously as any general election, so even the most trivial event or utterance was likely to come to the delegates' notice. Yet, in the welter of speeches and promises, it soon became clear that there was really only one important issue—the Conservative delegates desperately wanted a leader who would take the party to power, and the developing campaign was increasingly shaped by this imperative.

The search for a winner soon effectively eliminated all but the big three candidates. Gamble and Fraser were never taken seriously by anyone, Pocklington was perceived as too right-wing, Crombie as too left-wing, and Wilson as so uninspiring that he couldn't win even in his own Toronto backyard. Only Clark, Crosbie, and Mulroney seemed to have the ability to command the substantial personal support necessary in a national party leader while at the same time appearing to be to the conservative side of the well-trodden political center. Clark urged delegates to keep the party on its current course (behind him), and argued that the polls proved they would soon be back in power. Implicit in his appeal was the claim that the party's incessant regicide was damaging its appeal to ordinary voters, who could not be expected to support a party that constantly attacked its own leader. Crosbie's claim to the leadership rested on his considerable personal appeal and on his record as a minister of finance who would recognize and face up to the country's difficulties. He was portrayed as the man of experience and competence. Mulroney, the outsider, quickly became a serious candidate because he proved he could build an organization capable of mobilizing support among young Conservatives, especially in populous Ontario and all across Quebec, and because he offered the party the opportunity to end its long alienation from French Canada.

It was French Canada that ultimately doomed Crosbie. More accurately, it was Crosbie's unwillingness or inability to cope with the changed political imperatives in a Canada that had become a self-consciously bilingual political community that did him in. In the years since his entry into national politics John Crosbie had not learned French. Since he had been known to parry with Prime Minister Trudeau in Latin and Greek across the floor of the House of Commons, few could believe he could not have mastered French. It appeared that he simply had not bothered. As the campaign wore on he was increasingly confronted by journalists demanding to know how he could appeal to Québecers when he did not speak their language. Finally, in a moment of exasperation during a scrum with reporters, he blurted out he didn't speak Chinese or German either but that didn't mean he couldn't deal with people in those communities, and that party leadership was not restricted to the minority of Canadians who were bilingual. This apparent coupling of French with foreign languages was a disaster, for it reminded the Québecers why they had been shunning the Tories for several generations. And English-speaking Conservatives began to realize that a unilingual leader was unlikely to lead them to power. The episode dramatically confirmed that national party leadership in Canada had indeed become the preserve of the bilingual.

As the delegates gathered in Ottawa in early June, no candidate commanded a majority of the delegates and it was widely expected that several ballots would be required to determine a winner. By this stage of the race 8o percent of the delegates had made a commitment of first-ballot support. Clark's people were primarily tied together by organizational loyalties, while Mulroney's supporters were more likely to declare a personal commitment to their candidate.[28] It remained to see which of these coalitions would hold together and then grow in the heat of the convention.

Table 3.2 Progressive Conservative Convention Ballot Results, 1983 (percentages in parentheses).

	Ballot			
	1st	2nd	3rd	4th
Clark	1,091 (36.5)	1,085 (36.7)	1,058 (35.8)	1,325 (45.5)
Mulroney	874 (29.2)	1,021 (34.6)	1,036 (35.1)	1,584 (54.5)
Crosbie	639 (21.4)	781 (26.4)	858 (29.1)	
Wilson	144 (4.8)			
Crombie	116 (3.9)	67 (2.3)		
Pocklington	102 (3.4)			
Gamble	17 (0.6)			
Fraser	5 (0.2)			

The Decision   Although the convention stretched over three days, as if to justify bringing people from the far ends of the country, and time was filled by talk and partying, everything waited on the results of the first ballot. On the eve of voting the candidates all made their final appeals to the convention, and though Crombie stirred the crowd with a passionate reminder of their Tory traditions of community and social justice, and Crosbie confronted his nemesis by promising to become bilingual, there were few delegates left to be moved. Perceptive observers noted that they heard more French being spoken than at previous Conservative gatherings, perhaps a signal that the party was finally changing.

It took the convention three ballots to winnow the parade of leadership hopefuls and force a showdown between Clark and Mulroney on a final, fourth ballot (see table 3.2). While there may have been a few surprises on the first ballot in terms of the numbers of votes individual candidates received, the general result was as expected. Clark led, but with just 36 percent was far from a majority. Mulroney and Crosbie followed, both in contention with over 20 percent of the vote. The three second-tier candidates all had between 100 and 150 votes (3–5 percent), while Gamble and Fraser managed to win but twenty-two votes between them. Clearly all five of them were out of the race.

At this point all but Fraser, who was automatically eliminated, had to decide where their political future lay. Gamble withdrew and with Fraser signaled his support for Crosbie. More important were the decisions taken by the other three. Both Pocklington and Wilson also withdrew from the ballot but they moved to join the Mulroney camp. Their decision was entirely pragmatic and based on the premise that Clark had to be removed as leader. Mulroney was simply the candidate best placed to defeat him. Though only about half their supporters followed them to Mulroney on the second ballot (many going to Crosbie), their action indicated the strength of the ABC feeling.[29] Crombie decided to stay on the ballot, a decision that would prolong the process but also allow the three major candidates an opportunity to discover how the delegates would react once the field had been cleared.

Clark continued to lead on the second ballot but he won no new support, while Mulroney and Crosbie both saw their vote rise considerably. Crombie was now eliminated and most Conservatives expected him to move back to Clark, who shared many of his moderate views. Instead he moved to Crosbie, further evidence of the widespread conviction among those who had declared against Clark that his reelection would be intolerable.

By the third ballot it was evident that Clark was in serious trouble but his supporters, demonstrating unexpected loyalty, stood by him. John Crosbie had hoped that enough Clark supporters would desert to his camp—in an attempt to stymie Mulroney—to put him on the last ballot, but the language fiasco had probably killed all hope for that scenario. Too many of Clark's supporters came from Quebec. Left off the last ballot, Crosbie made no attempt to indicate his preference or direct his supporters, and the convention moved to its now inevitable outcome.

When Joe Clark lost to Brian Mulroney on the fourth ballot he stood alone. Not one of the four M.P.s, three of whom had served in his government, had rejoined him, nor had the only other Albertan in the race. Their rejection, and that of the convention, was proof that both the parliamentary and extraparliamentary party were convinced that he could not lead them back to power. They preferred to trust themselves to the untried outsider.

The Mulroney Party   Mulroney won partially because he was an outsider for, despite spending most of his adult years as an active partisan, he was not part of the party's elected or appointed establishment. This strengthened his appeal to the large number of Conservatives who felt themselves outsiders, both in terms of the country's and their own party's leadership. The delegates at the convention reflected the widespread view in the parliamentary and extraparliamentary wings of the party that the Clark team had to go. Of all the candidates Mulroney attracted the broadest coalition of support because he was seen as the man best capable of putting a new face on the party and getting it elected.

This was an invitation to build a Mulroney party. Implicit in the choice was a recognition that the party had to come to grips with its past and bridge the gap between French and English. The election of a bilingual Irish Catholic from a small town in Quebec signaled a determination to bury the specters of Riel, conscription, and the British connection. For it was only if Brian Mulroney could accomplish this remolding of the party that Conservatives could expect to become regular contenders for power. And in the meantime they would wait to see who the Liberals would put up against their new leader.

The Governing Party: 1984

Pierre Trudeau had retired as party leader once before, but when, on February 28, 1984, he announced his decision to step down, few doubted that the end of an era had really come.[30] Most Liberals were pleased and agreed that it was time for a change.[31] If the party was to stay in office, (its natural vocation according to most Liberals), it had to be renewed and rebuilt. After sixteen years its leader was very unpopular in many parts of the country and was thought by many to personify every evil in the land; its policies had drifted off the center and it was trailing badly in the polls; and its organization in western Canada was nonexistent.

Despite having invented national party leadership conventions, the Liberals have held only half as many of them as the Conservatives. The party prided itself on its discipline and was wont to note that, unlike the Tories, it stood loyally behind its leaders. Liberals didn't play dirty tricks on one another and the orderly selection of Trudeau's successor would be offered to the voters as another instance of why they should continue to support the party. In the past something like an "apostolic relationship" had characterized Liberal successions and some party members feared that their convention would look more like a coronation than a genuine contest, hardly the thing for a party that saw itself as *the* manifestation of Canadian democracy.

But two aspects of the 1984 Liberal leadership struggle marked it off from previous ones. First, there was no heir apparent in the government, and John Turner, a favorite of many in the party, was obviously disapproved of by Prime Minister Trudeau. There would be no laying on of hands this time. The second difference touched on French-English relations, which Liberals saw as their special preserve. The party's leadership had alternated between French and English speakers but many were questioning whether the party ought to feel bound by this "rule." Trudeau himself intervened in the campaign to defuse the issue by declaring the party ought to choose the best person irrespective of language, a move widely interpreted as legitimating the candidacy of Jean Chrétien, the sole French-speaking Québecer in the race.[32]

Candidates With no obvious successor in the parliamentary party many of the Liberal ministers who might otherwise have been more modest about their leadership potential were encouraged to consider their chances. In the end, six decided to enter the contest, though five were never taken very seriously from the moment they announced their intentions. These soon-to-be also-rans included Donald Johnston, a slightly donnish tax lawyer from anglophone Montreal; John Roberts, an urbane academic from Toronto, whose career gave the impression of having inexplicably stalled; Mark MacGuigan, a former dean of law who, despite holding the senior portfolios of justice and external affairs, had not managed to emerge from the prime minister's shadow; John Munro, a Hamilton party boss whose record and style demonstrated a real attachment to his working-class constituents; and Eugene Whelan, a farmer and populist who prided himself on his ability to masticate the Queen's English (never mind the nation's other official language) and the large green cowboy hat that was his trademark.

What encouraged these men to run is not clear. Few members of the Liberal caucus supported them, and none of them had the backing of a single fellow cabinet minister. Ego must have played a considerable part, but some were seeking to shift the direction of party policy (Johnston to the right, Munro to the left), some were attempting to establish their political weight in the party, while at least one, Whelan, was running simply to oppose John Turner.[33] Two others who probably would have made stronger candidates chose not to run. Lloyd Axworthy, the only powerful elected Liberal in western Canada, threw in with his old mentor Turner; Iona Campagnola remained neutral in her role as national party president.[34] Though realistic, those decisions ensured that there would be neither a western nor a woman candidate.

From the beginning the race was dominated by two men, Jean Chrétien and John Turner. Chrétien liked to portray himself as the little guy from Shawinigan, and in his accented English would remind audiences that he was a typical pea-souper who had spoken only French when first elected to Parliament in the sixties. His deliberately populist personal style stood in sharp contrast to Trudeau's image as an aloof intellectual out of touch with the worries of ordinary Canadians. In fact, Chrétien had been at the center of power in Ottawa for a decade and a half, holding a succession of critical portfolios: he had been the first French Canadian minister of finance in the nation's history, and he had led the federalist forces in Quebec at the time of the Parti Québécois government's referendum on sovereignty-association.[35] By conventional standards his record should have made him the classic insider candidate.

Turner had been, by choice, an outsider for almost a decade. He had been a senior minister (justice, and then finance) in Trudeau's first governments after finishing third in the 1968 leadership race. Apparently unhappy over his role, and the direction of government policy, he had resigned in 1975 to go into private business. While working in the boardrooms of the country he maintained his party membership and continued to nurture his personal political networks. It was not long before he emerged as a silent (and sometimes not so silent) critic of the Liberal's drift to the left, and a rallying point for the party's disaffected. The media continued to report his widespread appeal to many Liberals so that by 1984 most observers took it for granted that he was a primary contender to succeed the man he had broken with a decade earlier.

The Liberal party establishment, like its Conservative counterpart, was preoccupied with winning elections. For them, the best leader would be the man who could restore the party's position in the polls and then defeat Brian Mulroney. Turner looked to be that man. He offered a new, but experienced face; he was a Liberal, but well distanced from Trudeau; his roots in British Columbia meant he could credibly seek to regenerate the party's appeal in the west.[36] Not surprisingly the party elite abandoned Chrétien and came down heavily for Turner. Only six of his cabinet colleagues supported Chrétien, while more than three times that many, accompanied by the bulk of the caucus, declared for Turner. As the struggle started, the insider was running as outsider, while the outsider had been made the candidate of the machine.

The Liberal Race   Most Liberals had enjoyed the spectacle of the Conservatives falling out over their leadership and assumed that they would do it differently. After all, they were choosing a prime minister; they did not have the Tories' long history of organized faction fighting; and the outcome of the Liberal race looked the most predictable of any leadership contest since the 1950s. But in fact the structure and character of the Liberal contest was remarkably like that of the Conservatives. With basically identical rules governing the two selection processes it was almost inevitable that this would be so. The candidates' strategists insured it by emulating all that they had seen work successfully for Tory candidates the year before.

Just over half the Liberal delegates (54 percent) were selected by local constituency associations, with the rest coming in a wide variety of ex officio capacities or as representatives of some interest in the party. With his enormous backing in the party hierarchy Turner was able to have many of his supporters chosen as nonconstituency delegates early in the campaign and he quickly jumped into the lead. The same was true to some extent in local constituency delegate selection meetings, and he managed to win about 60 percent of the delegates who were known to be declared supporters of one of the candidates when they were chosen. In this the Turner campaign was virtually identical to the one Clark had conducted in the Conservative party.[37]

Running against the party elites forced Jean Chrétien to organize a much more personalized campaign. It soon became clear that he was the best-liked candidate and that he had a surprising amount of strength all across the country. As it gradually became clear that Turner's organization was not going to be able to capture enough delegates to be sure of a first-ballot victory, the campaign for the delegates' second preferences heated up. The five other candidates each claimed that the two leaders would stalemate and that he would emerge from third place as the compromise winner. But no one really believed that.

The cross-country campaign for delegates' votes was very similar to the one the Conservatives had staged the previous spring. The Liberals tried to focus debate on the issues by instituting all-candidate policy sessions in five major cities across the country. But these sessions soon degenerated into just another platform for the candidates' set pieces. While each of the seven men attempted to define the direction in which the party needed to move (with Roberts and Johnston "vying for the title of campaign intellectual"[38]), a basic conflict soon emerged between Turner and Chrétien.

In his promise to recenter the Liberal party, to set it on a course of greater financial prudence, and to open communication links between the leader and the grass roots party organization, Turner was effectively repudiating much that had gone on in the party since he had left active political life. He was telling Liberals that under his leadership they could reestablish the party of St. Laurent and Pearson—Canada's natural governing party. This was an ill-disguised attack on Pierre Trudeau's leadership, and the prime minister responded by publicly disputing Turner's version of the events that had led to his resignation almost a decade earlier, to let Liberals know what he thought of Turner. But it was Chrétien who defended the record of the government. He repeatedly reminded Liberals of their accomplishments, declared he was proud to have played a major part in most of them, and promised to keep the party and government on the same course. He wrapped his appeal in an emotional and patriotic promise to keep Canada "number one."

As they approached the June convention, Turner's early lead among committed delegates had shrunk to something less than 50 percent. His supporters, like Clark's the year before, were primarily tied through their organizational commitments, while the Chrétien delegates had developed personal loyalties to their man. But without the strong antipathy to the leading candidate that had characterized the Conservative battle, Chrétien's chance of duplicating Mulroney's come-from-behind victory seemed slim.

The New Prime Minister   The results of the first ballot left little doubt that the Liberal delegates were going to make John Turner the next prime minister (see table 3.3). With over 46 percent of the vote he was almost certain to be returned on the second ballot, the easiest party leadership victory since the 1950s. As if to signal this inevitability Mark MacGuigan quickly moved to the Turner camp. But then, in a gesture rather uncharacteristic of Liberal ministers, Roberts, Munro, and Whelan all walked over to join their doomed

Table 3.3 Liberal Convention Ballot Results, 1984 (percentages in parentheses).

	Ballot			
	1st		2nd	
Turner	1,593	(46.4)	1,862	(54.4)
Chrétien	1,067	(31.1)	1,368	(40.0)
Johnston	278	(8.1)	192	(5.6)
Roberts	185	(5.4)		
MacGuigan	135	(3.9)		
Munro	93	(2.7)		
Whelan	84	(2.4)		

colleague. Johnston stayed in the race, a gambit that allowed him to avoid choosing between the two factions of the party that lay exposed on the convention floor.

Although Chrétien's support increased sharply on the second ballot, he could not overtake Turner, who won handily. The Liberals had decided to entrust their party and government to a man whom they believed would renew both before engaging Brian Mulroney and the Conservatives in electoral battle. The Gallup polls in the weeks immediately following the convention gave the Liberals a ten-point lead among decided voters, convincing them that this strategy was going to work. And in the aftermath of the reelection that was sure to come, there would be plenty of time and opportunity to heal the divisions produced by the leadership struggle.

Within three months Turner had lost the prime ministership and was reduced to leading the smallest Liberal caucus in Canadian history.[39] The party appeared to face a long period in opposition and a major rebuilding from the ground up if it was ever to emerge again as the country's governing party. Turner's leadership will ultimately be judged by how well the Liberals cope with this new challenge. Given the power of the extraparliamentary party to depose the leader, the undiminished ambitions of other leading Liberals, and the example of the Conservatives when in the same position, the amount of time Turner has to revive his party is probably limited.

The New Party Leaders

Eighty years ago André Siegfried pointed out how much Canadian party organization and electoral politics revolved around the party leaders. Leaders were chosen by their colleagues because they personified the party and symbolized its policies.[40] Now, parties choose leaders in the hope that they will give them new policies and a new persona. Mulroney and Turner were expected to make their parties over, to give them a new face and direction, and so lead them to electoral victory.

The process by which these men were chosen cannot be said to have structured a coherent debate over the direction of party policy, nor did it provide a mechanism for accommodating the competing strains within each of these ideologically diverse parties. But the long preconvention campaign, much of it conducted in the full glare of the media, did provide a severe testing of the candidates and forced partisans to confront their political futures. In choosing Mulroney (and rejecting Crosbie) as Clark's successor the Conservative party was turning its face to French Canada for the first time in generations. In electing Turner the Liberals were seeking to disown some of the policy impulses of the Trudeau government and restore their appeal (or at least acceptability) in western Canada.

Political outsiders appear to have an inherent advantage in this kind of leadership politics. They offer the freshest faces, unsullied by past compromises or unpopular policies. And the outcomes of the party leadership battles of 1983 and 1984 suggest that this dimension of the process has become more important than ever before. Both Turner and Mulroney were seen by the extraparliamentary party as men with the skills needed to take over the leadership of the parliamentary caucus and put it on the right course. But this also means that such leadership is vulnerable and subject to challenge. In office this has not proved a problem, given the electoral orientations of the two parties. In opposition, as the recent history of the Conservative party demonstrates, it can have a profoundly destabilizing and divisive effect. Party leaders, in their relations with the parliamentary and extraparliamentary parties, are rather like an individual dancing with two partners, doing different steps to different rhythms. It takes skillful leading to avoid putting a foot wrong or seeming to be out of step. And there is always someone wanting to cut in.

To the extent that this system of leadership selection is defended, it is done so on the grounds of being open, representative, participatory, and hence democratic. John Courtney has called this one of the "sustaining myths" of Canadian politics.[41] There is little in the experience of the conventions of 1983 and 1984 to suggest that we need to revise that judgment. The process is largely orchestrated by highly personalistic organizations in an uneven and ad hoc fashion. For the most part it seems to engage and involve only the most politically interested of the middle classes. The numbers taking part remain relatively low; but the numbers participating as spectators are quite high. National leadership conventions are now major events in the calendar of electronic party politics.

Both of Canada's two major parties got the leaders they wanted in 1983 and 1984. Only time will tell if they got the leaders they deserved, and what the consequences for the country's political life will be.

Notes

1. Patrick Weller, "Labour in 1980," pp. 64–68, and "The Anatomy of a Grievious Miscalculation: 3 February, 1983," pp. 253–56, 268–73, in Howard R. Penniman, ed., *Australia at the Polls: The National Elections of 1980 and 1983* (Washington, D.C.: American Enterprise Institute, 1983); Paul Kelly, *The Hawke Ascendancy* (Sydney: Angus and Robertson, 1984).
2. Anthony King, "Politics, Economics, and the Trade Unions, 1974–1979," in Howard R. Penniman, ed., *Britain at the Polls, 1979* (Washington, D.C.: American Enterprise Institute, 1981), pp. 39–45, 58–69.
3. British practice is now in flux. In 1981 the Labour party decided to have the parliamentary party share its power to choose the leader with constituency parties and affiliated trade unions. See Austin Mitchell, M.P., "A College Education: Electing Labour's Leader," *The Parliamentarian* (1984), pp. 104–16; and Henry Drucker, "Intra-Party Democracy in Action: The Election of Leader and Deputy Leader by the Labour Party in 1983," *Parliamentary Affairs*, (Summer 1984), pp. 283–300. The new British Social Democratic party has deliberately opted for choosing their leader by postal ballot of their members to emphasize the difference between it and the old parties. On New Zealand, see Stephen Levine, "New Zealand's Political System," in Howard R. Penniman, ed., *New Zealand at the Polls: The General Election of 1978* (Washington, D.C.: American Enterprise Institute, 1980), pp. 16–17. For Ireland, see Brian Farrell and Maurice Manning, "The Election," in Howard R. Penniman, ed., *Ireland at the Polls: The Dáil Elections of 1977* (Washington, D.C.: American Enterprise Institute, 1978), pp. 162–163; and Joe Joyce and Peter Murtagh, *The Boss: Charles J. Haughey in Government* (Dublin: Poolbeg Press, 1983).
4. King, "Politics, Economics, and the Trade Unions," p. 43. For a comparative overview see Patrick Weller, "The Vulnerability of Prime Ministers: A Comparative Perspective," *Parliamentary Affairs* (Winter 1983), pp. 96–117. For an intimation that leadership selection processes vary across western Europe see Leon D. Epstein, "Political Parties: Organization," in David Butler, Howard R. Penniman, and Austin Ranney, eds., *Democracy at the Polls* (Washington, D.C.: American Enterprise Institute, 1981), pp. 67–68.
5. The standard source is John C. Courtney, *The Selection of National Party Leaders in Canada* (Toronto: Macmillan, 1973). My observations in this chapter are limited to the Liberals and Progressive Conservatives. For the New Democratic party see chapter 7 of Courtney. In the summer of 1985 the Parti Québécois experimented with a fourth method by selecting their new leader by a vote of all party members. As there was no real contest for the leadership, it is difficult to assess how successful the process was. As yet, no other party in the country appears to be planning to adopt a similar system.
6. For a study of the way leadership has bedeviled the Conservatives see George C. Perlin, *The Tory Syndrome* (Montreal: McGill-Queen's University Press, 1980).
7. D. D. McKenzie of Nova Scotia (who went on to run a poor fourth at the 1919 convention) has been lost to history, largely ignored by academic and party literature alike. At the 1984 Liberal leadership convention the party propaganda circulated to the delegates to remind them of previous leaders didn't even include McKenzie in a footnote.
8. C. G. Power, *A Party Politician: The Memoirs of Chubby Power* (Toronto: Macmillan, 1966), p. 371.

9. For a stimulating analysis see Ian Stewart, "The Ins and the Outs: Status Cleavages at Canadian Leadership Conventions," in George C. Perlin, ed., *Party Democracy in Canada* (Scarborough, Ont.: Prentice-Hall, 1987).

10. Norman Snider, *The Changing of the Guard: How the Liberals Fell from Grace and the Tories Rose to Power* (Toronto: Lester and Orpen Dennys, 1985), provides a vivid account of what conventions are like.

11. D. V. Smiley, "The National Party Leadership Convention in Canada: A Preliminary Analysis," *Canadian Journal of Political Science* (December 1968), pp. 373–97; Robert Krause and Lawrence LeDuc, "Voting Behaviour and Electoral Strategies in the Progressive Conservative Leadership Convention of 1976," *Canadian Journal of Political Science* (March 1979), pp. 97–135.

12. John C. Courtney and George C. Perlin, "The Impact of Regional Cleavages on Convention Politics," in Perlin, *Party Democracy in Canada*. For a full list of all delegate categories see John C. Courtney, "Leadership Conventions and the Development of the National Political Community in Canada," in R. K. Carty and W. P. Ward, eds., *National Politics and Community in Canada* (Vancouver: University of British Columbia Press, 1986).

13. These figures come from delegate surveys conducted by G. Perlin. A full analysis will be found in his *Party Democracy in Canada*.

14. For a comparison of the attitudes of delegates to the Liberal and Conservative conventions with each other, and with the public, see Donald E. Blake, "Division and Cohesion among the Major Parties," in Perlin, *Party Democracy in Canada*.

15. Power, *A Party Politician*, pp. 396–97. Patrick Martin, Allan Gregg, and George Perlin, *Contenders: The Tory Quest for Power* (Scarborough, Ont.: Prentice-Hall, 1983) provides a comparative measure of the extent of preconvention campaigns in 1967 and 1983, appendix B, table 10.

16. The question of the financing of these campaigns—how the money is raised and on what it is spent—has yet to be investigated. In 1984 the Liberals imposed a limit (unenforceable) of $1.5 million on each of its candidates, a sum reached only by the two leading contenders. In total the Liberal candidates probably spent about $5 million. These are considerable sums by the standards of Canadian political money and it all falls outside the purview of existing party finance legislation.

17. George Perlin, "The Progressive Conservative Party in the Election of 1974," in Howard R. Penniman, ed., *Canada at the Polls: The General Election of 1974* (Washington, D.C.: American Enterprise Institute, 1975), pp. 103–07.

18. Clark was the first person to win a national leadership convention who had not led on the first ballot.

19. For accounts of the tumultuous events of 1979 and 1980 see John C. Courtney, "Campaign Strategy and Electoral Victory: The Progressive Conservatives and the 1979 Election," and William P. Irvine, "Epilogue: The 1980 Election," both in Howard R. Penniman, ed., *Canada at the Polls, 1979 and 1980* (Washington, D.C.: American Enterprise Institute, 1981).

20. For a book on the 1979 general election that cast Clark as a wimp see Dalton Camp, *Points of Departure* (Toronto: Deneau and Greenberg, 1979). This was the same Camp who led the charge against Diefenbaker in the 1960s. In the 1983 struggle he was perceived as a Clark partisan.

21. For the Gallup poll results between the 1980 and 1984 elections see table 4 of Courtney, chapter 9 in this volume.

22. By contrast, Diefenbaker had not indicated until the very last minute whether he would be a candidate to succeed himself in 1967, and that had probably worked against his cause. For

a superb account and analysis of the Conservative leadership struggles in 1982–83, from which I have taken much, see Martin, Gregg, and Perlin, *Contenders*.

23. The morning after the vote that forced Clark to call a leadership convention the Conservatives changed their rules so that they now have a leadership review only at the first general meeting following an election defeat. (It takes the form of a vote on the question "Do you wish to have a leadership convention?") Had the rule been in effect the day before, there would have been no vote and Clark would probably still be the party's leader.

24. Once the campaign started, Clark was pressured into resigning as leader of the parliamentary party so that he would not appear to have undue advantage. Erik Nielsen, a senior parliamentarian with no leadership aspirations was designated interim caucus leader. However, for a number of legal reasons having to do with party finance and the designation of official party candidacies, Clark remained as leader of the Progressive Conservative party of Canada. This episode was just another illustration of the bifurcated character of Canadian party leadership.

25. William Davis, who had been Ontario's premier since 1971, was being urged by many to run. He remained noncommittal for the first three months of the campaign (February through April) and then decided not to become a candidate. A key factor in his decision is reported to have been the strong opposition of Alberta's premier, Lougheed, and the unwillingness of Saskatchewan's premier, Devine, to support him publicly.

26. The Amway (read American way) Corporation is a pyramid sales operation that depends upon individuals who are totally committed to free enterprise and the benefits it can offer individual effort. Many of their people were deeply involved in the New Right politics of the United States.

27. R. K. Carty, "Campaigning in the Trenches: The Transformation of Constituency Politics," in Perlin, *Party Democracy in Canada*.

28. Carty, "Campaigning in the Trenches," (see especially tables 3 and 4).

29. Martin, Gregg, and Perlin, *Contenders*, pp. 170–71. They report that virtually all these delegates eventually moved to Mulroney for the final ballot.

30. See Irvine, "Epilogue," pp. 355–56 for the resignation and restoration of Trudeau between the 1979 and 1980 general elections.

31. Fully 82 percent of the delegates at the Liberal leadership convention reported that they thought it was a good idea that Trudeau had stood down; only 15 percent would have preferred that he stay on as leader.

32. Delegates at the Liberal convention proved to be divided on the matter. Six percent thought the alternation principle should be followed, 50 percent reported it ought to be a consideration but not a rigid rule, while 43 percent said it ought to get no consideration at all.

33. Whelan was apparently still bitter about Turner's "desertion" of the government in 1975 and determined to do what he could to keep him out of the party leadership.

34. Twenty percent of the delegates to the Liberal convention claimed that they preferred Mrs. Campagnola over any of the candidates who were actually running.

35. The Parti Québécois was pledged to achieving the independence of Quebec. Their long-awaited referendum presented voters with a wordy proposition about the desirability of negotiating sovereignty-association with Canada, but it was widely interpreted as being about the more general proposition of Quebec independence.

36. Turner had graduated from the University of British Columbia (where he won a Rhodes scholarship) and often portrayed himself as a westerner. But in his earlier career he had sat for Montreal and Ottawa ridings, and since leaving Parliament had lived in Toronto, so it is unlikely that many westerners saw him as a regional candidate.

37. Carty, "Campaigning in the Trenches."

38. Snider, *The Changing of the Guard*, p. 72.
39. Only Sir Charles Tupper who, like Turner, never met the House of Commons as prime minister, served a shorter period in office (in 1896). Ironically, Turner chose to be nominated for the Vancouver Quadra constituency (which he won) in a secondary school named after Tupper.
40. André Siegfried, *The Race Question in Canada* (1906; reprint, Toronto: McClelland and Stewart, 1966), chs. 20 and 22.
41. Courtney, *Selection of National Party Leaders*, p. 126.

4 Opportunity Regained: The Tory Victory in 1984

GEORGE PERLIN

———— Throughout this century the Progressive Conservative (PC) party has had a record of recurring electoral defeat. When Brian Mulroney assumed the party leadership in June 1983, the Conservatives had held office for only five brief periods (two of them of less than a year) totaling only twenty out of the previous eighty-seven years. Over that span the party had lost seventeen out of twenty-five elections. In the previous forty-nine years the Conservatives had lost twelve out of sixteen elections and had held office for periods totaling less than seven years.

The Legacy of Conflict

The biggest challenge Mulroney faced in seeking to overcome the Conservatives' electoral weakness was to master the fractious nature of his own party. Internal conflict has been a persistent characteristic of Conservative party politics over the past century, and the party's problems with internal conflict have had an important bearing on its recurring defeats in three ways.

First, its inability to find accommodation on major issues has contributed to its alienation of key social groups—most importantly French Canadians. The Conservative party had dominated federal politics in the first thirty years of confederation largely because of its success in managing conflict along the cleavage between French-speaking and English-speaking Canadians. The party's electoral problems began with a series of decisions in the 1880s and 1890s that cost it the support of most of the country's francophone voters. The alienation of francophones became a self-perpetuating process. The reduced presence of francophones in the Conservative caucus left it in the control of an anglophone majority unsympathetic to French concerns, with the result that when new issues arose touching on these concerns the party took positions that led to further francophone defections. In the twenty-five elections before 1984 the Conservatives won a majority in Quebec only once, and on only three other occasions did their share of Quebec's seats exceed 15 percent. Since Quebec elects one-fourth of the members in the House of Commons, the effect was to put the Conservatives at a permanent national disadvantage.

Second, internal divisions have impaired the party's effectiveness in government. Every Conservative government since that of Sir John A. McDonald, the party's first leader, has been at least partly immobilized by its inability to find workable accommodations on key issues, and on three occasions on the party's defeat has been precipitated by major public splits in the cabinet.

Third, the persistence of conflict has helped create an enduring image of the Conservative party as one that is unable to manage its own internal affairs and therefore not to be trusted to manage public affairs. Since survey data were first gathered on this subject the Conservative party has consistently been perceived to be less competent than the Liberal party—even when the general level of dissatisfaction with the Liberals has been higher. The problem has been aggravated by the fact that the conflict has invariably focused on the party's leadership. Every Conservative leader since McDonald has faced at least one serious challenge to his authority, some have had to live with continuous attempts to unseat them, and most of them have ultimately been driven from office by open or incipient revolt.[1]

The tenure of Joe Clark, who preceded Mulroney, was particularly troubled. The challenges to Clark's authority began within a few months of his election as leader in February 1976, when he became involved in an embarrassing conflict with a back-bench member of the party caucus over his constituency nomination. Over the next two years his chief rival for the leadership, Claude Wagner, fought with Clark over the party organization in Quebec and ultimately resigned his seat in the Commons to accept a Senate appointment from the Liberals; another leadership candidate, Jack Horner, left the party to accept a Liberal cabinet appointment; a back-bench member also crossed the floor; and several prominent members of the parliamentary caucus retired. By 1977 Clark's control of the party was so impaired that he was forced to accept as party president a man who belonged to a wing of the party opposed to his leadership and whose opinions on several issues were clearly an embarrassment to Clark.

Clark's problems within the party created an image of him as an ineffectual leader and journalists began to scrutinize everything he did, consciously or unconsciously, looking for evidence consistent with this stereotype. The Conservatives won the 1979 election despite Clark's image, but they were denied an overall majority in Parliament and seven months after they came to office they were forced into a new election by the defeat of their budget. In this election the burden of Clark's image and the party's reputation were added to by mistakes the government had made in its few months in office. Clark had had to reverse himself on well-publicized commitments, ministers had made conflicting statements on major issues, and the government had been slow to develop and present its policies. In February 1980, only nine months after it came to power, the Clark government was defeated.[2]

The loss of power led to renewed attacks from within the party on Clark's leadership. With close to half of the members of the parliamentary caucus in outright opposition to him and the continued support of many others uncertain, Clark's leadership suffered a serious blow at the party's biennial meeting in January 1981, when one-third of the delegates voted to call a leadership convention. He was compelled to promise the caucus that if he did not do better in the vote on his leadership at the next general meeting he would agree to the calling of a convention. Over the next two years, even though the Conservatives overtook and passed the Liberals in public opinion polls, there were persistent attacks on Clark's leadership, and at the biennial meeting in 1983 he was denied the vote he felt he needed to retain the support of the caucus. As a result, he asked the party to call a leadership convention and announced his intention to seek reelection. Six months later he lost the leadership to Mulroney.[3]

While Clark's difficulties may in part be explained by idiosyncratic factors, they also reflected more enduring factors in the structure and internal culture of the party—cleavages and patterns of behavior that Brian Mulroney would also have to deal with. One of these has been the tendency for factional cleavages to persist long after the issues that originally gave rise to them have been settled. One of Clark's problems was opposition to his leadership based on his association with the group that forced John Diefenbaker from the leadership in 1967. A small group of Diefenbaker loyalists in the caucus, who had constantly harassed Diefenbaker's successor, Robert Stanfield, was responsible for the most embarrassing challenges to Clark's authority in the first two years of his tenure, the period in which his image as an ineffectual leader was first imprinted on the popular consciousness. One element in this form of factionalism has been the general importance of personality in Conservative politics. This is a result both of the central role of leadership in the party, which has produced a tendency to relate all of the party's successes and failures to the strengths and weaknesses of its leaders, and because affective ties of personal friendship and loyalty to a particular individual have had a special importance in the formation of support networks within the party.

There has also been a broader, social basis to factional cleavages in the party over the last three decades. Most of the Diefenbaker loyalists came from social groups outside the centers of economic and social power in Canada.

They were people who harbored antielite feelings because of their social marginalization. Over the past fifty years there has been a natural tendency for such people to be attracted to the Conservative party because it has been the party of opposition. But it was Diefenbaker, the only populist to hold the leadership of one of the major parties, who most effectively articulated their feelings of alienation and became the particular object for their loyalty. Thus, the overturning of Diefenbaker's leadership was an event that reinforced their sense of social marginalization. In issue terms, in the debates within the party's parliamentary caucus this group has been distinguishable primarily by what it has stood against rather than what it has stood for. In particular, its frustrations have found expression in resistance to the policy, now widely accepted in the party, of seeking to accommodate the linguistic and cultural concerns of French Canadians and the province of Quebec.

Another source of instability in the party that has been of growing importance over the past fifteen years has been the presence of a group outspokenly critical of its pragmatic attitude toward state intervention in the economy. The prevailing opinion in the Conservative party has always been interventionist. The party has supported the use of public ownership to further national development, the building of the country's extensive social security system, and the extension of the regulatory activities of the state.[4] While there have always been some Conservatives who have opposed these policies, they have never been of sufficient significance to divert the party from its general course. Since the late 1960s the party as a whole has been shifting toward a more negative view of the interventionist state. But, notwithstanding this movement, both Stanfield and Clark were criticized by people who wanted the party to take a more right-wing position. This group played a significant part in organizing and financing the campaign that deprived Clark of the vote of confidence he sought at the biennial meeting in 1983.

In facing the problem of party unity Brian Mulroney had a number of advantages that neither Joe Clark nor Robert Stanfield had possessed. First, in winning the leadership Mulroney had had the support of most of the social outsiders in the party. For the first time since Diefenbaker's removal from the leadership they were in a position of real power and could be counted on to give their loyalty to the leader. Second, since it was in this group that most of the anti-French feeling in the party was located and since he himself was a fluently bilingual native of Quebec, committed to establishing a base for the party in French Canada, Mulroney was in a strong position to build accommodation across the language cleavage. Third, although his own views were in the tradition of pragmatic Toryism, Mulroney had taken a conciliatory attitude toward and won the support of most of the party's right wing. Thus, he was equally well placed to build accommodation across the ideological cleavage. Fourth, there was a clear determination by Joe Clark and among the group that had backed him to avoid the kind of factionalism that had so often harmed the party in the past.

Mulroney quickly signaled his own intention to seek consensus within the party. In his appointments to the shadow cabinet he provided representation for every significant interest, cutting across all of the factional divisions within the party, while in his appointments in the party organization he left in place or found new positions for most of the people who had held key positions under Clark's leadership.

In the interval between his selection as leader and the calling of the 1984 election, Mulroney's consensus-building strategy faced only one major test, but it was critically important in that it clearly established the effectiveness of his leadership. The issue, ironically, was that of the linguistic rights of the French-language minority in Manitoba—an issue that had played a major part in the events that led to the Conservative party's alienation of Quebec in the nineteenth century. The test came when the Liberals asked the other parties in Parliament to vote for a resolution supporting a proposal of the NDP government in Manitoba to recognize French as an official language of the province. The provincial Conservative party in Manitoba was vehemently opposed to the NDP proposal and several Manitoba members of the federal Tory caucus, with support from some other western members, were reluctant to support the resolution. Mulroney put his leadership on the line in confronting the caucus rebels and ultimately secured their compliance in his decision to support the resolution. In a further display of his firmness on the issue, he subsequently went to Manitoba to state his support for bilingualism in the province. His strong stand and his success in holding the caucus together on this issue symbolized both the party's commitment to his policy of making the Conservative party a credible political force in Quebec and its determination to master its fissiparous tendencies. With this issue behind him, Mulroney had established his ascendancy over the party.

As a result of the broad base of Mulroney's support in the party, the party's new sense of self-discipline, and Mulroney's skillful management, the Conservative party passed the twelve months between the leadership convention of 1983 and the calling of the general election of 1984 without any of the major breaches of party discipline that had been so harmful to it in the past. This was a major achievement and an important factor in the party's strength as it entered the 1984 campaign. A second factor in the party's strength in 1984 was the high level of its organizational sophistication and preparedness.

The Modernization of Tory Organization

The groundwork for the organization the Tories put in place in 1984 had been laid fifteen years before by Robert Stanfield. When Stanfield assumed the leadership in 1967 he found the party's only permanent national structure, the national headquarters, to be a decrepit and ineffectual institution. Constituency organization was of uncertain quality and the party's communications with the constituency associations were so sporadic that no one even knew how many of them were active and how many were purely paper organizations. Worse still, there was no campaign-planning structure and there was no one on headquarters staff with knowledge of modern electoral research and communications techniques. As a result, the 1968 campaign had to be fought with an ad hoc, ill-prepared, and uncoordinated organization that was badly overmatched by the incumbent Liberals. Stanfield was determined that this should not occur again and set out on a course of organizational modernization.[5]

The main obstacle to his achievement of this goal was the party's straitened financial condition. Inadequate funding, particularly in the interelection period, had always been a major problem for parties in opposition. As Stanfield launched his modernization drive, money was in such short supply that the party was hard-pressed to maintain even a minimal office staff to support the work of the national director. There was an effort to apply the new electoral technology in the campaigns of 1972 and 1974, but this effort was constrained by the money problem. The critical factor in overcoming this problem was the enactment, following the 1974 election, of electoral finance reforms that provided parties with public subsidies for campaigns and allowed tax credits for contributions to parties. The latter provision was particularly important for two reasons. First, it substantially increased the flow of money in the interelection period, permitting the development of the planning infrastructure and communications services needed to support the new approach. Second, it created the opportunity for fund-raising at the constituency and regional levels which, by providing purposeful activity to engage the interests of members, led to a broadening of the organizational base of the party.

Another factor that contributed to the increased strength of the Conservative organization was the development of a cadre of campaign professionals who learned how to apply the new techniques of electoral politics through their activities in provincial election campaigns. A key role in this respect was played by the provincial party in Ontario, which had held office continuously since 1944. The Ontario party organization, under the direction of advertising executive Norman Atkins, was the first to use the new campaign technology. Atkins or people who had worked with him were soon involved in provincial campaigns right across the country, introducing the organizational principles and techniques they had developed in Ontario. In this way there developed across the country a body of volunteer "professionals"—people who worked in other fields but had made the mastering of the new campaign technology a professional commitment—who could serve in the new organization being developed by the federal party.

The full effect of the transformation in federal party organization was first felt during the leadership of Joe Clark, who put in place a regular survey research program, increased the party's fund-raising activities through the adoption of direct mail techniques, and built national headquarters into a major bureaucratic support structure for the party's continuing organizational and campaign activities. In the elections of 1979 and 1980 the Conservatives, for the first time in twenty years, were able to mount national campaigns as technically competent and as well financed as those of the Liberals.

Despite the defeat of 1980, the transformation of party organization continued. A measure of the change that was taking place is the fact that in 1981 and 1982 party fund-raisers were able to collect some $5 million a year, nearly ten times the amount the party had normally been able to collect in even a good year in earlier interelection periods. And this money was put to good use as the party expanded its knowledge and ability to make use of the most advanced campaign techniques.

Planning for the next election campaign was already well advanced at the time that Clark's leadership was overturned. Ironically, although the leadership convention interrupted campaign planning, it provided a new stimulus to the process. The mobilization of people to participate in delegate selection meetings led to a new infusion of activists at the mass level and, through the organizational requirements of the leadership candidates, to the expansion of the number of experienced campaign professionals available to help in an election campaign. One of Mulroney's first acts as leader was to persuade Norman Atkins to become national campaign chairman, an appointment that insured both that the 1984 campaign would make full use of the new organizational resources that were available and that the corps of campaign professionals that had grown up around Atkins would be at the party's service. Thus, while the Liberals entered the 1984 election in a state of organizational disarray, the Conservatives were better organized for a national campaign than at any other time in their history.

The campaign crafted by Atkins incorporated the full range of modern election campaign techniques.[6] Daily tracking of public opinion through a rolling national poll was used to inform the broad national strategy. This was paralleled at the local level by intensive polling of swing constituencies and the use of the data gathered in this way to support direct mail and computer-assisted telephone campaigning to key groups in the targeted ridings. Candidate schools were established to inform candidates and their campaign managers how to make effective use of the latest campaign techniques, and a computer mail network linking each of the riding associations to national headquarters was used to effect instant communication between the national and local campaigns and thus ensure consistency in the application of the national strategy.

The 1984 Campaign

The broad dimensions of Conservative strategy for the 1984 campaign had begun to be defined by evidence from party surveys as early as 1982. These surveys had detected an important change in the political attitudes of Canadians. For the first time since such data had been gathered more than twenty years before, the number of self-identified Liberals in Canada was smaller than the number of self-identified Conservatives. But this was symptomatic not so much of a shift toward the Conservatives as a shift away from the Liberals. The hard core of Tory support had remained constant while the hard core of Liberal support eroded.

Behind this movement lay widespread dissatisfaction with economic conditions (which did not seem to be as central in the Trudeau government's agenda as the public's), coupled to dissatisfaction with the confrontational style of the Trudeau government. Allan Gregg, president of Decima Research, the party's polling firm, concluded from analysis of a series of surveys that the critical dimension in the public mood was a widespread and profound desire for change that focused on issues of process. Voters wanted change "in the way government works,"[7] and it was around this theme that the Conservatives decided to build their campaign.

While they had identified the thrust of their campaign, the Conservatives realized they still had serious problems to overcome. First, the party still bore the burden of its past. Voters continued to entertain considerable doubt about the Conservative party's competence to govern. Second, despite his success in managing the party, Mulroney's own image had not been clearly defined in positive terms as a prospective prime minister. His personal image was not strong enough to compensate for doubts about the party.

The third problem was that much of the discontent with the Liberal party was tied to its incumbent leader, Pierre Trudeau. Thus, when the Liberals changed their leader public perceptions of the party changed. Most voters expected John Turner to produce the change they wanted.[8] As a result, when Turner was chosen Liberal leader, the Tories lost the lead that they had held in the polls since 1982, with both uncommitted voters and former Liberal identifiers shifting their preferences.

Events in the early stages of the campaign seemed to further weaken the Tory position. An apparent conflict within the party over the cost of Conservative campaign proposals became public, and the party's shadow finance minister, John Crosbie, allegedly leaked figures to journalists showing that the party's promises would add $20 billion to the federal deficit. In addition, Mulroney was forced to retract comments he had made to journalists aboard his campaign plane about Liberal patronage appointments and his own position on the distribution of patronage to Tories. The Tories' rolling poll showed that for the first two weeks of the campaign they continued to trail the Liberals.

The turning point came with the leaders' debates in the third week. In the first debate, conducted in French, Mulroney's fluency in French and his greater sensitivity to the French political culture established his credibility to the Quebec electorate. In the English debate on the following night, a blunder by John Turner cut away the basis of his advantage over Mulroney. When pressed by Mulroney as to why he had agreed to make a widely criticized series of patronage appointments requested by his predecessor, Trudeau, Turner extended his arms in a gesture of seeming futility and said, "I had no choice." The image and words, which were to be shown in film clips on national television night after night and evoked in mocking humor by Mulroney in every subsequent speech as he crossed the country, destroyed the stereotyped contrast between Liberal competence and Tory incompetence. At the same time Turner's statement was an admission that he could not produce change; he had had to give in to Trudeau, the prime minister whose political style a majority of Canadians had rejected.

The effects of the debates were immediately apparent in the Tories' rolling poll. The belief that Turner could produce change was held by 60 percent of a national sample polled by the Tories on the day before the English debate and by only 40 percent two days later. And there was a shift of vote intentions from the Liberals to the Conservatives. Three days after the debates the Conservatives overcame the Liberal lead and ten days later they led by thirteen points.

Before the debates the Conservative strategy had been to run a two-stage advertising campaign, using the first stage to undermine the notion that Turner's government was or could be different from Trudeau's. As a result of the debates they were able to pass over this negative stage and go directly to the second stage, the building of Mulroney's image as a credible alternative prime minister, who represented a genuine form of change and could be expected to be more in touch than the Liberals with popular concerns. As this part of the campaign progressed, the PC lead in anglophone Canada was consolidated. In every poll published after the end of July the Conservatives were reported to be substantially ahead outside Quebec. And in Quebec the Tories' polls showed that more and more voters were coming to expect a Conservative victory.

At the beginning of the campaign the Tories' expectations in Quebec had been modest. Mulroney himself had known that he was taking a calculated risk in choosing to run in a Quebec riding. Following the French debate, as Quebec voters' expectations of a Conservative victory began to grow, their commitment to the Liberal party began to weaken.[9] At first this change was expressed in a substantial increase in the number of undecided voters. Noting this increase, the Conservatives amended Mulroney's national tour schedule to concentrate his efforts in the final four weeks of the campaign in the province of Quebec. Within days it was apparent in their polls that they would make a major breakthrough in Quebec.

Thus, in the final stage of the campaign, the Conservatives had only to guard against mistakes to maintain their momentum. The only issue that seemed likely to trouble them was a Liberal attack on the credibility of their claims about the costs of their campaign promises. And the Tories, informed by their polls that most voters didn't care about this issue, dealt with it by delaying a response until the last few days before the election. In its final two weeks, the Tory campaign proceeded as a triumphal progress, with the only issues in doubt the number of seats they would win in Quebec and the size of their overall majority.

Mulroney's Image

Among the specific components of the Conservative campaign, Brian Mulroney's personal image and style had a central role. At the beginning of the campaign certain aspects of Mulroney's image worried Tory strategists. Mulroney's rhetoric tended to the excess of hyperbole. As a result, his efforts to convince people of his sincerity seemed insincere. Surveys found a lingering public doubt about Mulroney—a trust problem that persisted throughout the early stages of the campaign. Journalists pressed him hard, testing this aspect of his personality. Many believed that he had a tendency to lie to them, even about small matters, and they pursued him aggressively, seeking evidence to support their opinion. This negative dimension of Mulroney's image was so significant that even after he had clearly mastered John Turner in the leaders' debates there was a discussion among party strategists as to whether his image should have a central role in the party's television advertising.

In the event, the television advertising campaign was constructed around Mulroney and the positive aspects of his image became the central vehicle for transmitting the party's message. Mulroney's working-class background was used to show his understanding of the concerns of "average Canadians" and to establish that a Conservative government would be in touch with the people, while his record as a successful negotiator for business in labor relations was used to give credibility to the Conservative claim that the party would bring a more conciliatory approach to the style of government. Mulroney's personality also served the general theme of the campaign. In contrast with both his predecessor as Tory leader, Joe Clark, and Liberal leader Turner, Mulroney seemed at ease in public appearances and on television and his personal self-assurance under scrutiny created a style that fit well with the general message of the campaign: "Nearly everything about the Mulroney style seems designed to signal confidence, calm and authority. When he walks, the upper part of Mulroney's body seems to glide, as though the lower half moved not on legs but on some kind of well-oiled machinery. At the same time, his easy informality and liquid-gold speaking voice regularly sooth and sway his audiences." [10]

The Campaign in the Constituencies

For all the importance of the leader's role and the national campaign, an election can be won only by winning the 285 separate elections in the individual constituencies. The first concern of Conservative strategists in this respect was the candidate nomination process. There is some debate in the scholarly literature about the impact of local candidates on voting behavior in Canada. The prevailing view seems to be that local candidates have only a marginal impact on electoral outcomes. [11]

Whether or not this is true, party strategists believe the quality of local candidates affects their chances, and journalists' commentaries on the national parties frequently use impressionistic judgments of the quality of a party's candidates to comment on the leaders' ability to attract able people to the party. Thus, the national campaign committee took a profound interest in the nomination process.

But it is difficult for a national party to influence the nomination process because it has no clearly defined right and only a limited opportunity to intervene. In fact, because constituency associations carefully guard the principle of local autonomy in the nomination process, where there is an active local constituency membership the national party can do little to influence nominations. In constituencies of this kind the national committee confined itself to the distribution of a booklet guiding the constituency associations in the establishment and running of candidate search committees. There was, however, a national effort to try to get certain candidates to run and in some cases the person who agreed to run was given both advice on how to organize to win the nomination and a list of names of people in his or her prospective constituency who might help in the nomination campaign.

In ridings where there was a sitting member of Parliament, the national committee scrupulously avoided any form or appearance of intervention because, apart from any other consideration, the party had to be wary of provoking conflicts that would be construed by journalists as evidence of a renewal of factionalism. All but two sitting members of Parliament who sought renomination were successful and in the two cases in which incumbents were overturned the party quickly accorded recognition to the new nominees.

The biggest effort at a province-wide level to find candidates was in Quebec. This search was directly under Mulroney's control because he dealt personally with the Quebec campaign. Mulroney had a special reason for concern about the quality of candidates in Quebec because his ability to rebuild the party in that province was one of the arguments on which his campaign for the leadership had been based, and he had a strong personal commitment to the achievement of this goal. The difficulty in Quebec was that a Conservative nomination was hardly a sought-after prize; the party had not elected more than two out of the seventy-five members from Quebec in sixteen years. In fact, Mulroney himself had had to choose a by-election in Nova Scotia as his own means of entry to Parliament after his selection as leader and it was not until after the formal calling of the election in July that he announced his decision to run in his native province. The recruitment strategy in Quebec was not to try to find high-profile "star quality" figures, but to look for promising people with solid reputations in the local community. In this way the party hoped to find candidates whose personal networks at the local level would compensate for the party's own weakness. On the whole, the party's national committee was satisfied with its candidate recruitment activities. The list of candidates contained few names of high-profile people attracted to candidacy for the first time, but neither was the party embarrassed by the nomination of a large number of controversial figures.

The coordination of campaigns in the constituencies with the national campaign was less difficult to deal with than candidate recruitment, but none-theless required careful planning. External involvement in local campaigns has always been viewed suspiciously, both because of the concern of local offi-cials to avoid any tampering with their autonomy and because national officials intervening at the local level have frequently blundered as a result of their insensitivity to regional and local conditions. The party had made an impor-tant change in its structure to try to deal with this problem in the campaigns of 1979 and 1980, when separate campaign committees were established in every province. This change had the effects both of making it easier to get national objectives and techniques accepted at the local level and of insuring that the national committee itself was better informed about regional and local concerns. As a result, in 1984 there was a more congenial environment for the coordination of the national and local campaigns and, from the perspective of the national campaign committee, the process of integrating the two levels of the campaign worked flawlessly.

The Party Platform

The component of the Conservative campaign that in some ways posed the most serious problems was the party platform. Mulroney had launched the process of platform development soon after his selection as leader by assigning responsibility for the development of party policy to caucus committees. But because of the wide spectrum of views represented, it was not easy to achieve consensus on policy in the Progressive Conservative party. Another factor that inhibited effective policymaking in the party was a lack of support staff for policy research. The party's parliamentary research office, funded from the budget of Parliament, has been used primarily to provide general support to members of caucus in their day-to-day activities in the House, and the party had no separate funds of its own assigned to policy research, preferring to commit all of its resources to the needs of campaign preparation, organizational development, and interelection communications. Some effort was made to compensate for this weakness by securing participation from the private sector in various policy advisory structures, but it was not easy to coordinate this activity with the work of the caucus committee. Mulroney was dissatisfied with the first product of the efforts of the caucus committees and ordered them to redraft their position papers. As a result, it was not until April 1984 that the drafts were approved by caucus.

The platform that emerged from this process suffered from a number of problems. In some areas it was cast in such general terms that it was not at all clear how a Conservative government would proceed, while in others it identified goals without explaining how they would be achieved. But the most glaring defect was that it contained clearly incompatible objectives— most notably promises to a wide range of interests that implied or explicitly required substantial increases in public expenditures, the sum of which, if they were fulfilled, would clearly vitiate the party's pledge to reduce the federal deficit.

There were some distinctive elements in the party platform. At the most general level it was distinctive in its emphasis. The issues of foreign policy, economic nationalism, and cultural and linguistic policy that had been central to the Liberal agenda were dealt with, but they were not the focus for the Conservative platform. The party's policy book for candidates instead focused on economic policy, social policy, and issues related to the process of government.

Economic policy was at the center of the platform. Party research had identified unemployment as the substantive issue that most concerned the electorate and it was on this issue that the Conservatives focused their attention. In Mulroney's evocative phrase, the central priority of the Conservative party was "Jobs! Jobs! Jobs!" To create new employment, the party's platform proposed to shift responsibility for the stimulation of the economy from government to the private sector. Government would remain active, but its programs would involve less direct intervention in the economy, taking the form of providing support to encourage private initiatives and creating a more attractive investment climate. The more "conservative" (economic-liberal) cast of economic policy was most clearly reflected in proposals to remove controls on foreign investments, to curb direct government ownership in the economy, and to reduce the scope of government regulatory activities.

Social policy, in contrast, stressed the maintenance and extension of the existing structures of the welfare state. There was a guarantee of the maintenance of the principle of universality in social programs and there were proposals to extend the national pension plan to include homemakers and to work with the provinces to develop programs for the provision of child-care services.

The third area of emphasis in the policy manual focused on issues related to the process of government. Its central place in the program reflected both the importance of populism in the Conservative party and party strategists' assessments of the underlying mood of the electorate. The platform contained proposals for accommodating provincial positions in order to settle a number of outstanding issues in federal-provincial relations and promised to end "confrontation and antagonism" in federal relations with the provinces. In addition, there were promises to reform Parliament, to increase scrutiny and control of the executive branch, to reform administrative practices in Revenue Canada (the tax department), to reduce the burden of bureaucratic demands on small businesses and to impose more effective controls on the management of government-owned corporations.

These proposals were linked in Mulroney's speeches to a general theme emphasizing the need to mute conflict and promote cooperation among governments and between government and the private sector. This emphasis on cooperation and harmony provided the underpinning for all the pieces of the Tory platform. A conservative government would give the private sector more freedom to provide the impetus for economic growth, maintain the network of social programs to promote equality of opportunity, and facilitate effective action to deal with national problems by serving as a conciliator and broker among conflicting interests.

The PC Victory

The PC victory in 1984 was striking both for its size and its breadth. The Tories won 211 seats, carrying majorities in every province (something no party had ever done before), and winning large numbers of new voters across all divisions on every politically relevant dimension of social cleavage. The election had provided the Conservatives with an opportunity to establish themselves on a broader base, but their majority rested on a very fragile foundation.

As the volatility of voter preferences right up to the middle of the campaign suggests, short-term forces, not fundamental realignment of partisan preferences, had produced the Tory majority. The critical factor in the election outcome had been a shift to the Conservatives by 1980 Liberal voters with weak partisan attachments. "Outside Quebec, a combination of weak attachment, negative evaluations of John Turner, attraction to PC policies, and the desire for change Turner did not represent seemed to explain the decision to defect to the PCs in 1984. . . . In the province of Quebec . . . the leadership issue dwarfs almost all others in the voting equation." [12] Thus, the Conservative majority rested on votes the party had won from members of the electorate whose continued support was contingent entirely on the new government's performance in office.

Postscript: The Tories in Office

Eighteen months after the election of 1984 the ephemeral nature of the Tory majority became stunningly apparent when national polls showed the Conservatives had fallen behind the Liberals in voter preferences. At least four factors may be cited to account for this dramatic decline in the party's support.

First, the Conservative campaign had roused expectations that no government could fulfill. Every group had been encouraged to expect beneficial changes, either by specific policy commitments the party had made or by the general theme of the Conservative campaign. It was impossible for the government to meet the specific claims of all the groups that had supported it—both because some of the claims were incompatible with one another and because severe financial constraints left the government with little policy flexibility. This problem was compounded by the fact that the party had articulated no sense of vision and found no dramatic policy initiative around which to mobilize national commitment. There was no common goal it could use to build support across the diverse range of specific interests embraced by its broad social base.

Second, while the government could not fulfill the expectations the campaign had generated, it tried desperately to avoid creating disappointment—with equally negative consequences. "The most powerful motive underlying the Mulroney style is a desire to be liked, to please—and not give offence. But what that has meant in policy terms is that whenever the Mulroney government finds itself under attack or saddled with an unpopular position, it tends to surrender its position." [13] The government thus very quickly came to be seen as indecisive and directionless.

This contributed to a third problem. The Tories had been able to win voter confidence in 1984 because, for once, they had been perceived to be more competent than the Liberals, but that perception was shaken by their performance. In addition to its indecisiveness, the new government was plagued by a series of individual ministerial blunders. In its first twenty months four ministers were forced to resign (one because of allegations that his personal conduct while on a ministerial trip might have created a security problem, another because of a controversy over the administration of his department, another because of a series of administrative embarrassments, and yet another because of an allegation that he had breached the government's conflict of interest guidelines).[14] In addition, the credibility of several other ministers was damaged by problems in their handling of their portfolios or by allegations of patronage awards that seemed to exceed the bounds of prudence. In the words of one assessment of the government's performance, written in mid-1986: "Scandal and misadventure have followed scandal and misadventure and it seems as if a week cannot go by without some further story of a conflict of interest, a ministerial indiscretion, or a judgement that seems to fly in the face of common sense."[15] The situation became so bad that the prime minister completely reconstructed his cabinet in the summer of 1986, replacing several ministers, including the deputy prime minister, who had been his chief spokesman in Parliament and his principal lieutenant.

Fourth, the image of the prime minister became a problem for the government. In media analyses the government's lack of clear direction was attributed directly to Mulroney's lack of a "strong personal agenda,"[16] and its indecision was explained as an expression of his own personal desire to be liked.[17] He was blamed for creating problems within the government by centralizing power in his own office while surrounding himself with personal staff who were not competent to exercise it.[18] He was also accused of lying to deflect criticism and of making exaggerated claims in an attempt to build up his personal image.[19] The accusations about the prime minister's truthfulness were particularly harmful because they touched a point of vulnerability—his trustworthiness—observed in public perceptions of Mulroney that had been a problem even before the election.

Some commentaries on the Conservative government's decline in popularity have ascribed it entirely to Mulroney's personal conduct and personality. Given the prime minister's central role in the Canadian system this is hardly surprising. The prime minister defines policy, makes all of the principal appointments in government, and represents the party to the country. Thus the prime minister's personal goals, style of leadership, and personality have a profound impact on the direction of any government.

But whatever the impact of Mulroney's personality on the government, it is important to recognize that his entire political experience until his election as leader had been in the internal politics of the Conservative party, while his leadership must be exercised within the constraints of the character of the party as it is now. From this perspective, the Mulroney government's problems need to be seen in the context of the party's problems.

Thus, it may be argued that: (1) the Mulroney government came to office without a coherently defined set of objectives around which to mobilize national purpose because of the internal fragmentation of the party, in particular its internal ideological divisions; (2) the need to represent all of the factional interests and cleavages within the party and the persistence of interfactional suspicions adversely affected the quality of Mulroney's initial ministerial appointments; (3) the pool of ministerial talent was limited, particularly in Quebec, because the party (because of its historic weakness and its general reputation) has had difficulty in recruiting people of outstanding ability or with records of outstanding accomplishment in other fields to run for it; (4) effective cooperation among members of the government took time to develop because party members tend to interact on the basis of attitudes bred by persistent factionalism; (5) many members of the government were slow to make effective use of advice from the public service or had problems with their departments because, having been so long in opposition, they were suspicious of the public service; (6) members of the government, many of whom had never even sat in Parliament before, made mistakes because of their inexperience; and (7) collectively, the government was overly cautious and tentative in its approach to office because of the obsessive concern among Conservatives with their failures in the past.

If this line of argument is accurate, some of the problems of the Mulroney government may be expected to correct themselves as its members become more accustomed to and socialized in their roles as members of a government, and as weak ministers are replaced by other members of the parliamentary caucus who have had an opportunity to acquire experience and demonstrate their ability. The party still has serious problems related to the nature of its internal cleavages, but in the short run there is reason to believe that its decline in popular support is not irreversible. Both the volatility of voter preferences in published polls over the past decade and a half and national election study data suggest that a large proportion of the federal electorate (perhaps as much as 55 percent) constitutes a floating vote without any strong partisan attachments.[20] In this context the Mulroney government still has some advantages—among them the resources of incumbency, the superb and well-financed organization of the Conservative party, and the fact that its tenure has been accompanied by a modest (although regionally uneven) economic recovery. The opportunity for electoral realignment that the Conservatives had hoped might issue from the 1984 election has been lost, but they may still avoid the disaster of precipitous defeat that has befallen every Conservative government since World War I.

Notes

1. The analysis of the Conservative party's problems with internal conflict presented here is based on George Perlin, *The Tory Syndrome: Leadership Politics in the Progressive Conservative Party of Canada* (Montreal: McGill-Queen's University Press, 1980).

2. The problems of the Clark government are discussed in Jeffrey Simpson's *Discipline of Power* (Toronto: Personal Library, 1980).

3. The events leading to Clark's resignation and defeat are discussed in Patrick Martin, Allen Gregg, and George Perlin, *Contenders: The Tory Quest for Power* (Toronto: Prentice-Hall, 1983).

4. For a discussion of the extent of these cleavages, see Donald Blake, "Division and Cohesion in the Major Parties," in George Perlin, ed., *Party Democracy in Canada* (Scarborough, Ont.: Prentice-Hall, 1987).

5. For a discussion of the development of Conservative campaign organization in the Stanfield-Clark period, see George Perlin, "The Progressive Conservative Party in 1974, " in Howard R. Penniman, ed., *Canada at the Polls: The General Election of 1974* (Washington, D.C.: American Enterprise Institute, 1975); and John C. Courtney, "Campaign Strategy and Electoral Victory: The Progressive Conservatives and the 1979 Election," in Howard R. Penniman, ed., *Canada at the Polls, 1979 and 1980: A Study of the General Elections* (Washington, D.C.: American Enterprise Institute, 1981).

6. The discussion of the Conservative campaign presented here and below is based on interviews with several key participants in the spring and summer of 1985. Since some participants requested that the interviews be treated as confidential, none of them will be identified.

7. Allen Gregg, as cited in unpublished notes from Patrick Martin of the *Toronto Globe and Mail*. I am indebted to Mr. Martin for making these notes available to me.

8. Ibid.

9. Ibid.

10. "The Winning Ways of an Irish Magus," *Macleans*, May 6, 1985.

11. See William P. Irvine, "Does the Candidate Make a Difference?" *Canadian Journal of Political Science*, 15 (1982), pp. 755–82.

12. Steven D. Brown, Ronald D. Lambert, Barry J. Kay, and James E. Curtis, "The 1984 Election: Explaining the Vote," paper presented at the annual meeting of the Canadian Political Science Association, June 1986.

13. "The Winning Ways of an Irish Magus."

14. A fifth minister resigned because of an investigation into his compliance with the Election Expense Act, but he returned to the cabinet when the investigation cleared him.

15. David Bercuson, J. L. Granatstein, and W. R. Young, *Sacred Trust: Brian Mulroney and the Conservative Party in Power* (Toronto: Doubleday, 1986), p. 297.

16. "The Winning Ways of an Irish Magus."

17. See "The Tories Fight Back," *Macleans*, September 8, 1986.

18. Ibid. Also see "Mulroney's Uneasy Anniversary," *Macleans*, September 9, 1985.

19. See "Mulroney Under Fire," *Macleans*, October 7, 1985, and "The Tories Fight Back."

20. Brown et al., "The 1984 Election."

5 The Dauphin and the Doomed: John Turner and the Liberal Party's Debacle

STEPHEN CLARKSON

Politics is about *conjonctures,* about opportunities and
how they are seized.
—Reg Whitaker

──────── For the Liberal party of Canada 1984 was a year of opportunities—
some of them grasped but most of them missed. After leading his colleagues
and the public through a guessing game about his political intentions that had
gone on since his reelection in 1980, Pierre Elliott Trudeau finally consulted
the stars on the night of February 28, 1984: "I went out to see if there were
any signs of my destiny in the sky but there weren't—there was nothing but
snowflakes." [1] He concluded that, after sixteen years of swinging from spec-
tacular successes to dismal failures, the electoral fates would not smile on
him again. By contrast, John Turner, his successor as Liberal leader, inherited a situation pregnant with possibility but he misread the meaning of the
same snowflakes and led the Liberal party to its worst humiliation since the
conscription crisis of World War I.

Prologue: The Prince, Fortuna, and Virtu

This drama took on classic proportions that highlighted an archetypical theme:
how much an individual leader can exploit a political *conjoncture* or, in the
terms Niccolo Machiavelli used to instruct his prince, the extent to which Virtu
can master Fortuna. [2] For Machiavelli, Fortuna represented the unexpected in
politics, those uncontrollable factors and unforeseeable events that we now
call luck, good or bad. Not that Fortuna was all powerful. The more a prince
possessed Virtu—political knowledge, skill, prudence, strength of mind, good
judgment, and wisdom—the more he could vanquish unreliable Fortuna. [3] The
weak and imprudent leader who puts his trust in hope and luck will suffer the
malevolence of fate, but such an outcome is not necessary. The politician of
supreme Virtu can exercise political control, carefully preparing for the future,
acting decisively and with foresight through purposeful action that changes

what the unsuccessful blame as the malignancy of fate into the determined execution of well-considered plans.

Fortuna's role is not entirely negative; no potential prince can act unless he is given the opportunity to do so. The circumstances must be favorable for the would-be leader to get his start. But once Fortuna has smiled, what he makes of this opportunity is determined by his Virtu. When Pierre Trudeau announced his definitive retirement, the immediate question was whether the succession offered some new prince a chance to show his Virtu. That opportunity was defined by the way Trudeau's last ministry had left the affairs of state, the way the public perceived them, and the way the Liberal party related to them.

Trudeau's 1980–84 government had been everything his previous government failed to be. Disregarding the uncertain mandate received in 1980 after a campaign that had "low bridged" the Liberal party leader in order to let the Conservatives defeat themselves without reactivating old angers at Pierre Trudeau, the reborn Trudeau team set out to govern, knowing this was probably their last chance to achieve their goals. Judged provocative and reckless by their detractors, daring and courageous by their supporters, they implemented a clearly conceived strategy.

–They fought a crucial supporting role in the Quebec referendum campaign that, on May 20, 1980, decisively defeated the separatist option. They then proceeded to engage in a bitter federal-provincial fight that resulted by 1982 in the patriation of the Canadian constitution, complete with a new Charter of Rights and a hard-won amending formula.

–They unveiled the most interventionist economic strategy attempted by Ottawa in the twentieth century—the National Energy Program (NEP) of October 1980, which challenged the dominance of the oil and gas industry by Alberta and a powerful multinational oligopoly and provoked, as a by-product, a severe crisis in Ottawa's relations with Washington.

–They introduced a restrictive and egalitarian tax reform budget in 1981 that turned into a political disaster, not just because it coincided with the worst economic recession Canada had suffered since the 1930s, but also because it undermined the middle-class business support of the Liberal party.

–They grappled with such historically intractable problems as western grain transportation (by abolishing what to western farmers was the almost sacred Crowsnest Pass rate), the Atlantic fisheries (by implementing the Kirby Report), civilian control of spying (by pushing through the Canadian Security Intelligence Service Act), and East-West tensions (by the prime minister's bold peace initiative on the international scene).

–They held the line on social security programs and even expanded support for Canada's poorest citizens in the face of the demonstrated appeal of neoconservative ideas, expressed most vividly by the popularity of Reaganomics in the United States.

Although these considerable achievements garnered new supporters from the public—the Charter of Rights had proven popular; the NEP had been hailed by consumers; women and the poor had rallied to Trudeau's party—the Liberals were held in contempt by the various powerful interests Ottawa had confronted: the provincial premiers and their governments, big business, the western farmers. The combination of Trudeau's abrasive personality and the controversial nature of much of his government's legislation relegated the Liberals to second place in the polls, well behind the Progressive Conservatives who had ranked first in the public's voting intentions since mid-1981 under both Joe Clark and his successor as Conservative leader, Brian Mulroney. After years of confrontation politics, the public was fed up with the Liberals, particularly with their leader. They were, in the words of the respected survey researcher Allan Gregg, looking for a "new man with a new plan."[4] It was clear that the public wanted change. It was less clear whether the Liberal party could satisfy this desire.

If champagne flowed in Calgary's Petroleum Club upon the news of Pierre Trudeau's announced retirement, relief also spread through the Liberal party itself. Although the man who had won four of the last five general elections and strengthened the Liberals' grip in Quebec was still widely respected, there was a general recognition in party ranks that they could not win again under Trudeau and that the party had ossified under his leadership. Trudeau had never shown much more than reluctant interest in the health of the extraparliamentary party. There was no outstanding potential successor in his cabinet. The Liberal organization had been reduced to a handful of people scattered among a weakened party headquarters, the Senate, and the prime minister's office itself. Most serious of all, Trudeau was leaving the party with limited electoral options. Because he had delayed his retirement decision so long, the new Liberal prime minister would be forced to call an election within a year of his succession.

The succession involved three separate challenges: to take hold of the leadership of the Liberal party and redefine its long-range goals; to take command of the Canadian government and implement new policies in the short term; to go to the electorate and seek a formal mandate for a new government. The common thread in each of these three challenges was the need to represent the change so strongly desired by a majority of the public while demonstrating enough continuity to sustain the party's traditional base.

With the January 1984 Gallup poll showing Liberal support at 30 percent compared to a 53 percent rating for the Conservatives, there was no question that Fortuna was offering the new Liberal leader a party at a very low ebb.

Still, with 41 percent of the Conservatives' support motivated by hostility to the person of Pierre Trudeau and 29 percent of it due to a generalized desire for change, the opportunity for a Liberal successor who could offer the promise of genuine change was enticing.[5]

Act I. Leadership Renewal:
The Pack, the Savior, and the Party

The Liberal party's recent experiences with leadership renewal fell into two distinct categories. In 1948 and 1958 there had been a clear laying on of hands when the incumbent prime minister stepped aside (Mackenzie King, then Louis St. Laurent) and the long-acknowledged dauphin (Louis St. Laurent, then Lester Pearson) was duly crowned by the party establishment and endorsed by the partisan faithful. Since Pierre Trudeau had groomed no one to fill his shoes, it was natural for Liberals in 1984 to refer to the other model, that of 1967–68. When Lester Pearson announced his retirement the party was behind in the polls, facing a Progressive Conservative opposition with a new, apparently popular leader. At that point a pack of impressively experienced ministers had declared themselves candidates, only to be outshone by a relative outsider, Pierre Trudeau, who took on the allure of savior to the party. He redefined its ideological mission and regenerated the enthusiasm of the Liberals who, under his charismatic leadership, grasped the reins of government once more and went successfully to the people in a snap election that returned the Liberal party to power with a majority in the House of Commons. In 1984 all of these factors—the cabinet candidates, the savior from outside, the discussion of new directions and the renewed energy of the party, the chance to remold the new party leader as prime minister before making an electoral appeal to the public—could be discerned at least in potential, though their realization in practice fell uncomfortably short of the 1967–68 standard.

The pack of candidates who emerged from Trudeau's cabinet were experienced but not exciting. Donald Johnston had the most integrity in his advocacy of new policy approaches to old problems but was undynamic in their expression. John Roberts presented the most coherent and eloquent script for a "new Liberalism" but developed little support outside Toronto. Mark MacGuigan explicitly identified himself with Gary Hart's then-rising star but had difficulty squaring his economic conservatism with his social progressivism. John Munro's left-wing nationalism found almost no resonance and Eugene Whelan's single interest, advocacy of farmers' needs, was regarded mostly as comic relief. Only Jean Chrétien demonstrated enough strength within the party's ranks to mount a credible campaign for the succession, but his was still a wild card. Since the Liberal party had always alternated francophone and anglophone leaders, the principle of *alternance* was held against Chrétien by the party establishment. Although his frank expression of loyalty to the Trudeau record and his unashamedly patriotic appeals ("Canada is number one") had real resonance among delegates, his image as a somewhat folkloric French Canadian who seemed weak on policy matters undermined his dynamic campaign.

Four prominent Liberals outside the cabinet were eligible for the role of savior. Donald S. Macdonald, the candidate who had been almost a sure bet to win the leadership had Pierre Trudeau not returned in 1979 from his brief retirement, was politically immobilized as chairman of a royal commission that he could not abandon with its work unfinished. Iona Campagnolo, the incumbent president of the Liberal party and a former minister in Trudeau's government in the seventies, attracted considerable support among party activists because of her dedication, western roots, vivacious speaking style, and striking appearance, but she declined to stand. James Coutts, Pierre Trudeau's principal secretary from 1975 to 1981, and one of the shrewdest minds the party had ever attracted, still carrying the burden of party hostility from those years when he had been identified as the back-room boy who had kept Trudeau isolated and inaccessible, also decided not to run, despite a longstanding ambition to do so.

Given the political *conjoncture,* only the fourth "outsider" had a real chance for the savior role. His name was John Turner.

> In appearance, he is perfect. Looking for the man to play the Senator from Rocky Ridge, central casting would bring him into the part without hesitation. It's all there—the trim, exercised body, still, at 54, the body of an athlete; the face, handsome enough for a shirt ad, but not weak, dominated by a firm jaw, an engaging grin and those remarkable eyes— baby blue one minute, icy grey the next. He has the voice, the carriage, the manners, the polish, the brains. He is bilingual, charming and hardworking. He chats as easily with tycoons as with janitors, smiles a lot, laughs a lot, and is guaranteed not to fade, rust or drip on the carpet.[6]

In one further respect John Turner fitted the Liberal party's recruiting profile. In 1887 and again in 1968, when the party was in trouble in Quebec, it had chosen dark-horse candidates with real appeal among francophone Canadians: Wilfrid Laurier and Pierre Trudeau. In 1919, with labor unrest growing in the shadow of the Bolshevik revolution and an industrializing capitalist economy, the Liberal party had chosen Mackenzie King, an expert in labor-management relations. Now in 1984, having fallen to third-party status in western Canada and having been spurned for years by businessmen, it made historic sense for the party once again to lead to its weakness by looking to a figure in the business community who could claim western roots.

Only in one major dimension did Turner not conform to the party's renewal formula. He represented opposition to, not continuity with, the outgoing incumbent's record. Having resigned from Trudeau's cabinet as minister of finance in 1975 under a cloud that poorly concealed the two men's mutual antipathy, Turner had worked ever since as a corporate lawyer in Canada's financial capital, where he had absorbed the laissez-faire ideology of big business as well as its emotional opposition to the Trudeau government's interventionist stance. Unlike Trudeau, who had been a severe critic of the Liberals but had joined the party to become a member of Pearson's government, Turner had left Trudeau's government to become the personification of its extraparliamentary opposition while remaining a member of the party. For years Turner was the undeclared leader of the discontented within the Liberal party's ranks.

Despite his muted disloyalty over the past decade, in early 1984 he seemed so obviously the winner that the party establishment flocked to his support even before he declared, on March 16, that he was throwing his hat into the ring. On that day, flanked by seventeen ministers from Trudeau's cabinet and half the caucus, carefully chosen to display a balance of old Liberals and new, male and female, anglophone and francophone, it appeared that Turner's dissociation from Trudeau could only help clinch his claim to the savior role. Fortuna smiled, but enigmatically: Did Turner have the Virtu required to exploit this opportunity?

The successor to political leadership needs the capacity to be both an agent of continuity and an agent of change: his role as innovator will be accepted only after he has demonstrated that he understands and accepts the values of his group.[7] So strong was the antipathy of John Turner and his advisers to the whole Trudeau opus that he immediately made it clear, during the nationally televised press conference announcing his candidacy in Ottawa's historic Château Laurier hotel, that he was distancing himself from Trudeau's policy on bilingualism. Even though he was forced by the outrage expressed by Quebec Liberals and anglophone Trudeau loyalists to make subsequent "clarifications" of his position, he nevertheless had sown doubts about his leadership capacity. In his effort to stake out positions attractive to new constituencies such as westerners (on language policy) and businessmen (on economic restraint), the question was whether these moves would be at the cost of losing support among the Liberals' traditional strongholds. Did his difficulty in grasping the issues of the eighties, such as women's pressure for contract compliance and equal pay for work of equal value, indicate that he had become rusty in the comfort of corporate boardrooms? Was his cautious campaign, invoking the dreams of his own youth, too much an appeal for a "better yesterday," in columnist Jeff Simpson's phrase, to offer the Liberal party that renewed sense of mission it so badly needed? Did the small errors of his campaign—his refusal to resign his corporate directorships, his revival of the controversy about why he had resigned from the cabinet in 1975, the chaotic organization of his campaign headquarters in the early weeks—suggest that John Turner's charisma had lost its aura? These worries were expressed repeatedly through the media coverage of the fifteen-week campaign. They were not entirely laid to rest even when Turner dropped his more right-wing themes in order to burnish his appeal to the Liberal delegates by affirming his commitment to their left-leaning social reform values.

In the end the party delegates set their doubts aside, doubts about Turner's lack of passion, doubts about his political fumbles and his awkwardness on television, doubts about what were his real commitments and values. Turner was considered superior to Chrétien by margins of two to one on virtually all leadership qualities: his TV image appeal, his views on policy, his overall ability and competence, his ability to unite the party and make tough decisions, his appeal to different regions, his capacity to earn respect from international leaders. Only in answer to one question—who delegates personally liked best—did Jean Chrétien outshine Turner by more than two to one. In sum, 63 percent of the delegates felt Turner was best able to help the party win the next election, compared to 19 percent for Chrétien.[8]

As Liberal delegates poured out of the Ottawa Civic Center on June 16, 1984, after selecting John Turner their leader (by a vote of 1,862 to 1,368 over Jean Chrétien), they had reason to be satisfied that the government party's second leadership renewal scenario had been followed in the main. The party's new "savior" might have lost some of his gloss after emerging from exile, but he still had the demeanor of a prime minister and a winner. The party might not have been sure whether it had actually redefined its policy direction with Turner's ideas, but it had gained new energy from the delegate nomination meetings and the candidates' tours across the country. Even if the public, for its part, had not developed any "Turnermania" similar to the outpouring of emotion that Trudeau had generated in 1968, there had been enough excitement in the race, enough sympathy for the appealing Jean Chrétien, and enough sense of policy renewal conveyed by the five regional all-candidates' debates for Gallup to report in early June that the Liberals had climbed to a 10 percent lead over the Progressive Conservatives. The questions now uppermost were centered on the new leader's performance as prime minister. Would he use the powers of his office to heal party wounds opened up during the rival candidates' campaigns? How would he manage the transition from party leader to prime minister? And what would he decide was the most opportune time to go to the public for a new mandate? Fortuna still seemed to be smiling. Turner now had to prove his princely Virtu in the office he had striven for all his life.

Act II. The Transition to Government:
From Leader to Prime Minister

The Turner team's difficulty in striking a workable balance between assuring continuity and proclaiming change was demonstrated vividly during the brief process of transition in mid-summer of 1984 when the party leader became prime minister and established his new cabinet. Although the new leader and his staff received briefings from the clerk of the privy council, Gordon Osbaldeston, and the prime minister's principal secretary, Tom Axworthy, who had been a Turner supporter in the 1968 leadership campaign, the new team's arrival in office appeared more like the sweeping in of an opposition party than the maintenance of power by a political team that had merely changed leaders. The files of the prime minister's office staff were packed up and sent to the Public Archives. The officers and staff in the prime minister's office resigned and waited—in all cases but one, in vain—to be rehired. The detailed transition books prepared for the new team by the outgoing staff explaining the problems of governance were ignored. This dismissal of experienced staff indicated a near paranoia among the Turner cadre about maintaining any links with the Trudeau era.

Not coping with the Trudeau legacy bureaucratically was one thing; not effectively dealing with party rifts politically was quite another matter. Prolonged negotiations took place with Jean Chrétien, deeply wounded by his loss in the leadership campaign. A public compromise giving him symbolic but not real power in the Quebec party did not resolve the factional bitterness between the Chrétien camp and the Turner forces in Quebec led by André Ouellet. Where party unhappiness was not vocally expressed it was ignored, but at longer-term risk. Little effort was made to recruit the best workers from the other leadership candidates' teams and so bind up party injuries by rewarding and exploiting their valuable capacities. The fissures of party disunity were underestimated as the new party leader became absorbed by the process of cabinet making.

One firm criticism that John Turner had leveled against the Trudeau government during his eight years in political exile was the excessive complexity of its cabinet committee system which, in his view, had neutralized strong ministers and paralyzed the policymaking process of the government's basic line departments. In an effort to signal the change his new broom was bringing about, the newly installed prime minister made two significant moves. First, the cabinet was pruned from thirty-seven to twenty-nine positions. Though this gesture was meant to symbolize a concern for government austerity, it was a dangerously self-defeating initiative. Twenty-four of the new Turner ministers had served in Trudeau's last cabinet, eighteen in the same ministries. Only five new faces joined the cabinet, none of national prominence since all had been elevated from the caucus. None qualified as the major figures from the business community and the west that Turner had promised to bring into government. At the same time, the dropping of incumbent ministers, some of whom had actually supported Turner's campaign, could only create dissatisfaction rather than solidarity at the senior level of the party's ranks.

Less politically damaging, but more expressive of Turner's weak grasp of the problems of governance, was his major reorganization of the cabinet committee system. In one stroke of radical surgery two central organs of Trudeau's finely tuned system were amputated. Since the late 1970s the ministries of state for social development and economic development had acted as central agencies coordinating the decisionmaking process of most government departments. Turner gave little indication that the essential functions of these central agencies would be filled elsewhere in the government structure. This action was portrayed as a decisive step by the new prime minister but cognoscenti of government shook their heads, wondering why such a potentially disruptive reorganization was being made if there were at most a few summer months available to make it work before the next election. While only close observers suspected that Turner's implementation of a decade-old personal agenda indicated he had no clear strategy for government, it soon became plain for all to see that the new prime minister also had no clear strategy for getting elected. Before he had secured himself in office and shown the country his capacity to govern wisely as prime minister, he plunged, exhausted and unprepared, into the next act of his drama of downfall. In circumstances that were fully under his control, he had neither assured continuity between the two Liberal administrations nor introduced convincing changes by the time he called an election on July 9.

Act III. The Federal Election:
From Prime Minister to Campaigner

On the face of it, there seemed every reason for John Turner to delay his election call and prolong his political honeymoon in the prime minister's residence until the autumn. For simple public relations reasons, taking a few months to act as head of government—welcoming the queen on her scheduled visit to the Maritimes and Ontario, greeting the pope on the first papal visit to the country, congratulating Canadian medalists at the Olympics, cutting ribbons, announcing projects—would have given the public a chance to firm up its image of John Turner as prime minister. Meanwhile, the Turner team could establish firm control of the machinery of government and clarify the content of their policy agenda. Party wounds would have time to heal, the troops time to rest, and the party cadre time to recover from the leadership campaign and prepare funds and plans for the general election.

Campaign preparation was desperately needed. No campaign planning had been done either at the general level of staffing headquarters or in such specific details as choosing and renting an airplane for the leader's tour. The election preparedness committee that Trudeau had set up under the cochairmanship of Senator Keith Davey and Finance Minister Marc Lalonde had done little, waiting first for Trudeau's decision to run again or retire and then waiting through the long spring leadership process for the party to decide which candidate would be prime minister. The executive of the Liberal party of Canada had done little, the president having fired her national director, Gordon Ashworth, one of the few people in active party service who had campaign experience. At the prime minister's office, where Ashworth was taken in, election preparation had been initiated with a heavy emphasis on developing policy themes for a new Trudeau platform and developing a research model produced by the party pollster, Martin Goldfarb, who offered the future campaign a state of the art system of monitoring public attitudes to policy issues. Although Goldfarb had briefed the leadership candidates on his work, the new Turner group decided to pay his ideas scant heed.

It was not because the new prime minister's staff had arrived with a coherent new agenda of issues and techniques that it disregarded the old staff's material. Turner had taken various positions during the leadership campaign, moving from the political right to the political center, but without articulating consistent new policies for liberalism in the 1980s. Even at a less lofty level, no slogan had been thought through, no logo designed, no ad campaign sketched out. In British Columbia, Alberta, and Saskatchewan there was virtually no party organization. As a consequence of the freeze on riding nominations decreed by the Davey-Lalonde committee, candidates had been nominated in only 40 of the 282 ridings, a figure that compared ominously with the Conservatives' 240 candidates and the NDP's 155 nominations already in place. For all of these reasons Jean Chrétien advised Turner to resist pressure to run, show his stuff, and wait for a better moment later in the year.

Chrétien's was the minority position among the Liberals surrounding the new prime minister. The Quebec caucus desperately wanted to seize the moment. Published polls had indicated the Liberals had a 10 percent lead, but the party's private pollsters reported that this support was soft. An immediate election was also the advice of the minister of finance, Marc Lalonde. Economic prospects for the fall were poor. If Turner waited and had to bring in an autumn budget, he might run into difficulty. Senator Davey concurred: Turner could take it as front-runner the way Trudeau had in the winter election of 1979–80.

Turner's acceptance of this advice against his better judgment indicated how far his hubris had taken him. He ignored the fact that Trudeau was known to the public and experienced in campaign battle, having run four times before as party leader. He held Brian Mulroney in low regard, as a lightweight in politics as he had been in business. Turner seemed to nurture an overriding belief in the power of his own public persona. After all, he was devoting himself, a man of superior talents, to the mission of government. His word alone should be enough to guarantee to the public that he was bringing a new broom to government. The very fact of his ascendancy would surely reverse years of discontent. When offered the choice between the untried Mulroney and the experienced Turner, surely the public would choose the better man.

In effect, John Turner consciously forfeited a situation whose main variables were under his control and threw himself into Fortuna's hands, hoping that his luck would hold and the Canadian public would endorse the Liberal party's recent decision. He took a weekend to fly to England and ask the queen, who refused to visit Canada while a federal election campaign was in progress, to postpone her visit to the fall. By the time he had returned to Ottawa the final decision had been made to ask the governor general to dissolve Parliament and issue the writ for a new election. The gamble had been taken. The outcome would depend on Turner's generalship, his campaign strategy and its policy expression, the leader's personal performance on the hostings and on television, and the capacity of his new campaign organization. In each respect the prince blundered or was the victim of serious errors by the staff he had appointed.[9]

Campaign Generalship Contrary to practice in every party, John Turner insisted that he would run his own campaign as if he were its chief executive officer. Rather than perch on top of an organizational hierarchy that was managed for him by a designated appointee, he sat in the middle of a participatory circle, exposed not to the consistent counsel of his chief of staff but to conflicting advice coming from many advisers whom he had chosen less for their experience or political astuteness than for their loyalty during his period in exile and their dissociation from the Trudeau regime. While Turner said he wanted to be open to advice, he established a campaign decisionmaking structure that inhibited the flow of information. William Lee, the manager for Turner's leadership campaign, was put in overall charge of the election campaign and had to start from ground zero to recruit staff. A complex policy structure was created to consider elements for the party platform. Regional cochairmen were appointed in such numbers that they made the campaign hierarchy topheavy. These processes of decisionmaking were too elaborate to produce either strategy or tactics expeditiously. Still, the lethargy that characterized the first three weeks of the Liberal campaign was due mainly to the prime minister's flat refusal to campaign during July. In waiting for Brian

Mulroney to self-destruct, Turner lost control of the political agenda and let the media concentrate on the mistakes, small and large, that he proceeded to make.

Strategy   Although Turner structured his decisionmaking system so as to generate a plethora of advice, he had great difficulty resolving the contradictory counsel he received. One of his two competing pollsters, Angus Reid, warned him against becoming the candidate of continuity; on the other hand, Senator Jerry Grafstein, an old Turner supporter who had also worked actively in Trudeau's campaigns, warned him against alienating the basic Liberal coalition. Turner and his strategists had still not resolved the conundrum of how to handle the Trudeau legacy and at the same time turn the public's desire for change to his own advantage. His key advisers wanted him to swing back to the right and appeal to the west. Yet if he ran against his own party's record in government, the danger was that the voters might agree that this record was not supportable and reject the Liberal party. Unlike Trudeau campaigns, which were directed according to a strategy hammered out by senior campaign officials, no strategic debate was carried on and finalized. With Angus Reid finding in his polling research that Turner was more popular than the Liberal party and ahead of Brian Mulroney on such leadership criteria as experience, trustworthiness, and competence, the campaign strategy centered by default on simply promoting the leader. No clear line of attack on the opposition leader was worked out. How Turner was to incarnate the public's desire for both change and strong leadership was not spelled out for the guidance of the campaign organization.

Policy   A leader-centered campaign requires that the leader have something to say. Neither John Turner's policy instincts nor his speech-writing infrastructure rose to the occasion. Instinctively, John Turner headed for what had traditionally been Conservative turf. Speaking like a corporate manager, he sounded the chords of fiscal responsibility, the need to eliminate waste from government and, above all, the priority of reducing the federal deficit. Ignoring the fact that his party had won four out of the five previous elections by appealing to an evolving Liberal coalition of francophones, ethnic minorities, the poor, women, youth, and the aged, Turner took the "high road" of responsible leadership, pledging not to bribe the public with promises to spend its own money as Brian Mulroney was doing. This did not stop him from making many old-style promises, particularly in the west, where he announced a number of emergency measures to combat a prairie drought. He did make pledges that his commitment to capitalism would not be at the price of his commitment to social programs, but did not clarify how this circle was to be squared. In shying away from Trudeau's recent Liberal issues of social justice, independence, and energy self-sufficiency, he failed to remind the basic Liberal vote why it should stay in his fold.

While no one else could be blamed for his failure to articulate his over-arching vision, the weak content of his major speeches resulted from a break-down of the policy process that had been set up in the prime minister's office. Although Torrance Wylie, Senator Michael Kirby, and Tom Axworthy—three left Liberals from the Trudeau era—were hastily recruited to produce solid theme speeches for the leader's tour, their material arrived late and was so inadequate that the speeches were written mainly on the leader's plane by one staff person without research support. A large youth apprenticeship program; grants for young entrepreneurs; a doubled tax writeoff of capital losses; a tax credit for living in the north; a new organization, Small Business Canada, to harmonize programs for small entrepreneurs; a dozen commitments on women's issues: it was a scatter-shot production that did nothing to clarify the confusing personal message that Turner was transmitting through his own campaign performance.

The Leader's Performance During the leadership campaign Turner had brushed aside criticism of his policy vagueness by maintaining that he would be judged by his actions, not his words. The first act of his election campaign was the notification given at a press conference that, in accordance with an agree-ment made with the former prime minister, seventeen members of Parliament were being appointed to various positions ranging from senator to judge to ambassador. At one stroke, Turner tarred himself with the brush of patronage politics with which Trudeau, in a rash of appointments made during his last weeks as prime minister, had been painted. Having been forced by Trudeau to sign an agreement to make the appointments of these outgoing members of Parliament at the time the next election was called (on the politically dubious grounds that Turner needed these M.P.s to maintain his majority in the House), Turner failed to put these appointments into perspective for the public. Offered the chance to reject dramatically the Trudeau style (as his campaign manager had advised), Turner instead implicitly associated the new regime with the old, causing voters to question their evaluation of the new Liberal leader. Dwelt upon by the media for lack of other news of the campaign, exploited by the opposition who worked it into a major campaign issue, Turner's patronage appointments became a symbolic factor, indicative of the norms of public life being violated by a man who proclaimed it his mission in life to restore them.

This major error in the opening moments of the campaign reminded reporters of the repeated slips and clarifications that had characterized Turner's leadership campaign and alerted them to further pratfalls. Turner proceeded to oblige them with the help of his party colleagues. When, on a public platform,

Turner patted the posterior of Iona Campagnola, the party president reacted by patting him back, in full view of a television camera, thereby turning a quirk that lingered from his boardroom days into a major public incident. Brian Mulroney had committed a far worse breach of decorum by talking to reporters about the appointment to an ambassadorship of Bryce Mackasey in terms of there being "no whore like an old whore." But unlike Mulroney, who had swallowed his pride and apologized to the public, Turner stubbornly refused to address his unacceptable behavior, sloughing off the incident for several weeks, until just two days before his appearance at a leaders' debate on women's issues.

Other errors—his claim, for instance, that Mulroney would fire 600,000 civil servants when there were but 500,000 in the federal government's employment—kept undermining Turner's original asset, his reputation for competence. Far from displaying his dominance of Fortuna, Turner's performance indicated his incapacity to make issues work for him and prevent problems from working against him. While he needed to reject the style but not the policies of Pierre Trudeau, he was in fact rejecting the policies while endorsing the patronage style, and becoming an object of public derision in the process (the media christened his tour plane *Derri-Air*). Rather than offering the public "a new man with a new plan," he appeared in the relentless spotlight of daily campaign coverage to be an old man with no plan at all. At no moment was this ineffectiveness transmitted more immediately and dramatically to the public than in the first two of three national debates Turner had with the other two party leaders.

The Television Debates   In a situation where both Turner and Mulroney were running their first election campaigns as party leaders, a televised debate offered voters a chance to observe and assess directly these newcomers' political skills. In a devastating set of back-to-back debates in the third week of the campaign, first in French on July 24 and then in English the next day, Turner laid out his weaknesses in full public view. No precedent required the Liberal leader to engage in more than one debate. In 1980 Pierre Trudeau had refused to participate in any such event. Presumably confident in his Paris-learned French and his Rhodes scholar–certified intellect, Turner had accepted the challenge to a French-language debate with the faultlessly and colloquially bilingual Brian Mulroney. Where Turner was stiff, Mulroney was fluent. Turner spoke in arid generalities; Mulroney spoke with apparent sincerity and concern for Quebec's specific political problems. Mulroney affirmed his affinity with Quebec, Turner communicated his distance in both time and space.

Since these two untested leaders had not yet been brought into well-defined focus, the public was looking for signs of their humanity and competence. In his English-language debate Turner proceeded to forfeit what had been meant to compensate for his lack of campaign organization—his claim to superior leadership qualities such as decisiveness and intelligence. In sharp contrast to Mulroney's ease, Turner appeared frozen and nervous, referring to his notes and pronouncing with a rehearsed air sentences that had nothing special or personal to say to Canadians across the country. Asserting confidence but communicating unease, he showed no intellectual dexterity and had none of that combative quality that voters could remember in the performances of Pierre Trudeau. Indeed, Turner let Mulroney dominate the bulk of the debate. At one point he attempted to rally with a counterattack that handed the patronage issue to the Conservative leader, who proceeded to put Turner totally on the defensive. Claiming he had "no option" but to accept the deal that the former prime minister had imposed on him, Turner let himself be branded as the errand boy of Pierre Trudeau, in no way a break from the Liberal past. Alone on stage on the third Wednesday of the campaign, Turner was politically finished. He had faltered in full public view, partly because the cumbersome campaign organization he had himself set up continued to give him conflicting advice. During the last-minute preparations for the debate, Keith Davey was urging him to sound like a reformer and William Lee was telling him to distance himself from the Trudeau record.

Campaign Organization Lee had neither wanted Turner to call the campaign in the summer nor did he feel inclined himself to direct the operation. When Turner prevailed upon him to take on the formidable task of setting up and directing an organization, with no time for preparation, he did this assuming he would have full operational control from his office at the party's temporary campaign headquarters. His control was illusory. Even as Lee was setting up the campaign office and worrying about installing electronic communications with the ridings, most of which still had to nominate their candidates, the prime minister's office was establishing an organization to direct the leader's tour, bringing in people who were leery of Lee from the previous weeks of the leadership campaign. Torrance Wylie was brought in by principal secretary John Swift as the counterbalance to Lee. Stephen LeDrew, who was put in charge of the tour, was explicitly told to report to Swift, not Lee.

Although the chief players from headquarters and the prime minister's office met every morning at eight to consult on decisions large and small, a gradual breakdown of communications between these two centers developed. Lee complained that a parallel campaign was being waged from the prime minister's office, which in turn complained that Lee was withholding vital polling data. Other tensions developed, many focusing on the campaign chairman.

Policy material for candidates. Although the policy director of the party, Audrey Gill, had handled candidates' policy needs in previous elections, Lee brought in Gordon Kaiser, a lawyer who had been active in the Turner leadership campaign, as campaign policy director. Although he had no experience in the job, Kaiser rejected the large briefing books that had already been prepared by Gill and her staff. After many days of inaction by Kaiser, Marc Lalonde in exasperation sent out to candidates a policy briefing book prepared in his office in the Department of Finance. Later still, John Turner's final leadership campaign brochure was sent out masquerading between new covers as a policy agenda. After a month of campaigning, it was too little and too late to be of use to the candidates in the field. With communications deteriorating between the prime minister's office and campaign headquarters, crucial correspondence addressed to the prime minister was not forwarded to the party office. As a result, a number of questionnaires sent by interest groups for policy responses languished unanswered in a huge pile. This accounted for further bad press when, for instance, a South Asian group announced the Liberal campaign was the only one not to have responded to its questions.

The advertising group. The public learned only indirectly of the organizational paralysis on the policy side of the campaign. The tension between William Lee and Senator Jerry Grafstein's advertising group was played out in full public view, thanks to the leaking of the protagonists' internal memoranda. In previous campaigns Grafstein had enjoyed a very free hand in the setting up of Red Leaf Communications as the Liberals' umbrella advertising group. This time Lee insisted on exercising his authority and demanded full accountability from Grafstein concerning his budget and his program. The ensuing bickering delayed the production of the commercials, whose impact was blunted by the bad publicity this internal feud had generated.

Pollster versus pollster. Another conflict arose in the Liberals' campaign, between an old hand at Liberal campaigns, Martin Goldfarb, and a new figure brought in from the Turner campaign, Winnipeg pollster Angus Reid, an associate of Turner's leadership campaign cochairman, Lloyd Axworthy. Goldfarb's elaborate issue-monitoring model, which had been worked out for Trudeau, was set aside by the new group in favor of Reid. With his reputation and future government contacts at stake, Goldfarb fought for his turf. As a result, the campaign had two pollsters giving two sets of interpretations of their somewhat differing data.

Turner was unwilling or unable to resolve the bitter infighting and personality clashes in time. Whatever was going on behind the scenes, it was clear from the campaign's chaos in the field that this organization was the most amateurish observers could recall. Events were poorly planned, failing to display Turner to best advantage. Crowds were small and the ridings he visited were often neither key constituencies nor those where he owed the candidate a favor. Bickering seemed contagious: on the tour plane, a small DC-9 where the leader's group was in full view of the press personnel, the disarray had reporters agog. In the crucial campaign for Metro Toronto, no one seemed to be in charge to pull the organization together. Open disputes between the supporters of John Roberts and those of David Smith, who replaced him as political boss of Metro, came to the surface in nomination struggles through the northwestern ridings of the city. Around the country half of the provincial chairmen selected by Keith Davey had been replaced and had to start from scratch.

The cumulative impact of this organizational shambles was devastating. If the party could not put together a well-organized campaign, if it could not deal with the issues of the day, if it could not coordinate its personnel, it was bound to sacrifice that aura of competence on which its electoral success had been based for decades. The Liberal mystique was disintegrating within days of the campaign's launch, thanks to the willing efforts of the media to report that the white knight had fallen off his horse. Keith Davey wrote an angry letter to the *Toronto Globe and Mail* complaining of its "yellow journalism" and accusing this prestigious newspaper and flagship of the Thomson press empire of being "just another Thomson newspaper." [10] Elizabeth Turner, the prime minister's daughter, vented her rage at the media in general by screaming "Screw 'em all." [11] Lloyd Axworthy complained that, while Turner and the Liberal organization had been subjected to highly exacting scrutiny, Mulroney and the Conservative machine had been treated uncritically.[12] It was true that the press gallery was reporting with unprofessional glee every quirk of the prime minister, from the way he licked his lips to how he harrumphed and cleared his throat after making a joke. The press, displaying the pack mentality so often observed in election campaigns, picked on the faltering colossus. Like a band of tormentors, the reporters watched out for every error or mannerism that could be added to their repertoire of Turner gaffes. Trivial Pursuit was ardently played in front of a national audience.

Unfair though this treatment seemed, the Liberals had only their leader to blame. John Turner had failed utterly to respond to the changed nature of the press corps. Having been described for years in flattering terms by reporters who built up his myth as dauphin in exile, he was unnerved by their switch to a more critical stance once he reentered the political ring. The pathetic spectacle Turner made on the evening news and in the morning papers showed the prince at Fortuna's mercy, having lost all control of how and what he was communicating to the public. The reality of Turner the politician so clashed with the previous image the same media had sustained that reporters could barely disguise their contempt. A palpable dislike of the Liberals, rekindled from Trudeau's time, infused the whole coverage of the campaign.

The impact of the Liberal imbroglio on public opinion was unprecedentedly swift. By the end of July the Liberals had already lost their lead and were heading for a rout. In this rapid shift, supported by the generally critical coverage of the media, the debates were crucial. John Turner squandered his opportunity, leaving Brian Mulroney and the Conservatives as the only alternative. Responding quickly to its disappointment with Turner, the public reverted to its basic attitude as revealed in poll after poll over the previous two years, identifying the need for change with support for the Conservative party. By mid-August, 49 percent of the support the Liberals had commanded in June had turned elsewhere.[13] The Liberal coalition crumbled as the party lost popularity among every group of its constituents. The highly educated and high-income voters who had moved to the Liberals in June moved back again to the Conservatives. Research showed it was the debates that crystallised the party leaders' images with the public. Turner was seen to be insensitive to the needs and aspirations of Canadians. Though Turner had been considered the best prime minister in June by a margin of two to one over Brian Mulroney, by mid-August it was Mulroney who was preferred as prime minister by a margin of two to one over Turner.[14]

Nowhere was the turnaround more dramatic or devastating for the Liberals than in Quebec. A Southam Press poll published in June indicated that the Liberal party still enjoyed 61 percent of the public's support in Quebec. By all indications, Brian Mulroney would lose the seat he was contesting in his home riding of Manicouagan. But with the departure from the scene of the powerful Trudeau the Quebec electorate had become potentially volatile, as it had when previous overwhelmingly popular leaders such as Maurice Duplessis and Saint Laurent had died or retired. Turner made further errors about Quebec that accentuated the doubts about his commitment to the defense of the French language and culture that he had raised on the first day of his leadership campaign. He declared he would not negotiate a deal for Quebec to sign the constitution with the separatist government of René Lévesque. He attacked the Conservatives for running three candidates who had supported the Yes side in the 1980 referendum campaign. At a time when Quebec wanted to heal its wounds from the referendum and constitution struggles, Turner scratched off its scabs. He showed how badly he misunderstood the significance to Québecers of the referendum's defeat in 1980 and their humiliating exclusion from the federal-provincial accord on the constitution in 1981. When John Turner accepted Brian Mulroney's challenge to debate with him and Ed Broadbent in French on television, he gave the untried Conservative leader a windfall chance to present himself as Quebec's native son. Identifying himself with Quebec's interests and preaching reconciliation, the boy from Baie Comeau reached out for the mantle of Quebec's federal champion made available by Pierre Trudeau's retirement.

Turner raised doubts. Mulroney soothed fears. No organizational preparation had been made to deal with the transition after Trudeau's departure. Bitterness persisted between supporters of Jean Chrétien and André Ouellet, the Turner chief in Quebec. The allegedly invincible Red Machine turned out to be nonexistent. No theme was declared for the campaign. No signs appeared. On July 16 *La Presse* ran the headline: "Pas un seul candidat Libéral au Québec." The Quebec daily *Le Soleil* exemplified the switch by the Quebec media from the losing to the winning horse. Having supported Joe Clark over Brian Mulroney during the Conservatives' leadership campaign of 1963, having supported Turner over Chrétien in the Liberals' race the following year, *Le Soleil* shifted to Mulroney as its favorite for the 1984 general election. The Conservatives and Mulroney were ready to seize the chance that Turner had handed them in Quebec by running against the Liberals' record and by threatening to tear down what Trudeau had built.

Brian Mulroney, like John Turner, had directed his life toward the goal of becoming prime minister. Like Turner, he had been frustrated in an earlier attempt to win the leadership of his party. Unlike Turner, he left nothing to chance when Fortuna finally smiled on him. Indeed, the Progressive Conservative campaign was a study in contrasts with that of the Liberals. The campaign organization had been put in place months before the electoral call, staffed by professionals who were experienced in election campaigns and animated by a team spirit that resulted from bringing together talented organizers from all factions of the party. The Conservative leader's tour had been given a dry run while the Liberals were choosing their leader. No detail had been left to chance: the visual effects, the leader's speeches and themes, the way that the leader and his wife functioned together. The numerous members of the cast were rehearsed and practiced until their performance was letter perfect. Policy positions were worked out and held in readiness. Most important of all, a strategy was fashioned from exhaustive survey research and shrewd analysis of its implications. Mulroney carefully avoided the traps set for him by the Trudeau Liberals. Whether it was supporting the medicare system, defending French-language minority rights, or supporting Trudeau's peace initiative, Mulroney refused to be tagged as a reactionary right-winger, sticking so close to the ideological center that he could have passed for a Liberal himself. Having striven to reassure Canadians that a Progressive Conservative government would not attack the basic policy achievements of the Trudeau era, the Conservatives' task was to identify John Turner with all the unfavorable characteristics Canadian voters associated with the antagonistic person of Pierre Trudeau and, at the same, sell Brian Mulroney as prime ministerial in quality.

Mulroney and his well-practiced machine stuck to their strategy and, campaigning hard, kept the media busy but at arm's length. Mulroney emotionally attacked Turner's patronage appointments as a national scandal; Mulroney excoriated the Liberals' handling of the Canadian-American relationship, grossly exaggerating the ill will between the two governments. He lavished promises along the road. He raised the prospect of a brand-new era of federal-provincial and Canadian-American reconciliation dawning upon his election. He obfuscated difficult issues. He ignored contradictions in his own positions and he gave only three television interviews. Meanwhile, Tory ads, closely coordinated with intensive polling and Canada's most ambitious direct mail campaign, reinforced the message that only Mulroney could bring peace and prosperity to the post-Trudeau period.

In Quebec he courted the francophone vote by pledging to negotiate a constitutional veto for Quebec.[15] At the same time, he courted anglophone voters by supporting the defense of minority language rights in Manitoba. He flattered the nationalists and received enthusiastic support from the Parti Québécois political machine. He stroked the provincial Liberals, many of whom, including their leader, his friend Robert Bourassa, were happy to settle a grudge with the federal Liberals who had treated them with so much scorn and had been responsible for their defeat in the 1981 provincial election.

With their organization in a state of collapse, their strategy incoherent, and their leader in desperate straits, a consensus emerged among Turner's campaign advisers in early August that Bill Lee must go. Although opinions conflicted about whether he was actually responsible for all the ills attributed to him, Lee had become the scapegoat. Denied his leader's full confidence, Lee quit along with four key members of his staff. Keith Davey, who had been advising from the wings, was put in full charge of the campaign organization on August 4 with a mandate to redefine the campaign strategy, revive the organization, and restore morale throughout the party.

This desperate purge was in itself a further devastation of the Liberals' image of competence. Davey's return contradicted the whole thrust of the Turner effort to disassociate himself from the Trudeau legacy in general and the process identified as excessive back-room power, exemplified by Keith Davey, in particular. The change came too late to resolve all the backbiting that had developed in Quebec and between Trudeau and Turner loyalists. Nor could the promotion of Keith Davey stop the policy disarray caused when first Iona Campagnolo and then Turner's wife, Geills, disagreed with Turner on Canada's support of a nuclear freeze.

Davey did manage, despite these obstacles, to stabilize the campaign's thrust, restore morale in the campaign team, enhance the effectiveness of the tour and, most important, steady the leader enough for him to deliver his speeches effectively and gain more respectful press attention. By the final fortnight of the campaign John Turner seemed to have hit his stride, even generating reports that his campaign was catching fire with its new strategy.

Davey had prevailed upon the prime minister to rebuild his links with the Trudeau era by reactivating a left-of-center reform appeal to the old Liberal coalition of supporters. Turner pledged to maintain the thrust of Trudeau's peace initiative. He wrote a letter to Soviet First Secretary Chernenko and appointed retired diplomat George Ignatieff as Canada's ambassador for disarmament. He announced a multifaceted program of women's issues. He endorsed the notion of a minimum tax on the rich and started attacking Brian Mulroney's honesty by branding him a "let's-pretend Liberal." He claimed Mulroney had made 338 promises that would cost over $20 billion and castigated Mulroney's last-minute accounting as a snow job deceiving the Canadian public. Having ruled out negative advertising as unacceptable at the beginning of the campaign, Turner concurred when the Davey-Grafstein team decided to put commercials on the air that enraged Conservative supporters by their negativism: a shopping cart, for instance, being heaped by a Mulroney-like shopper with packages that were identified as Tory promises but bore no price tag until, at the cash register, the shopper was forced to admit he could not pay. The wheel had come full circle when Keith Davey prevailed upon Pierre Trudeau to make a formal appearance on behalf of the Liberals in an uncrowded hall in Montreal. "Requested in panic, given with reluctance, crafted in indifference," his speech was in Jeff Simpson's words, "a loon's cry before the terrible storm." [16]

Was the impact of the Davey rescue operation a further discrediting of Turner, who had made so much of his own honesty only to switch from a right-wing to a left-wing position? [17] Or had it saved the Liberal party from oblivion on the right in order to end the campaign at least in a position consistent with its previous principles of the center? These questions would only be answered after the immediate postmortems had been carried out.

Epilogue. Opposition Leader or Albatross

Considering that the Liberals started the campaign on July 9 with 49 percent support in the polls and received only 28 percent of the vote on September 4, falling from 146 seats (52 percent of the House) to 40 seats (14 percent of the House), 1984 must be seen as the worst electoral disaster in the history of the Liberal party of Canada. In the Atlantic provinces the Liberals fell eleven points in the popular vote from 45 percent in 1980 to 34 percent in 1984, returning only seven of the region's thirty-two seats. In Quebec the party fell thirty-three points in their traditional stronghold, receiving 35 percent of the vote and seventeen seats, with a loss of fifty-six to the Conservatives. In Ontario a loss of 12 percent of the vote left them with fourteen seats, thirty-eight less than they won in 1980 and just one seat more than the NDP obtained. In the west, where Turner had promised to restore Liberal strength, the party lost seven more percentage points in the popular vote, declining to a negligible 17 percent. It won only two seats, retaining Winnipeg-Fort

Garry, which it won in 1979 and 1980, losing St. Boniface, and picking up Vancouver-Quadra, which Turner himself contested in a symbolic gesture of solidarity with the west.

The Liberal party had lost touch with its basic electoral coalition and could only hope that, if the voters had been volatile in 1984, they could be volatile once more, as they had been after Conservative leader John Diefenbaker won a similar landslide victory in 1958. Having lost control of the political agenda, Canadian Liberals could do little but wait until the new government party faltered in its performance.

The Liberal party entered opposition with some assets whose husbanding could determine whether it would be able to turn its bleak situation to advantage. When Liberal senators appointed by Trudeau were added to the small group of Liberal members of Parliament, the party's caucus could be seen to boast considerable organizational and policymaking talent. The extraparliamentary party was far more substantial, legitimate, and active than it had been in the late 1950s after the rout of 1958. It provided the vehicle for recruitment of new blood and the forum for debating issues around which a new political content would have to be defined for Liberalism in Canada.

The party's liabilities were nevertheless substantial. The organization had been shaken by a political earthquake. Its troops were in shock. Its technology was behind the times. Its fund-raising capacity was inadequate to liquidate its large debt. Factionalism, the bane of opposition parties, had already broken out, particularly in Quebec, where disciplinary levers could no longer be pulled to keep order and maintain an electorally crucial facade of unity.

One last factor, John Turner himself, was classified by some as asset, by others as liability. For those who saw him as a liability, his winning the Vancouver seat of Quadra was the worst news of the night on September 4 because it ensured Turner would remain as party leader. It was he who had caused the electoral cataclysm by his amazing lack of political Virtu. Uncertain of where he stood, unsure in his political instincts, uncomfortable with the attacker role required of an opposition leader, in this group's perspective he was an albatross around the party's neck. Those who saw Turner as an asset pointed to his sense of personal mission to rebuild the Liberal party, his general decency, and his determination to emerge from his personal humiliation and fight his way back to power. It remained an open question whether Turner could acquire in opposition the Virtu he had so obviously lacked as prime minister. To outside observers it seemed that now, more than ever, Turner was in the hands of Fortuna. It would take many mistakes on the part of Brian Mulroney's Progressive Conservatives and an equally unskilled performance by the New Democrats' Ed Broadbent for John Turner's Liberals to find the fates smiling their way again.

Notes

The epigraph is from "The Liberal Party and the Canadian State," *Acadiensis*, 12, no. 1 (Autumn 1982), p. 159.

1. Carol Goar, "Canada after Trudeau," *Maclean's*, March 12, 1984, p. 20.
2. I am indebted to Johanna Superina for suggesting Machiavelli's relevance to John Turner's political performance.
3. Niccolo Machiavelli, *The Prince*, in Peter Bondanella and Mark Musa, *The Portable Machiavelli* (New York: Penguin Books, 1981), pp. 159ff.
4. Mary Janigan, "Turner's Race for the Crown," *Maclean's*, March 26, 1984, p. 11.
5. Mary Janigan, "The Political Shape of 1984," *Maclean's*, January 16, 1984, p. 11.
6. Walter Stewart, "The Natural," *Toronto Life*, June 1983, p. 30.
7. Léon Dion, "The Concept of Political Leadership: An Analysis," *Canadian Journal of Political Science*, 1, no. 1 (1968), pp. 4, 6.
8. "Liberal Leadership Convention Questionnaire," unpublished survey of 1,019 cases carried out for the Canadian Broadcasting Corporation; conducted by Professor George Perlin, Queen's University, June 6, 1984, p. 11.
9. This analysis draws heavily on some of the excellent postmortem analyses written by senior writers in the main national newspapers: Jeffrey Simpson, "Liberal Ruins Offer Clues to Party's Collapse," *Toronto Globe and Mail*, September 6, 1984, pp. 1, 8; Val Sears, "A Month Ago John Turner Admitted: 'I've Screwed Up'," *Toronto Star*, September 6, 1984, pp. A1, A8; Greg Weston, "Anatomy of Defeat," The *Citizen*, September 5, 1984, p. 9; Linda Diebel, "Why the Liberals Bombed," The *Gazette*, September 8, 1984, pp. B1, 4. Published after this chapter was written is Jeffrey Simpson, "The Vincible Liberals," in Alan Frizzel and Anthony Westell, eds., *The Canadian General Election of 1984: Politicians, Parties, Press, and the Polls* (Ottawa: Carleton University Press, 1985), pp. 15–28.
10. "Mr. Davey Protests," *Toronto Globe and Mail*, September 3, 1984, p. 6. The Davey letter was itself reported with editorial reaction in the same paper: "Davey says the Globe was Biased in Campaign," ibid., p. 5.
11. "Turner Contradicts Policy Adviser, Says All Must Pay Minimum Tax," *Toronto Globe and Mail*, August 27, 1984, p. 4.
12. Michael Tenszen, "Axworthy Rues Liberal Strategy," *Toronto Globe and Mail*, August 31, 1984, pp. 1–2.
13. Michael Adams, *The Focus Canada Quarterly Report*, (Summer 1984), p. 13.
14. Ibid., pp. 18–19.
15. "Mulroney Appeals to Referendum Yes Votes," The *Gazette*, August 7, 1984.
16. Jeffrey Simpson, "Last Hurrah," *Toronto Globe and Mail*, September 3, 1984, p. 6.
17. Jeffrey Simpson, "The Last Resort," *Toronto Globe and Mail*, August 28, 1984, p. 6.

6 Annihilation Avoided: The New Democratic Party in the 1984 Federal General Election

J. TERENCE MORLEY

──────── Relief, pride, and joy were the major aspects of New Democratic sentiment as the election returns unfolded on the evening of September 4, 1984. The relief was the obvious reaction to the party having survived with thirty seats in the new House of Commons when only a few months earlier, standing at a meager 11 percent in the Gallup poll, it had been confidently written off by most of the pundits. The pride was understandable given an almost perfect campaign that ran true to the form predicted in the election planning committee's script, and which featured a bravura performance by the party leader, a performance that attracted the media and, seemingly, impressed the public. The joy was natural for democratic socialist activists who, having imbibed the millenarian traditions of the left, were now certain that it could not be long before the Liberals, reduced to a scant forty seats, would conveniently disappear, leaving the opposition field to the New Democratic party (NDP) battalions.

The expectation that either the Liberals or the Conservatives would be reduced to impotence in like manner to the British Liberals has always been a fond hope of English Canadian socialists. This is hardly surprising since the Cooperative Commonwealth Federation (CCF), the forerunner of the NDP, was primarily led by middle-class Canadians educated at Oxbridge or elsewhere in England, and populated by members disproportionately made up of working-class Britons who came to help build the new Jerusalem in a more congenial New World environment. The hope and expectation that the NDP will one day become one of the two rivals for power in the land (as indeed it has in three western provinces) is central to the party's sense of itself as a genuinely important player in the political game, and central to its ability to sustain the morale of the membership given the harsh reality of third-place finishes and exclusion from power.

The Background

The NDP's defiance of harsh reality is not so difficult to understand, given an historical context: There have been many victories, although they have not generally been associated with the outcome of federal general elections. The mood of the country during the years of World War II established the basis for party optimism in the teeth of electoral setbacks. In 1943 a Gallup poll reported that the CCF was supported by 29 percent of those surveyed, with the Liberals and Conservatives at 28 percent each. That same year saw the CCF in Ontario jump from having no seats in the legislature of that province to thirty-four, only four shy of the number captured by the Conservatives, who were able to form a minority government. Nineteen forty-four saw the CCF come to power in the province of Saskatchewan. Thus, while the federal election results of 1945 (Liberals with 125 seats; Progressive Conservatives, 67; CCF, 28; and Social Credit, 13) were obviously disappointing, they were not devastating because these other victories were available to sustain the party faithful in their hope of eventual success. These same factors applied to each succeeding election fought by the CCF until the 1958 contest when, reduced to a mere eight seats and with both the leader and deputy leader defeated, there was a momentary despair. This despair quickly translated to an even more rampant optimism about eventual victory. David Lewis, later to become party leader, persuaded the key union leaders in the country to agree to a kind of merger between the CCF and the Canadian Labour Congress (CLC), the main labor central in Canada. This new arrangement was to formalize the relationship between the party and the unions and, as in Britain, a major benefit for the party would be the provision of union funds for political action. The Liberal party had also been devastated by the 1958 Conservative landslide, and a number of previous Liberal supporters were tempted to throw in their lots with this new political formation. A 1960 by-election in Peterborough, where a candidate running under the new party label won with ten times the vote obtained by the CCF only two years earlier, suggested that this new party might well be the key to electoral success for democratic socialists in Canada and so the New Democratic party, formed in 1961, began with exceedingly high hopes of making the British Labour party model a Canadian reality.

Those hopes were quickly dashed in the 1962 election. The Liberals charged back with 100 seats, to 116 for the Conservatives. The NDP elected only nineteen members and were ignominiously reduced to fourth place in the Commons as Social Credit elected thirty M.P.s. The party was back to third place in 1963, but with only seventeen members. Subsequent elections through 1980 confirmed this third-party status, yet party newspapers and the speeches of New Democratic luminaries continued to reflect the old belief that someday one of the "old-line parties" would fade away and the NDP would gain its rightful place in the sun. It is no wonder, then, that the party was relieved to find itself with thirty seats in the midst of a new Conservative landslide, and overjoyed to find the Liberals with only forty seats in that same contest. It is also no wonder that observers of Canadian politics with a sense of history are not quite so quick to write the Liberal epitaph or declare the NDP on the road to ultimate victory. The Liberals certainly have problems, but Liberal problems do not mean an end to NDP problems and so the pattern of consolation in provincial and Gallup victories, combined with disappointing national election results, may well continue.

The Effects of the Electoral System

The difficulties that faced NDP strategists prior to the 1984 election are structural difficulties that will not readily yield to a newfound near parity in Liberal and NDP seats. Indeed, one of the most important problems that faced these strategists was the effect of the "first past the post," single-member plurality electoral system on any party unable to garner more than 30 percent of the popular vote, a problem that will continue to plague the NDP even if they are "fortunate" enough to share it with the Liberals. Alan Cairns outlined the problem in a classic article on the effects of the electoral system in Canada in elections from 1921 through 1965.[1]

The CCF/NDP has been doubly handicapped by the operation of the system. First, the party, in an attempt to portray itself as the political arm of working-class Canadians, makes an argument that necessarily disparages appeals to regional interest and ethnic cleavage in favor of a national or binational appeal that emphasizes class differences and the need for a concomitant solidarity among workers no matter whether they are French or English, from Ontario, British Columbia, or Nova Scotia. The difficulty is that this appeal to class difference has a rather limited force in almost all parts of the country, and class partisans can rarely be mobilized in sufficient numbers to provide enough votes to place the NDP candidate "first past the post."[2] Consequently, as a party that garners much less than 30 percent of the national vote and yet attempts to make an appeal across the whole country, the CCF/NDP has invariably elected significantly fewer M.P.s than would be the case if Canada adopted any likely formula for proportional representation (PR). Second, and this is an irony, the attempt to make a cross-country, class-conscious appeal is hampered by the fact that the seats won by the party have, for the greater part, been disproportionately from the four western provinces.

The party, then, has come to be misperceived, particularly in Ontario, as a western, even prairie phenomenon, which has not assisted attempts to garner support in the industrial heartland. The electoral system now rewards the NDP when it makes a regional appeal, but a regional appeal contradicts the ideological attachment of the party to class politics. A class appeal, however, is not likely to provide enough adherents to ensure a vote across the country for the NDP in excess of the 30 percent necessary to guarantee the election of a sufficiency of M.P.s. Given the present electoral system, a regional appeal condemns the NDP to third-party status but a class appeal, the kind of national appeal that conforms to democratic socialist ideology, condemns the NDP to a fraction of the seats it would deserve in any kind of PR system. However, the NDP is unable to press vigorously for a PR system because several provincial parties, notably the British Columbia NDP, are adamantly opposed to any proselytizing for an abandonment of the plurality system since its retention, they believe, holds the key to the NDP gaining a majority in certain provincial legislatures. NDP strategists dimly recognize the conundrum but also know that there are no easy solutions.

No doubt the major reason why the party does not even attempt to approach a solution to the electoral system puzzle is that party mythology suggests that a solution has already been developed and only needs to be put into practice. That solution is the 1961 strategy of enlisting the support of the trade union movement. It is a solution that makes sense, given the ideological stance of mobilizing working-class consciousness to support the New Democratic party. Unhappily, union members have not, in practice, been very supportive. There are, of course, exceptions, in particular the Steelworkers' union and the United Auto Workers but, as Keith Archer points out, the grim facts for the party are that only 8.2 percent of unionists were affiliated in 1981 and the most recent data suggest that even unionized workers are more likely to vote Liberal than NDP.[3] Moreover, determined efforts by the CLC executive to produce a massive labor vote for the NDP, as in 1979 and 1980, have proved to be relatively unsuccessful.[4] The hope of breaking through the 30 percent barrier on a wave of working-class votes—as though the NDP were the British Labour party—remains, but the reality of election disappointment after election disappointment with a 20 percent barrier also remains, poignant though that reality has been following the hopes engendered by the formation of the NDP in 1961.

Six Fundamental Problems

Following the 1980 election more specific problems engaged party strategists and activists. Six were particularly important. The first was a general unease about the growing attention paid to conservative voices in Western democracies. In 1979 Margaret Thatcher had "climbed to the top of the greasy pole" by becoming Britain's prime minister, defeating both the Labour government under Jim Callaghan and the moderate or "wet" faction of her own party. Then, in November 1980, Ronald Reagan, a longtime hero of the fundamentalist right in America was handily elected as president of the United States. Other symbolic defeats for the left occurred during the early 1980s (although there were some victories as well, such as the election of Mitterrand as French president) and New Democrats began to feel hostility from various groups—a hostility that had not been a part of the electoral environment since the middle 1950s. Those few party members familiar with Philip Converse's argument that electoral shifts such as the one that saw Eisenhower replace Truman do not, in fact, constitute a coherent and conscious ideological change among the mass of the people could view Thatcher and Reagan with some equanimity.[5] For most party activists speculation in the media about a shift to the right, coupled with the spectacle of right-wing Conservatives successfully plotting the downfall of Tory leader Joe Clark, suggested that the traditional NDP message was going to be more difficult to deliver to a mass audience. Party leaders also believed that economic recession made it less likely that the electorate would be prepared to try democratic socialist solutions. Various polls had convinced them that most people were more easily persuaded about fundamental economic and even social changes in prosperous times when they could be reasonably certain that their own jobs would be safe. As Tony Pennikett, then party president observed, "we know that tough economic times are tough political times for a movement like the New Democratic Party."[6]

This sense of foreboding about the acceptability of the message was exacerbated by the continued adoption in convention of certain policies that were divisive and generally unpopular in the country. At the 1983 convention a majority of delegates voted to condemn the Manitoba government, the only NDP government in the country, for prosecuting Dr. Henry Morgantaler, who had established a clinic in Winnipeg at which abortions could be obtained in contravention to the procedures laid down in the criminal code. Abortion is a no-win issue for any politician. The NDP stand, that the decision to abort belongs to the woman alone and that no one else, neither the putative father nor a medical practitioner, is to have a say, offends powerful forces in Canadian society. The attack on its own government over such an emotional issue was a difficult action for party officials to defend, particularly since it was couched in language suggesting that the delegates would applaud a provincial attorney general who would conspire to nullify a significant law passed by Parliament.

Foreign policy issues also caused grave problems for the party leadership. At the 1983 convention the party voted for the establishment of a Palestinian state and to permit the Palestine Liberation Organization (PLO) to take part in the process; to support the anti-American Sandinista regime in Nicaragua and the anti-American guerrillas in El Salvador; and to have Canada withdraw from NATO. Some parts of this package would find favor with many Canadians, particularly the attitudes on Central America. The whole package, however, suggests an anti-American neutralist view that likely runs counter to the views of most Canadians and certainly runs counter to the views of the organizers of public opinion in groups and communities. Certainly, NDP leaders are able to defend particular policies eloquently, but they have real difficulty with the somewhat strident image that attaches to the whole package.

A third concern of the strategists continued to be the lack of support for the NDP in Quebec. Ever since Robert Cliche, leader of the party in Quebec in the late 1960s was narrowly defeated for a Commons seat by Liberal Eric Kierans, the party there had consistently lost support. In part it suffered the same fate as the Conservatives, who were unable to elect M.P.s as long as the Liberals enjoyed the votes of more than 50 percent of an electorate pleased to have, in Pierre Trudeau, a Québecer prime minister. What made the situation worse for the NDP was the growth of the Parti Québécois (PQ), advocating an independent Quebec plus social democratic welfare statism combined with a mixed economy. The PQ was easily able to recruit Québecers with social democratic leanings to the *independatiste* cause, while the NDP was forced to distance itself from its natural allies in the PQ for fear of alienating its English Canadian supporters. By 1983 the Conservatives were able to hope the tide would turn through their own choice of a fluently bilingual Québecer, Brian Mulroney, as party leader. The NDP were meanwhile reduced to a membership base of little more than 200 hardy souls. This dismal standing in Quebec was bound to hurt the NDP's credibility in the rest of the country.

A less important weakness, but one that also diminished the NDP's credibility as a genuinely national party, was a continuing lack of support in the four Atlantic provinces. The failure to elect any M.P.s from this region in 1980 was a bitter disappointment following an historic breakthrough in Newfoundland with the election of Alphonsus Faour in a 1978 by-election, which was repeated in the 1979 general election and combined with a general increase in the party's popular vote in the region. The catastrophic drop in the Newfoundland vote between 1979 and 1980, from 31 percent to 17 percent, was disheartening to say the least. A new strategy to revive NDP fortunes in Atlantic Canada was not obvious after this debacle.

Popular feelings in western Canada produced the fifth and potentially most serious problem for the strategists—how to heal the wounds caused within the party over a fundamental disagreement about the process for patriating the Canadian constitution. When Prime Minister Trudeau announced in the fall of 1980 that his government intended to "bring the constitution home" he received the immediate support and endorsement of Ed Broadbent, speaking as leader of the New Democratic party. Unhappily, Allan Blakeney, then NDP premier of Saskatchewan, was appalled by the Trudeau initiative. Blakeney felt that a new amending formula should not be imposed without some significant agreement from the provinces; that an entrenched Charter of Rights along the lines of the American Bill of Rights, while it might be applauded in principle, raised grave questions about the locus of power in a federal state and potentially substituted judicial judgment for the democratic political process; and, that for the federal government to proceed unilaterally would violate the federal principle so essential to the 1867 confederation bargain. Blakeney's opposition to the Trudeau package was given additional authority among party members in the four western provinces because it coincided with a popular regional distrust of all the works of Pierre Trudeau and the Liberals.

Broadbent was somewhat miffed by the hostile reaction to his endorsement of a proposal that had been CCF/NDP policy since the 1930s. Blakeney and others in the west were furious that Broadbent had acted in what they felt to be a precipitous fashion after inadequate consultation. In the end, with a little help from the Supreme Court of Canada and independent-minded British parliamentarians, the eight provinces opposed to the Trudeau package forced a compromise. The country, or at least the English-speaking part of the country, along with New Democrats, joined in hailing the compromise arrangement, but the scars of the battle remained and Broadbent was, by 1983, accorded only grudging acceptance in the western provinces.

Finally, party leaders faced the need, before the 1984 election, to sustain party morale in the wake of a devastating election defeat in Saskatchewan in the spring of 1982 and a bitter third consecutive defeat in British Columbia at the hands of Bill Bennett's Social Credit party a year later. The victory in Manitoba in 1981, the election of a second member of the Legislative Assembly (MLA) in Alberta in 1982 and four members to the assembly in Nova Scotia (up from only one) in 1984, along with the November 1982 by-election success of Bob Rae, the new party leader in Ontario, had all provided some consolation, but these smaller triumphs could not rid party activists of the sense of losing ground in the country as a whole—a sense compounded by the obvious difficulty of concocting a strategy that would be acceptable to the party and yet appeal to those who had not voted NDP in the past.

The 1983 Convention

It was with a growing consciousness of these intractable problems that the party assembled in Regina in the summer of 1983. Ed Broadbent and the other organizers of the convention hoped that the presentation of a new statement of principles, a new Regina Manifesto, would provide a modern ideological focus for solving the public policy problems of the eighties and nineties, and would thereby enhance the NDP's credibility as a vital and thoughtful political force. In turn, this new image would lift party spirits.

Unhappily, the convention proved to be a public relations disaster. A few days before it began Allan Blakeney, the former premier of Saskatchewan, and

Grant Notley, the leader of the party in Alberta, put forward their own version of the statement of principles. The act of proposing an alternative statement was interpreted by the press as a not-so-veiled attack on Broadbent's leadership from a dissatisfied western Canada, a region where the party had twenty-five of its thirty-one seats in the House of Commons.[7] In the end a compromise was reached, with elements of both documents incorporated in a final version, but the disagreement between eastern and western leaders had, in the process, been accentuated. Those differences inevitably tarnished Broadbent's image, particularly since one M.P., Douglas Anguish from Saskatchewan, publicly declared that he had seriously thought of challenging Broadbent for the leadership, while another M.P., Nelson Riis from British Columbia, admitted that he had been approached by a group to mount a challenge. An obscure party member from Ontario actually filed nomination papers for the leader's post though, under pressure from party officials and members of the left caucus, he withdrew and Broadbent was acclaimed.[8]

Acclaimed but not untroubled. The pro-choice stand on abortion coming in the form of a strident attack on the Manitoba attorney general was bound to alienate significant sections of the electorate; other voters would be disturbed by a decision to nationalize one of the five largest chartered banks (there was no decision on which bank—any of the five would do), and others by the anti-American thrust of various foreign policy resolutions. These problems were made more acute by the impression left even the casual observer that Ed Broadbent was only tolerated by party activists and that they would quickly rid themselves of him, perhaps for former British Columbia premier Dave Barrett, as soon as the next election delivered the expected poor result.[9] A fiery speech delivered by the well-beloved Tommy Douglas, premier of Saskatchewan from 1944 to 1961 and leader from 1961 to 1971, was a triumph for nostalgia and a boost for morale, but the present reality of party infighting and the unhappiness with Ed Broadbent, even though it was confined to only a few individuals, was more than a little worrisome for the strategists.

The Strategic Plan

In fact, the strategists, certainly those formally charged with planning the election effort, were already very worried about the very real divisions of strategic options. According to Terry Grier, the chairman of the Election Planning Committee (EPC), a meeting of the full committee held on May 27, more than a month before the convention, was "particularly troubling."[10] The meeting featured a long debate on the themes and issues that party spokesmen ought to pursue. It quickly became clear that there was little agreement among members of the committee, in large part because there was no consensus on

whether to focus on the governing Liberals or on the Conservatives now leading in the polls. The task was not made easier by the fact that Larry Ellis,
a newly acquired pollster from Saskatchewan, had run into operational problems and was unable to provide the committee with much hard information
about current public opinion. After a long and fruitless debate it was decided
to develop a short-term, six-month strategy for the fall to provide some preelection coherence to party activity.[11]

In late August the steering committee[12] of the EPC met to consider the
interim strategy. The debacle at the convention and its effect on party morale
made it even more imperative that some immediate activity be undertaken.
It was also felt that there was a need to reassure and even reactivate core
supporters. To this end it was decided to develop a significant preelection
campaign. At this point the total proposed central budget for the election was
approximately $3 million. (Under the provisions of the Election Expenses Act
the party reported spending $4.7 million, compared to approximately $6.3
million spent by both the Liberals and the Conservatives. The $1.7 million
difference was in large part made up of spending by provincial parties and
reporting the "in kind" expenses made by unions on behalf of the election
effort.) In a paper presented to the steering committee, Dennis Young, the
assistant federal secretary, and Leslie Turnbull, the director of organization,
proposed that almost 17 percent of this figure, $500,000, be spent in the
preelection period. They argued that this preelection campaign should involve
the party in a major effort to restore morale and that to do this the party should
expend sufficient funds to ensure significant media coverage, hire preelection
organizers, mount a canvassing effort, and conduct a direct mail blitz in key
areas. The major aim of this preelection campaign was to secure and reinforce
the base in priority ridings, generally those currently held plus a few others
located in the more favorable areas of the country. Young and Turnbull argued
that this would have the desirable side effect of raising morale across the
country.

This plan was approved at a meeting in late October. It was also agreed
that as part of the accelerated strategy, caucus research would be focused to
helping boost morale, and that the CLC would run a parallel campaign directed
by Pat Kerwin, a CLC senior staff person. The committee was aware that the
$500,000 expended over the winter and spring would not be available to the
party during the election campaign, but felt that the gamble was necessary.
Indeed, the need for some kind of dramatic act became much more acute after
the party lost a critical by-election in late August in the British Columbia seat
of Mission–Port Moody, which had been considered a safe NDP stronghold.
It was felt that the Young-Turnbull strategy of public campaigns in Manitoba,
Saskatchewan, British Columbia, and Ontario was the only way that the party

could halt the erosion of support. The strategy was adopted with a conscious commitment of no second-guessing and from this point Grier believed that the election planning process stopped floundering.[13]

Undoubtedly the point of departure for these public campaigns, and indeed for the election campaign itself, arose from a disagreement about how to interpret the polling data now available. This data revealed that the NDP had a low, often very low credibility rating on economic management issues, but enjoyed some considerable approval and much greater believability for its perceived stand on fair taxation, poverty, and welfare issues. The NDP was seen as an effective advocate for "the little guy." Ellis, in interpreting his own poll results, believed that the economic management issues were, in fact, the vote-determining issues, and that the NDP needed to focus its campaign on reversing the negative public perception. In large measure this had been Broadbent's strategy since his election as leader and for him personally the Ellis findings were more than a little distressing. Nonetheless, it was decided not to keep trying to pursue the will-'o-the-wisp of economic policy credibility, but rather to orient the campaign to portraying the party and its leaders as the champions of "ordinary people." It was felt, moreover, that emphasizing a theme rather than specific, concrete proposals would not only downplay the negative associations that many people had for NDP economic bromides but would also permit greater regional flexibility in advocating specific economic and other policies. M.P.s would have the ability to propose specific projects to benefit their regions which, while they would have to fit in with the overall theme of providing fairness for ordinary people, would have a greater immediate impact on voters than would an abstract analysis of the whole economy.

Ellis strongly disagreed with this November decision and wrote to both Grier and Gerry Caplan, the party's federal secretary and designated campaign manager, to put his views on the record. These were not well received and on January 13, 1984, the steering committee decided to look for a new polling firm. Vic Fingerhut from Washington, D.C., who had done some very useful work for liberal Democrats in the United States and for the Canadian Union of Public Employees in Vancouver, was hired. In order not to offend nationalist sensibilities it was decided not to make any public announcement about this appointment and though party officials were slightly nervous about being embarrassed, this view was outweighed by a feeling of relief in having a pollster with a proven track record on board. Undoubtedly one of Fingerhut's most important contributions was to show the strategists that there was a reasonable likelihood of holding incumbent seats even though support in the country was measured at an all-time low (for the NDP) of 11 percent. The incumbency factor plus the positive reactions of focus groups to the general theme that the NDP best represented the "little guy" gave the EPC the necessary encouragement to ignore the various media reports of shifting public opinion and instead concentrate on developing smooth-running public campaigns in the key provinces.

The Preelection Period

However, the party suffered one more blow before this "heads down" approach could be put into effect. James Laxer, who had resigned at the end of the year as federal caucus research director in order to return to teaching at York University in Toronto, hurled a parting thunderbolt. For much of the last several months as research director Laxer had been drafting a report analyzing NDP economic policies and on January 9 he delivered that report in the guise of a confidential document. The only problem was that it was also delivered to the *Toronto Globe and Mail* and its devastating critique of NDP policies was gleefully reported coast-to-coast in Canada's "national newspaper." Over morning coffee active New Democrats, along with active Liberals and Conservatives and a large section of the Canadian middle classes read that Laxer had described NDP policy as "seriously inadequate, contradictory, short-sighted and ideologically ambivalent." [14] At the beginning of his report Laxer wrote "The NDP's analysis of economic and social evolution remains locked in the 1950's and 1960's where it had its origins. . . . It is now so seriously out of keeping with the reality of the 1980's that it has become a serious impediment . . . to appropriate action rather than a guide to it." [15]

The worst part of this broadside was that many in the party thought that Laxer was right. As Saskatchewan M.P. Lorne Nystrom observed, "the NDP talks too often about creating jobs without paying attention to inflation and industrial competitiveness." [16] Yet by allowing the report to be given to the press and by employing colorful, inflammatory language in a first chapter which many, including Grier, felt was added as a polemical afterthought in order to attract media attention, Laxer reinforced this image. For the strategists this was the low point leading up to the election, even though the polls continued to show reduced support up to the end of June. The polls, after all, were produced by other, alien organizations; Laxer's findings were those of a man who had placed second to David Lewis in the 1971 federal leadership contest and who had been privy to caucus and party secrets. For many New Democratic activists this was proof that the party was on the road to dismembering itself before the watchful eyes of a disdainful press prior to being decimated in the forthcoming election.

Nor was this gloomy view a simple manifestation of a collective paranoia. The media generally accepted the view that the NDP was in serious trouble and a kind of deathwatch atmosphere characterized their coverage of the party, particularly the coverage in the print media. Party members suffered through headlines such as "The NDP's fading fortunes," "The NDP's fight for survival," "Tracing the decline of the NDP," "The NDP's slump," "For the NDP, the good times are just a memory." [17] The theme of these and many other stories was that poll results below 15 percent (the *Toronto Globe and Mail* CROP polls in March, April, and June only gave the party 11 percent, a clearly disastrous result) heralded the loss of all but a handful of seats and that to some extent this was deserved because the party, as Jim Laxer had so sagaciously noted, had lost its way and was now only capable of advocating 1930ish piety and utopianism. No doubt the country would mourn the party of J. S. Woodsworth, M. J. Coldwell, T. C. Douglas, and Lewis, but all good things come to an end and the future belongs to those who understand the present rather than the past.

This dismissal, whether haughty or sympathetic, was always unnerving. Grier and Caplan decided that the only course was to ignore the polls and the pundits and force the party to do likewise.[18] A media boomlet in April, suggesting that Broadbent might be replaced by Roy Romanow, the former attorney general of Saskatchewan, was quickly deprecated by the whole party leadership, including Romanow's Saskatchewan supporters. The watchword now was forge ahead according to plan by spending the time on filling in the details of the campaigns instead of worrying about the possible outcome of the election.

Some of these details were announced at a January meeting with a nervous caucus in order to repair their morale. The "ordinary Canadian" theme was outlined, though at this point the emphasis was on Mulroney's business connections, yielding the slogan "Now more than ever you need the NDP to stand up for you." It was as a result of the pretest during the preelection campaign that the "ordinary Canadian" theme became central. The decision to use this phraseology instead of the more class-conscious "working Canadians" was justified by the use of focus groups, which were used on several occasions to test the theme, slogans, and choice of issues. Although the abandonment of the industrial strategy approach was undoubtedly personally frustrating for Broadbent, given the time he had spent in developing it since he became leader, it was nonetheless agreed that the party should emphasize a fair taxation policy, youth employment, job security, and job creation. As well, the party should defend medicare as its own creation by condemning the practice of extra billing and would hope to win support for its disarmament emphasis by attacking the government's decision to permit the testing of the Cruise missile over Alberta.

The promotion of these issues during the preelection period was to feature billboards, a jingle, direct mail, radio spots, and print advertising. The M.P.s were pleased to learn that the money was to be spent largely in incumbent ridings, though there were a few nonincumbent priority ridings, particularly in Ontario. The decisions on priority seats were not made unilaterally by the

Election Planning Committee but rather after considerable consultation with counterpart committees set up in the provinces to manage the federal campaign in each province. Grier recalls that this process featured more cooperation between the two levels of committees than had been the case in the past.[19]

This concentration on developing and carrying out the chosen strategy was necessarily interrupted, even modified, by political events beyond the control of the NDP. The most important of these in 1983 had been the election of Brian Mulroney as leader of the Progressive Conservatives over former prime minister Joe Clark. The NDP had initially welcomed this change in the Conservative leadership, believing that Mulroney's ties to big business and to swashbuckling entreprenuers (in particular to Peter Pocklington, who supported Mulroney after his own leadership bid failed and then openly boasted that Mulroney as prime minister would appoint him as a one-man royal commission to bring the flat income tax to Canada) would mean that many "progressive" Conservative voters would desert, particularly in the western provinces, and vote NDP. This view faded as it became clear that Mulroney was not, in fact, a right-wing ideologue and would make the peace he needed within his own party to ensure that the PC remained well ahead of the Trudeau Liberals in the various voter surveys. With Mulroney in Parliament it seemed that any hope for resurgence that the NDP might enjoy must result from a Liberal failure.

That failure seemed particularly likely to New Democrats, certainly to Broadbent and his staff, if the Liberals should oblige by electing John Turner as Pierre Trudeau's successor. It was not that Broadbent was disdainful of Turner's personal gifts but rather a delicious sensation that with Turner, who had spent his time out of politics as a corporate "Bay Street" lawyer in Toronto, it would be possible to paint both the Conservatives (under the ex-president of the Iron Ore Company of Canada) and the Liberals (under this corporate handmaiden) as almost identical parties of the right, justifiably opposed by the NDP—the only party for progressive Canadians. Turner's selection over Jean Chrétien, a shrewd populist from a small town in Quebec who was well liked in small towns all across the country, was greeted with cheers in the NDP. Party strategists were now persuaded that the ordinary Canadian theme would be even more potent than they had originally believed. Even though the Liberals were enjoying a postconvention surge in the polls, and even though the NDP itself was still running a dismal third in June following that convention, the party leadership were more than anxious to have the campaign get under way.

The Election Campaign

John Turner was good enough to oblige. After a quick trip to England to visit the queen, a rather puzzling piece of piety for all the antimonarchists in the

Liberal party, Turner announced in June that the election campaign was under way. He had been prime minister for only days but clearly felt that the lead the Liberals now enjoyed in the polls might be dissipated if he waited overlong to obtain the electorate's blessing.

The NDP kicked off its own campaign on Bay Street, an unlikely venue but, as it turned out, a most inspired choice. As Canadians tuned into the television national news to watch the beginnings of the campaign dance they were treated to the spectacle of Ed Broadbent wending his way through Toronto's financial community denouncing John Turner and Brian Mulroney, the "Bobbsey Twins of Bay Street," for their neglect of ordinary people in favor of friends in the bank towers. It made good television and gave the Broadbent campaign a much-needed lift at the beginning of the campaign.

From this point on, NDP strategy was simple. Broadbent and the others who spoke for the party would keep repeating that the NDP stood for ordinary Canadians while the Bobbsey Twins of Bay Street could do nothing other than reward their rich friends in the banks and corporations. Every policy pronouncement was tied to this theme, as were party advertisements, and the senior strategists, in particular Gerry Caplan, the campaign manager and George Nakitsas, Broadbent's new research director, made certain that, despite immediate temptations, there was no deviation from this elemental thrust.[20]

As it happened, the campaign was more gratifying for the party than even the most optimistic activists had believed possible. As in 1979 and 1980 the housekeeping details were managed smoothly and with a minimum of mistakes. It looked professional, and this was critical in improving the NDP's "bungling amateur" image. Moreover, Broadbent himself went from strength to strength. There had been some considerable nervousness in the party about the effect of the first televised debate. This debate, though broadcast across the country, took place entirely in French and party strategists were worried that Broadbent, who had painfully learned his French during his time in the House of Commons, might be made to look slightly foolish by Mulroney, who had been bilingual since childhood, and Turner, who had learned his French at the Sorbonne thirty years earlier. They need not have worried quite so much. As Graham Fraser noted in the *Toronto Globe and Mail*: "He [Broadbent] may still have gained respect in the debate, questioning Mr. Turner closely on women's rights and pointing out that the NDP was the only party to call for Quebec to be given a veto during the constitutional debate." [21]

Everything looked even better for Ed Broadbent and the NDP campaign following the next evening's English debate. Broadbent was very much in command of himself and looked very much the equal of the other two leaders. As University of British Columbia political scientist Richard Johnston observed: "As a piece of theatre it wasn't very exciting but I think Broadbent was the winner. . . . The other two couldn't pretend the NDP weren't part of the campaign. He also articulated a position. The others couldn't. He pointed out where the emperor had no clothes. The others had to obfuscate. He was the net winner, although that may not mean much." [22] Other media commentary was in a similar vein. Hugh Winsor, a senior reporter with the *Toronto Globe and Mail* wrote that "as it happened in 1979, Mr. Broadbent's effective, sometimes witty, use of the stiletto helped him turn in the best performance in the strictest sense." [23] Equally positive comments on Broadbent's performance in the hastily organized August 15 debate on women's issues,[24] combined with substantial increases in support recorded for the NDP in the major surveys, did much to restore party morale. The revitalized party in turn was a much better prospect for NDP supporters who, at the start of the campaign, had considered abandoning ship. The core vote stayed on the social democratic homestead and the party kept a respectable number of seats in the wake of the Tory landslide. A few western incumbents were defeated but these losses were offset, certainly for Broadbent and his closest associates, by modest gains in Ontario, gains which would mean that the new federal caucus would inevitably be more sympathetic to Broadbent's leadership.

Lessons: Learned and Unlearned

Parliamentary seats are a precious political commodity. The NDP felt very good about winning thirty of them, and even better about the Liberals' collapse, which yielded a "mere" forty M.P.s. The party had once again survived and would live to fight another day. Of course, the Conservatives had the rather more tangible benefits of office to cheer them along, but New Democrats, expecting so much less, were equally elated by the result. Whether that elation would prove to be a kind of hubris, the tragic pride that goes before a fall, remains to be seen. Certainly the fundamental problems of the party were not transcended in the 1984 election results: the NDP remained hopelessly weak in Quebec and to a slightly lesser extent in the Atlantic provinces, and the party is wedded to a class-conscious set of attitudes that fit neither with the regional cleavages that characterize Canadian politics nor with the popular culture of North America. Worse, the party seems to have lost the ability to be self-critical and hence the ability to develop genuinely new policy initiatives. Such initiatives are generally viewed within the NDP as potential defilers of the holy writ of socialist doctrine as laid down in the Regina Manifesto.

In large measure the NDP is a victim of the "decline of party" that many scholars believe to be characteristic of all contemporary Western democratic political systems.[25] For the NDP, this new inability of political parties, including the NDP itself, to maintain the loyalty and support of even longtime adherents carries with it the potential for real devastation. If circumstances should again conspire, as they seemed to be doing at the call of the 1984 election, to confine the party to its reduced core electorate, then the Canadian electoral system might well only deliver a handful of seats to New Democrats. This, in turn, might so discourage the hard-core party faithful that the whole organization could well collapse. At present, however, the organization has not collapsed. On the contrary, it is well oiled and even, for a democratic socialist party, well heeled. The party enjoys a line of credit with its bank that would be the envy of many medium-size businesses. It had little trouble raising the necessary cash for the preelection and election campaigns[26] and this, combined with an experienced cadre of full-time functionaries, meant that the NDP in 1984, in the midst of many troubles, was nonetheless able to mount a well-planned, professionally executed campaign. This, in turn, could mean that the NDP could take advantage of some future constellation of circumstances within the new reality of party decline and uncommitted voters and use this party machine to capture a sizable portion of the new volatile electorate. Having survived one more time, the New Democratic party has still to overcome fundamental weaknesses: paradoxically it now owns the machinery that in some circumstances could provide not mere survival but a dramatic increase in electoral support.

Notes

1. See Alan Cairns, "The Electoral System and the Party System in Canada, 1921–1965," *Canadian Journal of Political Science*, I, no. 1 (March 1968), pp. 55–80, for a full discussion of the regionalizing effect of the electoral system, in particular the effect on the Conservatives in Quebec. Since the article was written the Liberals have experienced a similar problem winning seats in the western provinces, particularly Alberta, where with only 20–25 percent of the vote they elect no M.P.s and have been seen to pay little attention to the needs and desires of Albertans.

2. There is an extensive literature on the impact of class position, both subjective and objective, on vote determination. See, in particular, Robert Alford, *Party and Society: The Anglo-American Democracies* (Westport, Conn.: Greenwood Press, 1963), esp. chs. 5 and 9; John Meisel, *Working Papers on Canadian Politics* (Montreal: McGill-Queen's University Press, 1975); and Harold D. Clarke, Jane Jenson, Lawrence LeDuc, and Jon H. Pammett, *Political Choice in Canada*, abridged ed. (Toronto: McGraw-Hill Ryerson, 1980). Although this question has occasioned a very lively scholarly debate in Canada there is some consensus that objective class position has almost no impact on vote and subjective class identification only a modest impact.

3. See Keith Archer, "The Failure of the New Democratic Party: Unions, Unionists and Politics in Canada," *Canadian Journal of Political Science*, 18, no. 2 (June 1985), pp. 353–66.

4. Walter D. Young, "The New Democratic Party in the 1979 Federal General Election," in Howard R. Penniman, ed., *Canada at the Polls, 1979 and 1980* (Washington, D.C.: American Enterprise Institute, 1981), pp. 190–207.

5. See Philip Converse, "The Nature of Belief Systems in Mass Publics," in David Apter, ed., *Ideology and Discontent* (New York: Free Press, 1964), pp. 206–61.

6. *Toronto Globe and Mail*, July 1, 1983, p. 2.

7. *Toronto Globe and Mail*, June 22, 1983, p. 8.
8. *Toronto Globe and Mail*, July 4, 1983, p. 9. It should be noted that the federal NDP constitution provides that the leader must be formally elected at every convention. No distinction
is made between the post of leader and the other offices (president, vice presidents, etc.).
Invariably, incumbent leaders have been acclaimed but neither they nor their friends can do
anything to prevent a determined challenge, whether a frivolous attempt or a more serious
effort, aimed at changing the party leadership. Although the other major parties now elect
their leaders in convention, Liberal and Conservative leaders are not formally so vulnerable
to constant challenge, although in the Conservative party they have been subject to a more
active leadership review. (See R. K. Carty, ch. 3 in this volume.)
9. See *Toronto Globe and Mail*, July 4, 1983, p. 2, for a pessimistic view of the party's chances
in the forthcoming election from Howard Pawley, premier of Manitoba; and the *Calgary
Herald*, July 6, 1983, p. F10, for speculation about Barrett replacing Broadbent after that
election.
10. Interview with Terry Grier, February 23, 1985. Mr. Grier has long been a key figure in
the NDP. He was federal secretary, the chief administrative officer from 1962 to 1966, and
then was full-time assistant to the Ontario leader, Donald C. MacDonald, until 1969. He
has been the chairman of the Election Planning Committee since 1975 after serving as
campaign manager for Ed Broadbent's successful bid for the leadership. He was M.P. for
Toronto-Lakeshore from 1972 to 1974. In 1984 he was appointed vice president of Ryerson
Polytechnical Institute, where he has been a member of the Department of Politics since
1969. I am very grateful to him for his helpful and candid account of the internal party
election planning process.
11. Ibid.
12. The Election Planning Committee (EPC) was composed of the chairman, the party leader
and his senior staff, the federal president, the federal treasurer, the federal secretary and his
senior staff, a senior staff representative from the Canadian Labour Congress (these formed
the steering committee) plus one or two representatives from each federal election EPC set up
in the various provinces.
13. Grier interview.
14. *Toronto Globe and Mail*, January 10, 1984, p. 1.
15. Ibid.
16. *Toronto Globe and Mail*, January 11, 1983, p. 8.
17. These examples are from *Maclean's*, January 30, 1984, p. 9; *Maclean's*, April 23, 1984, pp.
14 and 15; Jeffrey Simpson in *Toronto Globe and Mail*, March 28, 1984, p. 6; and *Toronto
Globe and Mail*, April 7, 1984, p. 4.
18. Grier interview.
19. Ibid.
20. Ibid.
21. *Toronto Globe and Mail*, July 25, 1984, p. 2.
22. *Toronto Globe and Mail*, July 26, 1984, p. 1.
23. *Toronto Globe and Mail*, July 26, 1984, p. 5.
24. See *Toronto Globe and Mail*, August 16, 1984, pp. 1, 4, and 8.
25. See John Meisel, "The Decline of Party in Canada," in Hugh G. Thorburn, ed., *Party
Politics in Canada*, 5th ed. (Scarborough, Ont.: Prentice-Hall, 1985), pp. 98–114, for a
stimulating analysis of the possible fundamental and proximate causes for the displacement
of political parties as the central institutions of public life in Canada.
26. Grier interview.

7 The 1984 Federal General Election and Developments in Canadian Party Finance

KHAYYAM ZEV PALTIEL

———— Whether or not the Canadian federal general election of September 4, 1984, can be considered a realigning election, there is no doubt that the financial aspects of that campaign reveal significant differences between the three parties represented in the House of Commons. The lack of preparedness of the Liberals was underscored by the monetary shortfalls disclosed in the aftermath of defeat, which showed that the national party was almost $3 million in debt. By contrast, the well-endowed opposition Progressive Conservatives, after the nomination and installation of their new leader, Brian Mulroney, in early 1983, had mounted a sophisticated organizational effort in anticipation of the general election that had to be called by the spring of 1985. The governing Liberals, partly in deference to the sensibilities and dithering of their outgoing leader, but more seriously owing to an abortive attempt to present a modified image to the Canadian public and disarray at the national executive level, neglected the crucial campaign planning that had to be undertaken in view of the election to come. Furthermore, the new Liberal leader, John Napier Turner, anxious to capitalize on the favorable publicity generated by his successful leadership contest, was moved by a "blip" in the polls to request the dissolution of Parliament before he could assuage the hurt feelings of his recent rivals, whose support he needed, and much too early to galvanize his party's rusty machinery and reshape it in his image. The new campaign team he imposed on the Liberal national office did not have time to consolidate its position before it found itself on the campaign firing line.

Saddled with the legacy of the Trudeau regime and marked by a last-minute series of blatant patronage appointments, a sequence of unfortunate personal pratfalls, and tensions between his appointees and the remnants of the Trudeau team (which still dominated the central agencies), Turner was forced to turn to the very persons he had vowed to eliminate. Members of the team who had plotted strategy and tactics since the days of Lester Pearson were hastily reassembled to provide the organizational muscle lacking in the early phase of the campaign. It was too late, and the results are familiar to all.

On the other hand, the victorious Progressive Conservatives displayed that they had learned the lessons of earlier failures. The conciliatory approach of their new leader bridged the differences between central Canadian and western Conservatives that had contributed to the Pyrrhic victory of 1979 and the defeat of 1980. This enabled the recruitment and harmonization of the activities of skilled advertising men, professionals, and campaign organizers such as Norman Atkins, Patrick Kinsella, and Jerry Lampert, who had for so long successfully planned the victories of the provincial Tories in Ontario and their Social Credit allies in British Columbia. Brian Mulroney's Quebec origins and his portrayal of himself as "the kid from Baie Comeau" rallied the long-alienated francophones of "la belle province" to the Tory cause, thus creating a personal power base. Building on initiatives first taken under the former leader, Joe Clark, modern fund-raising techniques and campaign tactics acquired from friends south of the border close to the Republican party were put to good advantage. In contrast to the disarray in the Liberal ranks under Turner, the Conservatives used the fifteen months following the selection of Brian Mulroney to pull together a tightly controlled, centrally managed, and efficient campaign organization.

Even the New Democrats, consigned to near oblivion by many observers at the outset of the campaign, had spent the months prior to the writ of dissolution honing their organizational skills. The ambiguity of the Turner approach allowed the New Democrats to appeal to "ordinary Canadians," signaling a move toward the center, and to make an attempt to take over part of the electoral territory traditionally occupied by the Grits, who had previously been able to preempt their left-wing rivals, whom they had dubbed "Liberals in a hurry."

The financial and organizational crisis facing the Liberal party in the aftermath of the 1984 federal general election was foreshadowed and compounded by the debts that confronted most of the rivals for the leadership of the party at the conclusion of the June 1984 leadership convention. In addition to the erstwhile minister of finance, John Turner, six cabinet ministers entered the fray: Jean Chrétien, secretary of state for external affairs; Donald Johnston, president of the treasury board; John Roberts, minister of the environment; Mark MacGuigan, minister of justice; John Munro, minister of Indian affairs and northern development; and Eugene Whelan, minister of agriculture. Together the seven candidates spent about $6 million. Four emerged with no debts: Turner and Chrétien, who spent close to the party-imposed limit of $1.65 million, and MacGuigan and Whelan, whose costs amounted to $475,000 and $160,000, respectively. Three candidates were left with considerable debts after the convention: Johnston spent just under $1 million, Roberts over $550,000, and Munro $650,000; their respective postconvention debts were $225,000, $200,000, and $85,000. The latter trio were compelled to raise funds to cover these deficits, which were not recoverable from the party or the public treasury. As late as February 1985, John Roberts, for instance, was faced with a considerable burden that occasioned a lawsuit from one of his alleged creditors. These efforts to liquidate individual indebtedness clearly impeded the party in dealing with its own $2.8 million deficit.[1]

Little is known about the spending of leadership candidates for the Progressive Conservative party, which does not require any reporting or public disclosure of such costs. However, some inkling may be gained from the fact that the party admits to having collected $4 million during its two conventions in 1983. Furthermore, allegations by party notables such as Dalton Camp, and press reports concerning break-ins at Montreal Conservative party offices in the autumn of 1984, indicate that wealthy persons close to Mulroney provided funds to party organizers who appear to have been involved in meeting the costs of convention delegates opposed to the retention of the former leader, Joe Clark.[2] The New Democratic party is the only party that attempts to control the costs of leadership nomination contests by imposing a strict ceiling on the spending of aspirants. Canadian election law is silent on this matter.

The financial difficulties of the federal Liberal party are not new. As the longtime government party, it had been able to exploit the patronage opportunities of office to cover the gaps in its extraparliamentary apparatus. The advantages of incumbency permitted the party to cling to archaic and outmoded fund-raising practices and continued dependence on a relative handful of large corporate contributors, domestic and foreign, many of whom became estranged from the Liberals in the last, nationalist phase of the Trudeau regime.

The Progressive Conservative party, by contrast, had begun to exploit the fund-raising possibilities opened up by the Election Expenses Act of 1974.[3] Taking advantage of the incentive provided by the introduction of the tax credit for political donations, the PC Canada Fund, the party's fund-raising arm, pushed ahead with the electronically produced direct mail techniques introduced in the late 1970s. Donations from large corporate interests were not neglected, but their proportionate contribution to party funds fell in the years prior to the 1984 campaign in comparison to money from other sources. The PC Canada Fund systematically canvassed the small business community, many of whom were disaffected with the Liberals. More important, the Conservatives discovered in the young, upwardly mobile, technobureaucratic cadres of private industry and the free professions—doctors, lawyers, accountants, engineers, and the knowledge industries—a major source of financial support that could be mobilized by employing properly segmented mailing lists developed for private commercial purposes and acquired from "quality" magazines and publications. These direct mail techniques had additional advantages inasmuch as they enabled the targeting of specific groups who could be addressed in terms of their specialized concerns and aspirations. This personalized approach contributed not only to the success of the fund-raising effort but helped identify potential activists and supporters at the campaign and electoral levels. Framed in terms of the tax credits available to contributors, these mailings paid off politically as well as financially.

The New Democrats, for their part, continued to rely on the trade union movement and individual members and sympathizers in proportions that have remained more or less stable over the past decade.

The financial side of the 1984 federal general election campaign was marked by more than differences in the state of readiness of the principal competitors. Also noteworthy were significant changes to the ground rules in the form of amendments to the Canada Elections Act contained in bill C-169 adopted in the autumn of 1983.[4] These changes linked the expenditure ceilings to the variations in the Consumer Price Index since 1980, thus permitting a sharp rise in spending at both the party and candidate levels; reimbursements were fixed as a proportion of the sums actually spent by those who qualified. The method of allocating and administering purchasable and "free" time on the electronic media was revamped and the former subsidy of radio and television time costs for the registered parties was transformed into a refund of a portion of registered party expenses. The ceiling on the "personal expenses" of candidates was lifted, along with other administrative changes in the act. An effort was also made to eliminate advertising and spending designed to influence electoral outcomes by advocacy groups, single-issue organizations, and individuals during the formal campaign period. As it happened, these "third party" restrictions were challenged in the courts, and prior to the 1984 election were ruled unconstitutional as a violation of the Canadian Charter of Rights and Freedoms. The bearing of bill C-169 on the 1984 general election and its implications for future campaigns warrant detailed analysis.

Bill C-169—The 1974 Act
Amended and Challenged

Bill C-169 had its origins in a series of recommendations presented by the chief electoral officer, Jean-Marc Hamel, to the House of Commons as part of his report to Speaker Jeanne Sauvé, dated September 1, 1983.[5] It embodied thirty-seven proposals "unanimously agreed to" by the "Ad Hoc Committee composed of representatives of the chief electoral officer and the political parties represented in the House of Commons." This body, an extralegal administrative creation, consisting largely of nonelected, paid, full-time party professionals, has been the source of the bulk of the legislative amendments and administrative practices affecting the Election Expenses Act of 1974. It should occasion no surprise, therefore, that its suggestions tend to benefit established parties already represented in Parliament rather than challengers from outside.[6] The 1983 legislation, like the previous amending bill C-5 enacted in 1977, contained a number of clarifying technical and linguistic changes; however, its main provisions departed in a number of respects from the original 1974 act. Nevertheless, it was inscribed in the statute books without serious parliamentary debate or scrutiny, and with scarcely any comment in the printed press or the other mass media.

The bill was introduced in the House of Commons by Yvon Pinard, president of the Privy Council, on October 17, 1983, given First Reading, and ordered to be printed. A week later, on October 25, 1983, Pinard rose to move that the bill be given Second Reading; he was followed by spokesmen for the opposition Progressive Conservative and New Democratic parties who, despite some concern for its constitutionality, endorsed it. Within forty-five minutes the bill was referred to the Committee of the Whole House, which precluded the hearing of witnesses, and "by unanimous consent . . . reported, read the third time and passed."[7] Other than a straightforward news report of the bill's passage, the press took no notice of its content until a constitutional challenge to the validity of certain of its provisions was launched three months later in January 1984. The attempt by the Progressive Conservatives to distance themselves from the implications of the bill is belied by their spokesman's acquiescence, despite a few misgivings, during its passage through Parliament.

The bill was presented as an "updating" of the original act and as an attempt to take account of the inflation and experience accumulated in the previous decade. Changes in the spending ceiling were made, including an automatic escalator in party and candidate limits tied to the rise in the Consumer Price Index since 1980. Permitted spending per eligible voter for the 1984 federal general election was 1.318 times the initial base. In addition, the $2,000 limit on a candidate's personal expenses was removed. Furthermore, whereas formerly only candidates in twenty-five large, remote constituencies benefited from a modest upward adjustment in the spending limits, this number was sharply expanded to ninety-two constituencies by taking population density into account. Since 1983 candidates in ridings with less than ten electors per square kilometer benefit from a fifteen-cent per square kilometer increase in the expense ceiling to a maximum of 25 percent above the prescribed limit.

Similarly, the original formula for the reimbursement of the expenses of qualifying candidates was altered by setting this subvention at one-half the actual expenses, or a maximum of one-half the spending permitted. Under the initial scheme candidate reimbursements were linked to the cost of a first-class mailing and because of the rise in the latter were threatening to cover or even outstrip actual spending. In addition to these justifiable amendments, changes were made to federal election broadcasting procedures, the refund of registered party spending on the electronic media, the responsibility of party and candidate auditors, and the controls on "third party" spending during the campaign period. In all of these a weakening in the verificatory mechanism, a relaxation of spending limits, and a bias in favor of the three parliamentary parties are discernible.

The broadcasting amendments in bill C-169 transferred responsibility for administering these provisions from the Canadian Radio-television and Telecommunications Commission to a broadcasting arbitrator appointed by the chief electoral officer on the unanimous recommendation of two representatives appointed by the leader of each registered party represented in the House of Commons. The formula previously applied for the allocation of the six and one-half hours of purchasable prime broadcast time amongst the registered political parties was spelled out in legal terms: equal weight to both the percentage of seats won in the previous general election and the percentage of votes received, and half the weight of the above factors to the party's percentage of the total number of candidates at the previous election, with no party to get more than half the total time available for sale. The same principles are to be applied in the division of "free" time provided by broadcasters. While an additional potential of thirty-nine minutes of purchasable broadcast time was made available for allocation among "new" parties, the formula distinctly favors the established parliamentary parties. In the 1984 campaign the Liberals, Progressive Conservatives, and New Democrats were allocated 173, 129, and 69 minutes, respectively, whereas apart from the Rhinocéros, which was granted 8 minutes, no other party was accorded more than 5.5 minutes. This advantage has been accentuated by the change in party reimbursements. Until 1983 a registered party was only entitled to a refund from the federal treasury of one-half the cost of broadcast time purchased by it during the course of the campaign. On the surface this appeared to discriminate against the print and other media. The 1983 amendments converted the reimbursement of broadcasting costs into a general refund of up to 22.5 percent of the maximum permitted expenditure for any registered party *which had spent at least 10 percent of its maximum.* Since only the three parliamentary parties spent these amounts, smaller organizations that in the past could have benefited from the broadcasting subsidy were effectively eliminated as beneficiaries.

A serious weakening in the verificatory mechanism has also occurred. The 1974 act required that all party and candidate declarations be accompanied by an auditor's report verifying their authenticity: "The auditor . . . shall make a report . . . on the return respecting election expenses . . . and shall make such examinations as will enable him to state whether in his opinion the return represents fairly the financial transactions *required . . . to be detailed in . . . return"* (emphasis mine). While this was a heavy responsibility, it was seen by its authors and the Barbeau Commission as an essential element in the verificatory process. Nevertheless, the professional accounting associations mounted a successful lobby against this provision concerning possible omissions from the returns. The 1983 bill amended the clause to read that the auditor simply "state in his report whether in his opinion the return presents fairly the financial transactions contained in *the books and records of the candidate"* (emphasis mine). Furthermore, the auditors' reports appended to all party returns for the last general election contain the following or a parallel disclaimer: "The Act does not require us to report, nor was it practicable for us to determine, that the accounting records include all transactions relating to the . . . Party . . . for the general election held on September 4, 1984 . . . the Return . . . presents fairly the information contained in the accounting records." But these reports say nothing about the state or quality of these records.

The most important amendment included in the 1983 legislation was an attempt to impose an outright ban on promotional spending and advertising by "third parties" during the course of the formal election campaign. In order to fix the legal responsibility and accountability for the financial aspect of campaigns, the 1974 Election Expenses Act restricted the right to incur election expenses to candidates, registered parties, and their agents. However, expenditures during the campaign period "for the purpose of gaining support for views held by [a person] on an issue of public policy, or for the purpose of advancing the aims of any organization or association, other than a political party or an organization or association of a partisan political character" were permitted if made "in good faith" and not to circumvent the intent of the act.[8] Several efforts by the chief electoral officer to prosecute alleged contravenors were frustrated by the "good faith" defense.[9] Annoyed and discomfited by the confrontational tactics of advocacy and single-issue organizations, exemplified by antiabortion and pro-life groups during the 1979 and 1980 campaigns, and the stated intentions of peace, nuclear disarmament, and anti-Cruise missile movements, as well as environmental, ecological, and animal rights activists, the three parliamentary parties, acting through their directors on the ad hoc advisory committee, persuaded the chief electoral officer to request parliamentary repeal of this escape clause.

The authors of bill C-169 did not give adequate consideration to the validity of the amendment forbidding "third party" activity during campaigns. The chief electoral officer neglected to suggest an alternative, constitutionally acceptable wording. Parliament gave the matter short shrift. The press failed to note the civil liberties issue before it reached the courts; only then did public debate ensue. Given the far-reaching implications of the successful constitutional challenge, a detailed discussion is warranted.

"Third Party" Restrictions
Ruled Unconstitutional [10]

Within three months of passage and less than six months before the calling of the 1984 election, the right-wing National Citizens' Coalition led by Colin Brown attacked the constitutionality of those provisions of the clauses of bill C-169 which forbade them from employing the print or broadcast media to support or challenge a candidate or registered political party during an election. They alleged that sections 70.1(1) and 72 of the Canada Elections Act as amended in 1983 infringed on the rights to freedom of expression, the press, and other media of communication as well as the right to an informed vote guaranteed by the Canadian Charter of Rights and Freedoms and as such violated the principles of parliamentary democracy assured in the preamble to the Constitution Act of 1867.

The suit against the attorney general for Canada was heard in Calgary during the months of April, May, and June 1984. On June 26, 1984, Justice Donald Medhurst of the Alberta Court of Queen's Bench ruled the offending clauses invalid on the grounds that "on their face [they] do limit the actions of anyone other than registered parties or candidates from incurring election expenses during the prescribed time and in this sense there is a restriction on freedom of expression." Since there was very little evidence of abuses to justify such a restriction, it could not be argued that the 1983 amendments were "reasonable." Fear of mischief is not sufficient: "There should be actual demonstration of harm or a real likelihood of harm to a society value before a limitation can be said to be justified," he concluded. Technically, the judgement applied only to elections in Alberta; however, because of the forthcoming election, the attorney general for Canada decided not to enter an appeal and the chief electoral officer extended its application to the country as a whole in the interests of uniformity.

Failure to find constitutionally acceptable language to close the gap opened by this judgment may well lead in the future to unlimited election spending by advocacy groups, single-issue organizations, and interest groups, and presage the appearance of American-style political action committees on the Canadian scene. There were signs of "third party" activity throughout the country during the 1984 campaign but these were not monitored by any official agency. The National Citizens' Coalition—whose aims are reminiscent of the American National Conservative Political Action Committee—after its court victory announced through its vice president that it planned to spend $700,000 for campaign-period advertising and promotion as follows: $200,000 on radio and $100,000 on television in major markets, $224,000 on national and regional newspaper advertising, $100,000 in direct mail, and $60,000 for administrative support. Viewed by some observers as a right-wing front for the Tory party, it has been promoting such issues as the privatization of Crown corporations, the dismantling of Petro-Canada and the national energy program, the restriction of trade union rights, ending indexed pensions for civil servants and members of Parliament, legal obligations requiring balanced federal government budgets, and entrenching property rights in the Constitution.[11] Although a relatively minor factor in the 1984 campaign, such activities may well be a harbinger of things to come in the absence of acceptable legislative action.

National Party Finances, 1980–84

The pattern of ongoing party revenues and spending after 1979 diverged sharply from that of the previous five years.[12] Shifts in the public perception of the parties, notably the increasing disaffection with the governing Liberals and the growing attraction of the Progressive Conservatives to previous and potential contributors, help to account for this change. More important, it reflects the differential skill with which the major parties, particularly the Progressive Conservatives, were able to profit from the possibilities opened up by the tax credit system and modern sampling, electronic data processing, direct mail, and canvassing techniques. As tables 7.1–7.4 demonstrate, these interparty differences grew with the approach of the 1984 election.

The total income of the twelve registered parties in the period 1980–84, covering two federal election campaigns and expensive contests for the leadership of the Progressive Conservative and Liberal parties, amounted to over $140 million of which more than $137 million accrued to the three major parliamentary parties. Major party revenues in the 1984 election year totaled over $44 million, more than twice the funds raised by the Progressive Conservatives, the Liberals, and the New Democrats in each of the 1979 and 1980 general elections, which amounted to $19,419,030 and $21,121,932, respectively.

More significant, however, than the global figures are the interparty comparisons on a year-by-year basis. Rebounding from their defeat in 1980, the Progressive Conservatives more than doubled their national office income by the end of 1983. The New Democrats in the same period increased their resources by over 40 percent from a relatively static number of givers. But the governing Liberals raised little more than they had four years earlier. Part of the explanation for these disparities lies in the data contained in tables 7.1, 7.2, and 7.3. The Liberals were able to almost double the number of individual donations from 1980 to 1983 and increase their takings from this category by about one-half, but the Progressive Conservatives tripled the count of individual donors, who provided almost two-thirds of the party's income

Table 7.1 Progressive Conservative Party Fiscal Period Returns,
January 1, 1980–December 31, 1984.

		1/1/80– 12/31/80	1/1/81– 12/31/81	1/1/82– 12/31/82	1/1/83– 12/31/83	1/1/84– 12/31/84
Summary						
Contributions		$7,564,120	$6,949,797	$8,193,660	$14,108,012	$21,1 45,920
Other income		—	—	327,276	659,155	833,420
Total income		7,564,120	6,949,797	8,520,936	14,767,167	21,979,340
Operating expenses		3,759,282	6,800,348	7,307,662	10,977,197	18,155,542
By-election expenses		14,312	81,865	31,746	44,712	—
Transfer to party associations		1,148,998	659,334	1,181,686	2,177,281	2,620,938
Other expenditures		—	—	—	—	—
Total expenditures		4,922,592	7,541,547	8,521,094	13,199,190	20,776,480
Details of Contributions						
Individuals	No.	32,720	48,125	52,694	99,264	93,199
	$	3,043,829	4,319,604	5,181,016	9,105,732	10,142,398
Businesses, commercial organizations	No.	5,011	7,312	9,432	18,067	21,286
	$	4,367,936	2,573,208	2,922,661	4,819,737	11,003,522
Governments	No.	—	—	—	—	—
	$	—	—	—	—	—
Trade unions	No.	—	—	—	—	—
	$	—	—	—	—	—
Other organizations	No.	143	160	152	385	—
	$	152,335	56,985	89,983	182,543	—
Total	No.	37,884	55,597	62,278	117,716	114,485
	$	7,564,120	6,949,797	8,193,660	14,108,012	21,145,920
Details of Operating Expenses						
Salaries, wages, and benefits		$1,161,108	$1,822,696	$2,426,282	$3,011,310	$5,228,361
Traveling expenses		548,725	967,085	1,353,640	1,303,091	3,738,182
Party conventions and meetings		141,784	770,186	458,266	2,622,425	—
Rent, light, heat, and power		182,510	270,025	406,406	399,256	633,937
Advertising		110,599	131,563	69,795	64,049	1,148,097
Broadcasting		—	—	—	—	—
Printing and stationery		1,150,056	1,755,399	1,787,061	2,566,045	5,245,068
Telephone and telegraph		240,041	369,764	408,789	471,135	1,123,570
Legal and audit fees		48,477	59,886	80,883	75,652	67,447
Miscellaneous expenses		175,282	653,744	316,540	464,234	970,880
Total		3,759,282	6,800,348	7,307,662	10,977,197	18,155,542

Source: Report of the Chief Electoral Officer Respecting Election Expenses, Thirty-third General Election, 1984 (Ottawa, 1985).

Table 7.2 Liberal Party Fiscal Period Returns,
January 1, 1980–December 31, 1984.

		1/1/80– 12/31/80	1/1/81– 12/31/81	1/1/82– 12/31/82	1/1/83– 12/31/83	1/1/84– 12/31/84
Summary						
Contributions		$6,217,795	$5,095,158	$6,104,367	$7,285,115	$10,553,316
Other income		1,239,360	496,951	642,227	451,246	1,044,974
Total income		7,457,155	5,592,109	6,746,594	7,736,361	11,598,290
Operating expenses		3,306,955	3,428,162	4,107,781	4,616,117	11,205,819
By-election expenses		6,278	62,195	39,537	27,679	—
Transfer to party						
associations		388,572	1,625,925	2,633,578	1,633,213	793,487
Other expenditures		—	—	—	—	—
Total expenditures		3,701,805	5,116,282	6,780,896	6,277,009	11,999,306
Details of Contributions						
Individuals	No.	17,760	24,735	27,968	33,649	29,056
	$	2,277,650	2,101,350	3,195,283	3,261,950	5,181,097
Businesses,						
commercial	No.	4,420	6,039	5,652	7,536	6,494
organizations	$	3,730,983	2,705,385	2,521,810	3,542,895	5,339,729
Governments	No.	1	3	8	17	19
	$	92	592	1,428	2,268	3,496
Trade unions	No.	3	3	2	4	8
	$	1,697	1,627	2,745	3,223	2,499
Other organizations	No.	512	1,046	1,058	1,132	54
	$	207,373	286,204	383,101	474,779	26,495
Total	No.	22,606	31,826	34,688	42,338	35,631
	$	6,217,795	5,095,158	6,104,367	7,285,115	10,553,316
Details of Operating Expenses						
Salaries, wages, and						
benefits		$840,470	$1,000,032	$1,308,209	$1,320,118	$1,267,898
Traveling expenses		118,137	211,151	256,653	243,367	333,206
Party conventions and						
meetings		827,954	471,226	571,259	454,958	4,357,725
Rent, light, heat, and						
power		103,438	118,984	232,878	199,687	258,638
Advertising		121,965	128,691	18,950	8,130	154,027
Broadcasting		(22,943)	—	—	—	—
Printing and stationery		217,752	235,593	329,643	301,309	367,522
Telephone and telegraph		126,013	152,346	179,282	161,660	336,864
Legal and audit fees		87,166	64,355	112,864	95,803	109,633
Miscellaneous expenses		887,003	1,045,784	1,098,043	1,831,085	4,020,306
Total		3,306,955	3,428,162	4,107,781	4,616,117	11,205,819

Source: Report of the Chief Electoral Officer Respecting Election Expenses, Thirty-third General Election, 1984 (Ottawa, 1985).

Table 7.3 New Democratic Party Fiscal Period Returns,
January 1, 1980–December 31, 1984.

		1/1/80– 12/31/80	1/1/81– 12/31/81	1/1/82– 12/31/82	1/1/83– 12/31/83	1/1/84– 12/31/84
Summary						
Contributions		$4,646,090	$3,534,958	$4,537,112	$5,746,066	$6,549,680
Other income		1,454,567	2,467,624	2,571,085	2,922,586	3,963,016
Total income		6,100,657	6,002,582	7,108,197	8,668,652	10,512,696
Operating expenses		3,139,014	4,455,900	4,850,076	5,638,742	6,498,935
By-election expenses		11,505	17,648	21,458	25,214	—
Transfer to party						
associations		2,841,104	2,017,891	1,075,483	2,344,807	908,425
Other expenditures		—	—	—	—	—
Total expenditures		5,991,623	6,491,439	4,871,534	8,008,763	7,407,360
Details of Contributions						
Individuals	No.	62,428	56,545	66,665	65,624	80,027
		2,817,387	2,868,724	3,774,971	4,998,350	4,156,000
Businesses,						
commercial	No.	349	260	459	199	280
organizations	$	96,501	109,062	144,324	41,432	51,665
Governments	No.	2	2	2	2	2
		26,828	39,619	143,358	67,155	181,010
Trade unions	No.	903	759	766	1,203	947
		1,702,828	515,186	473,139	636,539	2,159,055
Other organizations	No.	17	14	8	30	5
		2,546	2,367	1,320	2,590	1,950
Total	No.	63,699	57,580	67,900	67,058	81,261
		4,646,090	3,534,955	4,537,112	5,746,066	6,549,680
Details of Operating Expenses						
Salaries, wages, and						
benefits		$1,543,162	$1,938,898	$2,387,559	$2,549,044	$2,536,516
Traveling expenses		481,589	627,315	708,293	654,668	554,687
Party conventions and						
meetings		51,539	527,770	93,022	571,228	615,212
Rent, light, heat, and						
power		104,998	119,391	122,335	149,887	12,704
Advertising		115,734	297,536	305,050	265,778	223,763
Broadcasting		—	—	133,955	—	226,052
Printing and stationery		358,809	423,956	546,174	826,205	911,051
Telephone and telegraph		87,019	121,064	189,432	192,549	229,242
Legal and audit fees		72,000	77,956	63,131	86,533	62,291
Miscellaneous expenses		324,164	322,014	301,125	342,850	1,127,417
Total		3,139,014	4,455,900	4,850,076	5,638,742	6,498,935

Source: Report of the Chief Electoral Officer Respecting Election Expenses, Thirty-third General Election, 1984 (Ottawa, 1985).

Table 7.4 Summary of Financial Activities of Minor Registered Parties, 1980–84.

Party	1980	1981	1982	1983	1984
Social Credit					
Total income ($)	162,297	68,153	66,325	54,808	27,577
Total expenditures ($)	75,574	62,044	67,065	50,067	18,327
Number of contributors	815	523	569	467	234
Communist party[a]					
Total income ($)	201,048	244,927	227,124	977,728	289,567
Total expenditures ($)	301,887	310,832	363,186	376,382	385,283
Number of contributors	606	675	601	596	774
Libertarian party					
Total income ($)	28,661	18,745	34,190	34,994	132,173
Total expenditures ($)	36,177	17,777	36,033	38,161	100,126
Number of contributors	61	236	272	290	697
Rhinocéros					
Total income ($)	7,501	160	270	100	N/A
Total expenditures ($)	283	52	822	1,700	N/A
Number of contributors	1	—	—	—	N/A
Parti Nationaliste du Québec (Union Populaire)					
Total income	42,237	21,532	10,292	151,345	258,457
Total expenditures ($)	54,616	13,462	5,497	89,621	293,685
Number of contributors	141	200	126	5,232	4,369
Marxist-Leninist					Deregistered
Total income ($)	756	932	2,315	2,565	
Total expenditures ($)	736	918	1,234	2,344	
Number of contributors	2	1	2	2	
Commonwealth party					
Total income ($)	Not re-	Not re-	Not re-	Not re-	16,245
Total expenditures ($)	gistered	gistered	gistered	gistered	16,319
Number of contributors					114
Green party					
Total income ($)	Not re-	Not re-	Not re-	Not re-	18,015
Total expenditures ($)	gistered	gistered	gistered	gistered	12,675
Number of contributors					232
Confederation of Regions Western party					
Total income ($)	Not re-	Not re-	Not re-	Not re-	30,075
Total expenditures ($)	gistered	gistered	gistered	gistered	106,992
Number of contributors					2,365

[a] Communist party income for 1983 includes party trust funds held in name of Tim Buck, Leslie Morris, and A. Dewhurst ($686,291.31) transferred to the party. It also includes transfers to provincial sections in its regular annual operating expenses.
Source: Report of the Chief Electoral Officer Respecting Election Expenses, Thirty-third General Election, 1984 (Ottawa, 1985).

in 1983, thus outstripping both in quantity and sum of such contributions the New Democrats, who in earlier years had led in this class of contributor. In addition, the Conservatives, because of their success in tapping funds from more than twice the number of smaller private corporations and businesses, were less dependent on a handful of large corporations than their Liberal rivals. Only in the trade union category did the NDP consistently outshine its opponents.

The 1984 election year witnessed a dramatic rise in major party income, with Conservative and Liberal revenues up by 50 percent and New Democratic resources up by 20 percent. Although fewer personal donations were made to the two older parties, this was offset by increases in amounts of gifts, particularly from business and commercial organizations. More people donated to the NDP and, although the amounts given were smaller, this was compensated by generous gifts from trade unions, whose donations more than tripled between 1983 and 1984. The financial advantage of the Conservative party in 1984 is indicated by the fact that its revenues rose from a position of near equality with the Liberals in the previous general election year of 1980 to twice the latter's resources in 1984; in contribution income alone the Progressive Conservatives outstripped their two parliamentary rivals combined by almost 25 percent.

These data lend substance to the conclusion that the Progressive Conservatives have been successful in discerning and carving out a new set of givers capable of being reached by appropriate techniques, given the proper stimuli. For the past seven years a systematic approach has been made to small business people, members of the professional classes, and the intermediate managerial levels of corporate enterprise through the use of personalized electronically produced letters from party leaders sent to subscribers to upmarket glossy magazines and business publications such as *Report on Business*. Commonly couched in terms of current neoconservative phraseology, these letters almost invariably remind recipients of the income tax credits available for contributions to the party and its candidates. Conservative party professionals claim that their percentage and per capita return on direct mail appeals are higher than those for their counterparts in the United States. In the past three years the New Democrats have also employed mail appeals to raise about one-fifth of their annual income, but these tend to be made to known supporters and previous contributors as reflected in the relative stability in the number of the party's donors. Electoral defeat and financial crisis have finally aroused the Liberals. A financial review committee headed by a former cabinet minister, Judd Buchanan, has recommended far-reaching reforms in the party's fund-raising procedures. Personnel have been engaged to run direct mail appeals; subscription lists from periodicals and magazines such as the *Financial Times*, the *Financial Post*, *Time*, *Life*, and *Reader's Digest* have been purchased, and provincial organizations have agreed to turn over their lists of party supporters for this purpose. In 1984 $250,000 net was raised by direct mail, after losses in the previous year. Furthermore, constituency, provincial, women's, and youth wings of the party will be expected to remit up to 25 percent of the money they raise to the national office; for its part, the Liberal national office has agreed to share half the proceeds of its direct mail appeals with the constituency and provincial associations of the party.[13]

In the four years prior to the 1984 federal general election the annual operating expenses of the nine registered parties more than doubled, from $10.5 million in 1980 to well over $21 million in 1983. In the 1984 general election year these expenditures amounted to $36.4 million, three and one-half times those incurred in the previous campaign year. Tables 7.1 to 7.4 demonstrate that the pattern exhibited with respect to contributions was repeated in the case of ongoing expenditures. Among the three parliamentary parties, the then governing Liberals did least well (although they were in a position to exploit the advantages of incumbency). New Democratic spending rose sharply. Progressive Conservative expenses tripled, signifying a vast expansion in the party's organization and capabilities. Even when the $2,622,425 spent on the two leadership conventions held in 1983 is taken into account, Tory spending in that year was double Liberal outlays. For their part, the Liberals expended over $4 million on the eve of the election party convention that chose John Turner as leader in June 1984.

The three major parties continue to make substantial transfers to their regional and local associations, a reflection of the fact that only the registered national party is entitled to issue official receipts for tax credit purposes in nonelection periods. The size of Conservative transfers in 1984 reflects the relative affluence of that party in comparison to its principal competitors.

Party Spending in the 1984 Campaign

The growth in the size of the electorate in the four and one-half years since the previous general election and the linkage of the basic expense limit to changes in the Consumer Price Index since 1980 increased the permitted spending in 1984 by a registered party with a full slate of 282 candidates during the formal campaign by 40 percent to $6,391,497.07. Total reported spending by the eleven registered parties in the 1984 campaign amounted to $17,617,972.92, a rise of more than 50 percent over the expenses totaling $11,707,402.97 reported by the nine registered parties in 1980. Over 98 percent of this money was accounted for by the expenditures of the three major parliamentary parties (see table 7.5).

An overview of the 1984 campaign reveals that actual party campaign costs were substantially higher than those reported to the chief electoral officer. Tables 7.6 and 7.7 reveal that all three parties doubled their expenditures on

Table 7.5 Registered Political Parties' Expense Limits and
Election Expenses Reported for the 1984 General Election.

Political party	Number of electors	Number of candidates[a]	Indexed election expense limits	Election expenses reported
Progressive Conser- vative party	16,164,636	282	$6,391,497.07	$6,388,941.00
Liberal party	16,164,636	282	6,391,497.07	6,292,983.00
New Democratic party	16,164,636	282	6,391,497.07	4,730,723.00
Social Credit party	3,230,017	51	1,277,148.72	5,155.00
Communist party	3,059,954	52	1,209,905.81	32,118.06
Libertarian party	4,230,140	72	1,672,597.36	45,818.43
Parti Rhinocéros	5,281,865	89	2,088,449.42	3,371.65
Parti Nationaliste du Québec	4,434,382	75	1,753,354.64	56,161.70
Green party	3,746,255	60	1,481,269.23	15,983.84
Confederation of Re- gions Western party	3,263,267	55	1,290,295.77	34,649.00
Party for the Common- wealth of Canada	3,954,773	65	1,563,717.24	12,068.24
Total	16,164,636	1,365	$31,511,229.40	$17,617,972.92

Note: Index factor is 1.318; basic limit is $0.30 per elector; indexed limit is basic limit times the index factor = $0.3954.
[a] In addition, there were eighty-four independent and other candidates not affiliated to a registered party.
Source: Registered Party Returns in Respect of Election Expenses (General Elections Only), for the election of September 4, 1984.

radio, and all but the Liberals drastically cut their spending on the print media. Travel by party leaders and officials also doubled, but only the NDP detailed the net cost of the tour of its leader, Ed Broadbent, which amounted to $393,652. In addition, the Progressive Conservatives outspent their nearest rival by eight times for the professional services of campaign consultants and organizers. The sharpest contrast between the parties, however, and one that reflects on the candor of these reports, lies in the treatment of campaign period national office expenses (item 8 in table 7.6) by the various parties.

The Progressive Conservative party allocated under 27 percent of national office expenditures as detailed in Schedule A of the above-mentioned reports to election expenses. Almost $1,700,000 of costs incurred were excluded. All $70,000 of advertising was included, in addition to the amount in table 7.6, but 50 percent of fund-raising costs, 42 percent of printing, almost 90 percent of salary and traveling costs, about 95 percent of telephone, and 80 per-cent of miscellaneous expenses in the election period (amounts ranging from

Table 7.6 Election Expenses Reported by Major Political Parties, 1984 General Election.

Category	Progressive Conservative	Liberal	New Democratic
1. Advertising	$ 206,651	$ 763,482	$ 153,846
2. Broadcasting			
Radio	1,236,075	1,069,248	494,466
Television	1,757,944	1,695,186	1,158,150
Subtotal	(2,994,019)	(2,764,434)	(1,652,616)
3. Rental of premises	9,372	41,092	107,505
4. Salaries and wages	137,283	202,760	702,275
5. Professional services	1,032,716	128,640	28,021
6. Traveling expenses [a] and rental of vehicles	1,129,512	880,817	539,436
7. Administrative expenses	253,946	431,321	367,582
8. National office expenses—	(2,302,761)	(1,579,337)	(1,179,442)
amount allocated to election expenses	619,160	1,080,437	1,179,442
9. Miscellaneous	6,282	—	—
10. Total election expenses reported	$6,388,941	$6,292,983	$4,730,723
Expense limit, 1984	6,391,497	6,391,497	6,391,497
Reimbursement claimed	1,437,512	1,415,921	1,064,413

[a] Includes the net cost of the national tours by the three party leaders.

Note: Total spending in 1984 by the eight other registered parties amounted to $205,325.92, as follows: Social Credit $5,155; Communist $32,118.06; Libertarian $45,818.43; Rhinocéros $3,371.65; Union Populaire/Parti Nationaliste $56,161.70; Green $15,983.84; Confederation of Regions Western $34,649; Commonwealth of Canada $12,068.24; none of these parties received reimbursements in 1984.

Source: Registered Party Returns in Respect of Election Expenses (General Elections Only), for the election of September 4, 1984.

Table 7.7 Election Expenses Reported by Major Political Parties, 1980.

	Party		
	Progressive Conservative	Liberal	New Democratic
Total election expenses reported	$4,407,206.93	$3,846,223.00	$3,255,152.95
Expense limit	4,546,191.60	4,546,191.60	4,531,561.80
Media advertising reimbursement	977,835.00	909,923.00	677,481.00

Note: In 1980 total spending by the six other registered parties amounted to $200,692. Of these, only Social Credit received a media advertising reimbursement of $1,749.

$150,000 to $400,000) were excluded. When added to "pre-writ" expenditures made in anticipation of the campaign, none of which are reported by any party as "election expenses," it becomes clear that the actual, as against the "official" costs of the Conservative party's 1984 campaign might well be the highest in Canadian history. Table 7.7 shows election expenditures in 1980 for comparison.

The Liberals also excluded all national office expenses incurred prior to the issuance of the writ of dissolution. Of such expenditures during the formal election period, over two-thirds were declared as election costs, but about $500,000 was excluded, comprising about $70,000 for travel, $50,000 for salaries, $90,000 for printing and stationery, $175,000 for telephone, and $112,000 for miscellaneous purposes.

The New Democratic party, on the other hand, included *all* costs incurred by its various offices during the campaign period as election expenses, but it too excluded pre-writ costs. More than half of its office costs were for salaries and benefits, one-seventh to cover fund-raising expenses, 10 percent for advertising, and not more than 5 percent for telephone, as compared to the enormous sums expended on this item by the other parties.

The glaring differences between the three parties in allocating their national office expenditures have two explanations. Clearly, the guidelines are very loose and the parties have broad leeway in the matter. As one party official put it: in 1979 and 1980 an "all-inclusive" definition of election expenses was employed, in 1984 a narrower "exclusive" definition was used. Nor does there appear to have been any consistency in applying the criteria for their allocation, each party doing what seemed best for itself. The New Democrats, whose spending fell well short of its permitted limit, wished to show that their expenditures were as high as possible so that they could claim the maximum reimbursement available under the new system, which refunded 22.5 percent of party spending. On the other hand, the Progressive Conservative party, which had spent to within $2,500 of the legal limit, was under the compulsion to reduce its actual costs to conform with the law, otherwise it would have been subject to severe legal sanctions (and in any case would not have received more in reimbursements). Similarly, the Liberals, who came to within $100,000 of their limit, could not attribute more of their national office spending to election expenses without falling afoul of the law.

The Progressive Conservative party had been gearing up for the campaign ever since the choice of Brian Mulroney as leader in the spring of 1983. Months before Parliament was dissolved the party machinery was set in motion. According to some party personnel interviewed by the author, at least 50 percent of the amount expended by the party for election purposes was spent in the pre-writ period prior to July 1984. The New Democrats, for their part, claim to have begun their campaign planning as early as September 1983, spending no less than one-third in addition to the amount expended during the official campaign. Only the Liberals, who had postponed their leadership convention until June 1984, failed to undertake the necessary precampaign effort with its accompanying costs. Taking all these factors into account, it would be no exaggeration to estimate that overall, national registered party spending above the constituency level for the 1984 election did not fall far short of $25 million.

Candidate and Constituency Campaign Spending

A total of 1,449 candidates presented themselves to the electorate on September 4, 1984, 1,365 of whom were endorsed by the eleven registered parties. Of the 282 declared elected, 211 were Conservatives, 40 were Liberals, 30 were New Democrats, and one was Independent. A total of 664 candidates (45.8 percent) received at least 15 percent of the valid votes cast in their constituencies, becoming eligible for the refund of their nomination deposit and the reimbursement of a portion of their election expenses. Included were all Conservative candidates, 238 Liberals, 140 New Democrats, three nominees from the Confederation of Regions Western party, and one Independent. No other candidate qualified for this refund. Andrew Roman, the lone Independent elected, was a dissident Conservative who had failed to win his party's official nomination in the Toronto area constituency of York North.

Total declared spending by the 1,449 candidates at the local constituency level in the two-month period from the date of the issuance of the writ of dissolution to polling day on September 4, 1984, amounted to $25,634,768, comprising $23,874,025 in formal election expenses plus candidates' personal expenses of $1,760,743. These figures may be compared with the sum of $16,707,959 spent by 1,497 candidates in 1980, representing $15,369,280 and $1,338,679 in election and personal expenses, respectively. To meet these local campaign expenditures in 1984, candidates raised a total of $24,326,590 in contributions from individuals, business, trade unions, and allocations from national and local party organizations. In addition, they received a total of $11,170,724 in reimbursements from the federal treasury. The comparable revenue figures for 1980 were $15,396,276 in contributions and allocations, and $8,523,768 in reimbursements. Over 95 percent of the funds raised and spent at the local constituency level in both the 1980 and 1984 federal general elections were attributable to the candidates representing the three major parliamentary parties.

The detailed analysis in table 7.8 demonstrates the preponderant financial position of the three major party candidates and the singular advantage of Progressive Conservative standard-bearers in 1984. The previously noted trend

Table 7.8 Summary of Candidates' Returns, 1984 Federal General Election.

Parties	Number of candidates	Contributions Number	Contributions $	Election expense $
PC	282	60,660	11,344,930	9,951,414
Liberal	282	29,915	8,391,346	8,835,787
NDP	282	20,106	3,723,537	4,226,974
Social Credit	51	404	34,116	26,150
Communist	52	592	64,385	54,077
Libertarian	72	318	93,080	84,316
Rhinocéros	89	612	32,681	22,424
Nationaliste	75	1,160	176,340	180,169
Green	60	761	59,421	47,499
Confed. of Regions	55	1,381	199,260	185,832
Commonwealth	65	25	3,533	3,576
Independents	61	271	94,933	139,180
Independents	23	448	109,028	116,627
Total	1,449	116,653	24,326,590	23,874,025

Details of Contributions to Candidates

Contributors	PC N	PC $	Liberal N	Liberal $
Individuals	42,247	4,714,002	21,185	2,384,4
Businesses/commercial organizations	17,639	4,488,161	8,052	2,316,7
Governments	7	11,073	13	28,5
Trade unions	14	7,209	9	2,8
Political organizations	339	702,258	168	719,5
Registered parties	297	1,233,549	381	2,765,8
Other organizations	117	46,922	107	69,3
Proceeds from fund-raising functions	0	141,756	0	103,8
Total number of contributors	60,660		29,915	
Total contributions ($)		11,344,930		8,391,3

Details of Election Expenses by Candidates

Expenses	PC $	Liberal $	NDP $	Others $	Total $
Advertising: Radio/TV	866,525	945,235	356,974	97,558	2,266,2
Other	5,046,369	4,193,935	1,794,919	534,336	11,569,5
Salaries	554,858	773,412	849,693	17,212	2,195,1
Office expenses	2,248,928	1,742,784	915,639	129,188	5,036,5
Travel expenses	261,880	267,394	147,797	26,939	704,0
Other expenses	972,854	913,027	161,952	54,617	2,102,4
Total	9,951,414	8,835,787	4,226,974	859,850	23,874,0

Source: Report of the Chief Electoral Officer Respecting Election Expenses, Thirty-third General Electi
1984 (Ottawa, 1985).

ending limits $	Candidates' personal expenses $	Reimbursements $
11,182,463	774,848	5,117,066
11,182,463	611,440	4,081,353
11,182,463	251,574	1,917,095
2,141,774	9,618	0
2,011,190	2,293	0
2,825,126	3,689	0
3,503,050	9,499	0
2,950,011	30,250	0
2,403,997	8,601	0
2,325,785	36,343	28,870
2,549,795	291	0
2,433,888	17,478	0
899,957	4,819	26,340
57,591,962	1,760,743	11,170,724

N.D.P.		Others		Total	
N	$	N	$	N	$
690	1,607,105	5,334	509,865	87,456	9,215,429
286	60,422	401	129,753	26,378	6,995,065
3	709	0	0	23	40,326
600	498,944	0	0	623	509,015
220	527,178	27	15,562	754	1,964,596
224	914,729	198	178,589	1,100	5,092,766
83	52,378	12	2,506	319	171,190
0	62,072	0	30,502	0	338,203
106		5,972		116,653	
	3,723,537		866,777		24,326,590

in the year-to-year financial activities of the national parties since 1980 was confirmed at the local level in the general election of 1984. Conservative candidates raised more money from more individual and corporate contributors than the other two major parties combined. Only in the trade union category did New Democratic candidates outpace their principal rivals. Liberal candidates were the most dependent on support from their national, regional, and local party organizations, receiving as much assistance from these sources as the Conservative and New Democratic candidates combined. These findings bear out the conclusion previously drawn concerning the primitive and outmoded condition of the Liberal party's national and local fund-raising apparatus, and confirm the observations made regarding the neglect of the party's organizational infrastructure during the Trudeau regime.

Summary of 1984 Campaign Costs

It may be possible to make a reasonable estimate of total spending by the registered national parties and all candidates for the 1984 federal general election using the following factors: the declared formal "election" expenses of the eleven registered national parties, the reported "election" and "personal" expenses of the 1,449 local candidates, and estimates of pre-writ and nonelection expenses. Declared spending at the national party level and by all candidates amounted to $17,617,974 and $25,634,768, respectively; pre-writ costs by the national parties may be estimated at about $8 million; and nonelection expenses incurred by parties and candidates during the course of the formal campaign period may be gauged to have been in the neighborhood of $3 million. A statement by the former director of the Progressive Conservative party to a leading Ottawa journalist concerning direct mail canvassing in the 1984 campaign confirms the high costs incurred. "In the campaign itself, the party used the computer data banks of its polling firm, Decima Research, to send letters to specially targetted voters in 30 ridings. Mr. Lampert says that cost $20,000 per riding." [14] (A figure certainly not reported in the party's election expense return!) These returns do not touch such matters as the alleged abuse of their franking privilege by outgoing members of Parliament to distribute election propaganda immediately following issuance of the writ of dissolution, nor do they cover the abuse of government-sponsored advertising during the course of the 1984 campaign when the Liberal government placed three times its normal summer advertising, about $21 million, mainly with agencies that were active in promoting the party's campaign. [15]

A reasonably conservative estimate of overall spending of $50 million to $55 million would clearly make the 1984 federal general election the most expensive in Canadian history.

Concluding Remarks

The 1984 federal general election and its aftermath highlighted a number of serious shortcomings in the enforcement, administration, and text of the Canadian election expense legislation. Allegations of overspending and omissions were made against about a dozen candidates, including elected members of Parliament from all three parties. One such allegation led to the temporary withdrawal from the cabinet of the minister of communications pending the outcome of the investigation. Although charges have been laid against a number of workers for different candidates, only one Independent member of Parliament has been formally charged with actual violations of the act. Nevertheless, rumors concerning certain members of Parliament from all parties have brought the enforcement sections of the legislation into disrepute. The commissioner of Canada Elections, who is responsible for the investigations, has claimed that delays, with concomitant damage to the candidates' reputations, are due to personnel shortages. This has prompted the chief electoral officer to request that he be provided with an independent staff to investigate allegations; even if this request is granted, it is likely that Parliament will move to decriminalize the sanctions provided under the act.

On the administrative level it is clear that the definition of "election expenses" must be spelled out, and that the "ad hoc committee" advising the chief electoral officer must be formalized to eliminate the taint that it is simply a mouthpiece for the interests of the three parliamentary parties. The legislation itself must be revised to eliminate abuses of the franking privilege and government advertising during campaigns. Furthermore, gaps in the act concerning pre-writ spending, the absence of control of local constituency association activities and finances, and the lack of cognizance of local candidate and party leadership nomination contest costs must be addressed. Finally, unless steps are taken to fill the void created by the Medhurst constitutional decision regarding "third party" spending, Canadian election contests in the future may well be dominated by political action committees on the American model.[16]

Notes

The original version of this paper was prepared for delivery to the Political Finance Panel of the Research Committee on Political Finance and Political Corruption at the XIIIth World Congress, International Political Science Association, Paris, France, July 15–20, 1985. I wish to thank the following for their assistance in providing material and information for the preparation of this paper: F. B. "Bud" Slattery, director, and Jerome Guertin, of the Election Financing Branch, Office of the Chief Electoral Officer of Canada. I am also grateful for the cooperation of Jerry Lampert, national director of the Progressive Conservative party, Gordon Ashworth, former national director of the Liberal party, and Dennis Young, federal secretary of the New Democratic party, who graciously agreed to be interviewed on March 5, March 8, and February 21, 1985, respectively. Interviews were also held with Senator Keith Davey, of the Liberal party, and Howard Stevenson, general manager of the Federal Liberal Agency. Needless to say, the opinions expressed herein are those of the author.

1. *Toronto Globe and Mail*, August 31, October 18 and 26, November 17 and 29, 1984, and February 11, 1985; The *Ottawa Citizen*, October 17, December 18 and 19, 1984, and February 2 and 11, 1985.

2. *Toronto Globe and Mail*, October 26 and December 10, 1984.

3. F. Leslie Seidle and Khayyam Z. Paltiel, "Party Finance, the Election Expenses Act and Campaign Spending in 1979 and 1980," in Howard R. Penniman, ed., *Canada at the Polls, 1979 and 1980: A Study of the General Elections* (Washington, D.C.: American Enterprise Institute, 1981), p. 237.

4. Bill C-169, An Act to Amend the Canada Elections Act (No. 3), received royal assent on November 17, 1983, First Session, Thirty-second Parliament, 29-30-31-32 Elizabeth II, 1980-81-82-83.

5. Chief Electoral Officer of Canada, *Statutory Report—1983*, Second Session, Thirty-second Parliament, (Ministry of Supply and Services, Canada, 1983), pp. 67–78.

6. Khayyam Z. Paltiel, "The Election Expenses Act of 1974: A Preliminary Study and Critique," paper presented at the annual meeting of the Canadian Political Science Association, Edmonton, Alberta, June 3, 1975; and idem, "Canadian Election Expense Legislation 1963–1985: A Critical Appraisal or Was the Effort Worth It?" paper presented at the annual meeting of the Canadian Political Science Association, Montreal, Quebec, June 1, 1985.

7. Canada, *House of Commons Debates, October 25, 1983*, 126, no. 572, 1st Session, 32nd Parliament, pp. 28295–99.

8. The Canada Elections Act (No. 3), Revised Statutes of Canada (1st supp.), c. 14 amended by c. 10 (2nd supp.), August 1982, sections 70.1 (1)(2)(3)(4) and 72.

9. For example, *R. v. Roach* (1977).

10. The paragraphs that follow are based on *National Citizens' Coalition and Colin Brown* v. *The Attorney General for Canada*, statements of claim, arguments of plaintiffs and the Crown, briefs and reasons for judgement, April, May, and June 1984.

11. *Toronto Globe and Mail*, August 8, 1984, and December 21, 1984.

12. Seidle and Paltiel, "Party Finance," pp. 235–50.

13. The *Ottawa Citizen*, December 3, 1984, and February 11, 1985; and *Toronto Globe and Mail*, October 22 and November 1, 1984, February 11 and June 3, 1985.

14. Jeffrey Simpson, "Oiling the Machine," *Toronto Globe and Mail*, November 30, 1984.

15. *Toronto Globe and Mail*, August 30, 1984.

16. For some of the legislative changes being considered see *Report of the Chief Electoral Officer of Canada on Proposed Legislative Changes, 1985* (Ottawa: Chief Electoral Officer, 1985).

8 The Media and the 1984 Landslide[1]

FREDERICK J. FLETCHER

———— The 1984 Canadian federal election, with its landslide victory for the Progressive Conservatives, has been described by one of Canada's most respected political analysts as "the boob-tube election." [2] Certainly, it was an election in which the national media campaign itself had a notable effect on the outcome. Many commentators have traced the landslide and the major shift in voter intentions during the campaign to the televised leaders' debates or to the media coverage in general. Indeed, the election coverage became a matter of controversy during the campaign and journalists have engaged in considerable public soul-searching since.[3] The purpose of this chapter is to review the coverage of the 1984 campaign and the criticisms made of it, with particular attention to trends over the past several elections.

That the campaign was important to the outcome in 1984 is widely accepted. Whereas the distribution of voter preferences among the major parties had changed little during the 1980 campaign, the 1984 shift was the largest since the beginning of national polling in Canada, a period spanning thirteen previous federal elections. The polls showed the Liberals with 49 percent of the decided vote in early July 1984, a 10 percent lead over the Conservatives. Within three weeks of the election call on July 9, Liberal support had dropped to 39 percent, ending up at 28 percent on election day (September 4). The previous high for change in voter intentions during a Canadian campaign was 8 percent.[4] In 1984 almost half the voters made their vote decisions during the campaign (more than half in Quebec), a significant increase over previous campaigns. Perhaps most important, more than half of the voters who had voted Liberal in 1980 made their decisions after the campaign began, and 56 percent of them defected to other parties. Overall, the Liberals were able to hold fewer than half of their 1980 voters.[5] In this context of unprecedented voter volatility the campaign became crucial to the outcome and media coverage was scrutinized closely by all parties.

The national campaign was important to all three established parties. The two major parties had new and untried leaders with relatively unformed public images, despite the publicity surrounding the leadership conventions that had selected them and John Turner's previous record as a high-profile cabinet minister before 1975. Both the Conservative delegates who chose Brian Mulroney and their Liberal counterparts had chosen leaders they thought could win the next election. Delegates gave both of them high marks for "winnability" and "television appeal." [6] Each of the new leaders had a reputation to live up to: Mulroney had to justify the coup that had displaced his predecessor, Joe Clark, while Turner had to bring renewal to a party long in office. The new Liberal leader also had to cope with the powerful image of Pierre Trudeau, who had left office with many devoted supporters, especially in Quebec, despite the low standing of his party in the polls.

The New Democratic party (NDP), despite having an established and popular leader in Ed Broadbent, was in serious trouble as the campaign began. Between June 1982 and June 1984 support for the party had fallen from 23 percent to 11 percent in the Gallup Report on Party Preferences. [7] Private polls showed support at an even lower ebb and the party faced the risk of losing more than half of its thirty seats, possibly even falling below the twelve needed to remain an official party in the House of Commons. Failure to retain party status in the House would have meant the loss of considerable public subsidies for caucus research and the leader's office, as well as status in the operation of the House. The 1984 campaign was a battle for survival for the NDP.

Changes in the Campaign
Communications System

The evolution of the Canadian campaign communications system continues to reflect the basic principles of fairness and proportional balance established in the 1930s. The key elements of free-time broadcasts, paid advertising (permitted only in the final four weeks of the eight-week campaign), partial reimbursement of costs from the public purse, and leaders' tours aimed at the national media (primarily television) remained in operation. There were, however, some modest adjustments for 1984.

As in the previous two elections, free-time broadcasts and paid advertising time were allocated among the registered parties according to a formula based on seats held in the House of Commons at dissolution, share of the popular vote in the previous election, and number of seats contested in the current election. Parties were permitted to purchase as much of their advertising allocation as they wished, within the overall campaign spending limits. The actual time allocations were negotiated by the agents of registered parties and the broadcasters, under the supervision of the Canadian Radio-television and Telecommunications Commission (CRTC). For the 1984 federal election a broadcast arbitrator was appointed by the CRTC, with the agreement of the parties and broadcasters, to resolve disputes. The CRTC had found that it was unable to deal with disagreements regarding time allocation, rates, and similar factors during the limited campaign period.

In 1984 twelve political parties were eligible for free time and paid advertising time. The formula can be illustrated by the allocation of free time on the Canadian Broadcasting Corporation (CBC), the public corporation that operates radio and television networks in English and French. Of the seven hours allocated, the incumbent Liberals received 41.4 percent, the Conservatives 31 percent, the NDP 16.5 percent, and the nine minor parties 11.1 percent (or five minutes each). The allocations were identical on the other networks, although the total time allotted was less. CTV, the private English network, provided three and one-half hours. Private broadcasters are not obliged to provide free time but must adhere to the formula if they do. They must, however, make paid advertising time available, during prime time, at normal rates. Normally, the parties are unable to purchase all of the time thus made available. In 1984 the parties targeted their media buying very carefully to gain most exposure in areas where they had the best chance to win seats. They devoted most of their resources to spot advertisements, which are the best means of reaching uncommitted voters, and used the free time to reinforce their central themes.

The patterns of party expenditure are set out in table 8.1. The bulk of the more than $12 million spent on advertising was allocated to television, despite a change in the regulations that ended the policy in force in the previous two elections of providing partial reimbursement for broadcast advertising only. The change, lobbied for by the print media, did not stem the flow of funds away from print advertising. Radio, however, did gain at the expense of television in 1984, primarily because it was thought to be more cost effective than television in reaching targeted audiences in the summer.

In an attempt to ensure equity in campaign spending Parliament in 1983 moved to prohibit anyone other than registered parties or candidates (and their agents) from expenditures designed to promote or oppose a particular candidate or party. The amendments precluded party or candidate-related spending by interest groups during the campaign. The fear was that unrestricted spending by single-issue groups or political action committees, such as those in the United States, would undermine the spending limits established in 1974. Just prior to the 1984 campaign the section was declared a violation of the Charter of Rights by an Alberta court and the federal government chose not to appeal. In addition, it did not enforce the rules in other provinces. One study indicates that there were few, if any, abuses during the 1984 campaign, perhaps because groups feared that direct endorsements would encourage further legislative restriction.[8] The concern remains, however, and the chief electoral of-

Table 8.1 Advertising Expenditures (%) by Medium and Party, 1979, 1980, and 1984.

	Party											
	Conservative			Liberal			NDP			Total (in millions of $)		
Medium	1979	1980	1984	1979	1980	1984	1979	1980	1984	1979	1980	1984
Print	10	19	7	24	16	22	24	23	9	18	19	13
										$1.2	$1.4	$1.1
Radio	34	21	39	23	22	30	19	13	27	27	19	33
										$1.8	$1.5	$2.8
TV	56	60	55	53	62	48	58	64	64	55	62	54
										$3.6	$4.7	$4.6
Total ($ millions)	2.7	3.1	3.2	2.4	2.6	3.5	1.3	1.8	1.8	6.6	7.5	8.5
% of total spending	71	72	50	62	67	56	61	59	38	66	66	49

Source: Calculated from returns submitted by the political parties to the chief electoral officer.

ficer commented in his 1984 report on the need to strike an acceptable balance between "adequate control of election expenses and the freedom of expression of Canadians."[9]

With respect to news coverage of the campaign the national media continued to dominate as they have in most recent elections, but there were some noteworthy changes in their structure and operation. In the period 1980 to 1984 two major dailies closed, journalistic competition declined, and concentration of ownership continued to increase. By 1983 twelve groups owned 89 of the 116 daily newspapers and the six largest accounted for nearly 80 percent of the 5.5 million total circulation. Many of the owners were conglomerates, owning broadcast stations and large-scale, nonmedia enterprises. By 1984 direct competition existed in only six cities, although the *Toronto Globe and Mail* had established itself as a national newspaper, competing for "elite" readers in all major centers. The Royal Commission on Newspapers, established to look into the increasing concentration of ownership, found no evidence of direct control of political coverage, but there were some indications that the ownership trend had reduced the diversity of perspectives on national politics.[10]

During the same period some new players entered the media system. Among these were a number of tabloid morning dailies modeled on the financially successful *Toronto Sun*. These newspapers, flashy and simply written, introduced a much more opinionated form of political journalism, nonpartisan and populist, that tends to be conservative and antigovernment. More important, perhaps, in the television age, was the introduction on the CBC English television network of "The Journal," a nightly forty-minute public affairs program. It was created to follow "The National," the network's major twenty-minute nightly newscast when it was shifted from 11:00 P.M. to 10:00 P.M. The move increased the audience to about two million for the twinned programs (and appears to have increased the overall audience for national newscasts in English, since its previous private network competitors also gained in the ratings). "The Journal" has become a national forum for political discussion and is now regarded as an indispensable outlet by party strategists.

The Parties and the Media

The three parties had in common their focus on their leaders, the use of sophisticated polling, and the regional targeting of their messages. The two larger parties also controlled access to their leaders and engaged in a contest with the media and with one another to establish the issues that would be central to the campaign. In addition, both Conservative and Liberal strategists were well aware of poll results showing that many Canadian voters were tired of the high levels of federal-provincial conflict and the economic difficulties that marked the Trudeau era. These voters wanted a change, though careful analysis demonstrated that they wanted a different style of governing, not a radical shift in policy.[11] As a consequence, both parties tried to sell their leaders as agents of change without espousing policies that would threaten a skittish electorate. The 1979 and 1980 campaigns had been about leadership.[12] Why should 1984 be any different?

The Conservative leader tour and advertising campaign strategies were essentially similar. The central themes were: (1) a contrast between Mulroney as the agent of real change and Turner, who was portrayed as "yesterday's man";[13] (2) Mulroney as concerned with the problems of Canadians; and (3) Mulroney as a man with a "prime ministerial image."[14] In Quebec the speeches and advertisements stressed Mulroney's Quebec roots and promised change without any direct attack on the Trudeau legacy. In English Canada there was more stress on change but the major focus was on promoting the "star quality" of the leader. In both 1979 and 1980 the Conservatives had emphasized the need for change (translated in 1980 as a real chance to govern). In 1984 the Conservatives returned to the "time for a change" theme and ran a series of commercials in which Mulroney expressed concern about an issue and closed by saying: "You help me and *we* will solve this together." Many of the spots were shown only in selected regions and the issues were chosen specifically for those regions. In both the spots and public appearances care was taken to ensure that Mulroney was photographed against a dignified backdrop (such as rows of law books). Taking a leaf from the book of Ronald

Reagan, Mulroney traveled with a portable backdrop, along with a lectern and sound system, which he used for all his public appearances. His strategists were anxious to grab the glamor factor that Trudeau had had and that appealed to many casual voters.

Similarly, the Mulroney campaign was carefully planned to set the media agenda. A good example was the Conservative leader's refusal to accept the media linkage of promises to costs without full cost-benefit analysis. The party resisted strong media pressure to put price tags on Conservative policy proposals and left it to Mulroney himself to provide a cost-benefit analysis in the last week of the campaign. Mulroney promised after pressure mounted that he would provide a full accounting before the end of the campaign and eventually named a date. This took the pressure off and made it difficult for the other two leaders to generate interest in the matter. The Tories could not have waited so long had it been a pressing issue with the voters, but party polls showed it was not.[15] The Conservatives were able to tie Turner to the record of the Trudeau administration and to link their theme of change to the economic issues concerning the voters.

For a number of reasons the Liberals found themselves on the defensive for most of the campaign. Turner was caught between the clear need in English Canada to establish himself as the candidate of change, requiring that he distance himself from the Trudeau legacy, and the continued popularity of that legacy in Quebec. In addition, he had to compete with a well-prepared and well-financed Conservative party, while relying on a rusty Liberal campaign organization and a rocky transition from the Trudeau staff to his own.[16] There was no clear strategy and the campaign twisted and turned as it tried to respond to the Conservatives. Indeed, one study concluded that "the Liberal campaign was very close to a textbook example of how not to run a modern media-oriented campaign."[17] The leader was poorly prepared, the party was short of funds, and the advance work was shaky.

The two major themes of the Liberal campaign—Mulroney's credibility and the cost of the Conservative campaign promises—did not gain much media attention. The latter was mentioned in only 2.6 percent of television news items and 2.5 percent of front-page stories in the daily newspaper sample. Similarly, the attempt to capitalize on voters' lack of trust in Mulroney, which showed up clearly in the polls, did not catch on (perhaps because Turner had trouble with his own image in this area). The late addition of slashing attacks on Mulroney in the advertisements cobbled together at the last minute by Red Leaf Communications and in the leader's speeches was ineffective, perhaps because they smacked of desperation, given the Liberal slide in the polls.[18]

Fighting for its life, the NDP opted for a survival strategy. It began the campaign with a fairly standard theme, stressing the essential similarity of the

Table 8.2 Relative Attention to Major Parties on TV Network News, 1980 and 1984, Compared to Popular Vote in Previous Election.

Party	1979 Vote[a]	1980 TV News Range[b]	1980 TV News Mean[c]	1980 Newspapers Range	1980 Newspapers Mean	1980 Vote	1984 TV News Range	1984 TV News Mean	1984 Newspapers Range	1984 Newspapers Mean
Liberal	40	35–39	37	28–46	38	44	41–46	44	36–55	42
PC	36	38–46	42	30–48	42	33	34–36	35	27–38	36
NDP	18	18–24	21	14–27	21	20	17–24	21	10–28	22

[a] Percentage of popular vote.
[b] Percentage of network news time and front-page space devoted to party, reported as a range.
[c] Mean percentage of time on network news/daily newspaper front-page space.

Sources: Calculated from table 3.3 in Soderlund, *Media and Elections in Canada*; table 1 in Romanow, "Television News"; and data from Newspaper Coverage of the 1980 and 1984 Federal Election Campaigns, described in the appendix.

two major parties and arguing that it was the only party that offered a distinctive approach to national problems. As the campaign progressed, however, the party made its initial theme secondary. The new approach dealt with a variety of issues grouped around a single theme: the need for a strong NDP presence in the House to represent the interests of ordinary Canadians. The second wave of commercials tacitly admitted that there was going to be a large Conservative majority, freeing voters who wanted the Liberals out from having to vote Conservative and stressing that ordinary Canadians would need active representation in a House dominated by Conservatives.[19]

The News Organizations and the Campaign

Despite reduced editorial budgets in many cases, the major news organizations devoted significant resources and attention to the campaign. For example, the major dailies devoted between 6 and 10 percent of their total nonadvertising space to campaign coverage, a healthy proportion of the space available for news.[20] Coverage on "The National" newscast on the CBC English television network was up nearly 10 percent over 1980, to 390 minutes, though it did not reach the peak achieved in 1979. However, if one adds the extensive coverage (582 minutes) on "The Journal," the total comes to more than twice that on the extended newscasts of 1979.[21]

As far as attention to the major parties and their leaders is concerned, the rule of proportional balance continued to apply. As table 8.2 shows, the television network newscasts adhered very closely to the formula for free-time broadcasts (and, therefore, to the popular vote in the previous election).

The major dailies were basically similar, though with a little more variation, derived primarily from regional differences in party support. The minor parties, however, got even less attention than the formula would suggest, especially on television news. Editorials and columns tended to focus even more heavily on the incumbent party than on news items, with the NDP getting less attention than in the news pages.[22] These patterns have been consistent over the past four elections and are, therefore, clearly a result of well-established journalistic practices. Because the major news organizations are committed to reporting at least one item from each leader every day, leaders can, by rationing access, control the agenda. NDP organizers were relieved to discover that the party continued to get a reasonable share of attention, despite its low standing in the polls. "The Journal," for example, followed a three-party format for most of its items, with the result that the NDP received as much time as the Conservatives and only a little less than the Liberals.[23]

The Conservative dominance of editorial endorsements observed in 1979 and 1980 continued in 1984, with the addition of support in the French press. As in the two previous elections, virtually all English dailies endorsed the Conservatives, as did most columnists. The *Toronto Star* was one of the few dailies to maintain its traditional Liberal loyalties. The important exception was in Quebec, where a number of editorials and columnists came out in favor of Mulroney's Conservatives, an historic breakthrough for the Tories. Interestingly, many of the English editorials expressed doubts about Mulroney but support for the party. In the French press that pattern was reversed. It was Mulroney who struck the responsive chord among Quebec journalists.[24] In general, it appeared that most editorialists and working journalists privately favored the Conservatives.

The trend toward adversarial journalism noted in earlier studies of campaign coverage accelerated in 1984. Reporters worked hard at trying to tell their audiences the political purposes behind leaders' statements and, as a consequence, provided more commentary and less reporting than in previous campaigns. One study reported that in 127 stories dealing with Mulroney and Turner on the CBC national news, only 12 percent of time was direct coverage of what the two leaders were saying, a total of forty-two minutes over eight weeks. The other 88 percent was taken up with reporters' summaries of leaders' statements and reactions to them by reporters and others.[25] This pattern was found in all media, but especially in the press, as newspapers attempted to regain some of the ground lost to television over the past several elections by attempting to go beyond the staged campaign to tell readers what they thought was really happening.[26] While some saw these developments as healthy for democracy and an antidote to manipulative party strategists, others saw it as the triumph of instant assessment and casual opinion, depriving voters a chance to hear the leaders and make their own judgments.[27]

Personal journalism, though not new in 1984, was more widespread. Among other things, it meant a shift in the focus of coverage. Along with less direct reporting of leaders' statements and more assessments of their performances, there was also an increase in attention to party strategies and organizational problems and a notable increase in direct reporting on party-media relations. There was, for example, an almost fourfold increase from 1980 to 1984 in news reports generated by statements by or interviews with party strategists (from 2.3 to 8.1 percent of all campaign reports, according to my study). Comber and Mayne found that almost 60 percent of news reports dealing with the party leaders on "The National" (CBC) and in the *Toronto Globe and Mail* contained at least one explicit assessment of the leader or his performance. Some phrases from CBC news reports illustrate their contention: "Turner's handlers are worried that he can't perform under pressure" (July 11); "terrible blunder" that "raises serious questions about [Mulroney's] sincerity," in reference to the Conservative leader's comments about patronage to a reporter on his campaign plane (July 22); "Turner fumbled on equal pay for equal work and had to be prompted," in the women's issues debate (August 13).[28] While some of these examples are less compelling than others, the general point seems well taken. The same authors interviewed a number of political journalists and found that many were comfortable with the adversarial role, with one arguing that his task in covering the campaign was to find the "chinks in the armor" of the leaders' images.[29] In addition, they found a substantial number of stories that dealt with the logistics of coverage, problems of media access to leaders, and even the opinions and antics of other reporters.[30] It is interesting to note that the English-language press was much harsher on all parties and leaders than the French press, even though French journalists have a longer history of personal journalism.[31]

John Turner's problems with media relations can be traced not only to his being out of touch after nearly a decade in private life, but also to the fact that he "faced a new and far more probing media."[32] He was surprised that there were no friendly advocates for the Liberal party in the press gallery, as there had always been in the past, and that the old rules about casual conversations were no longer accepted by reporters.[33] One such casual conversation led to an acrimonious exchange between himself and Trudeau that did his standing in Quebec considerable damage. Observers report that he was unnerved by the hostility he felt among journalists, engendered in part by the fact that reporters' needs were not as well served by Turner's shaky organization as by the other two parties. Indeed, Turner's problems with his speeches, throat clearing, and nervous gestures, were openly mocked by reporters on his plane, making the leader's tour a kind of trial by ordeal. Both Mulroney and Turner were "sandbagged," as Mulroney put it after he made unwise remarks to reporters that suggested a hypocritical attitude to patronage.[34]

Major Features of the Coverage

The most striking features of the media coverage of "Campaign '84" were the unprecedented attention to voter preference polls, the extremely negative treatment of John Turner and the Liberals, the centrality of the three leaders' debates, and the increased attention to the campaign process at the expense of issue coverage. After the volatility of party preferences over the previous four years, analysts could hardly avoid being struck by the strong and clear trend toward the Conservatives in the polls. It was not surprising that the focus was on the two new leaders and their performance, especially as Turner found himself unable to live up to the inflated expectations created by the media during his time out of public life, which portrayed him as an attractive leader in exile.

The Polls

The trend toward media-funded polls continued unabated in 1984. There were twelve national media polls, an increase of two from 1980, and many more regional and local voter surveys. The national polls were sponsored by five major news organizations and the results were featured in television specials and major news reports. Even more than in past elections, the polls were at the center of campaign coverage, setting the tone for much other coverage and commentary and affecting the morale of party activists. Poll results were featured in 20 percent of election items on national network television in 1984, an increase of 4 percent over 1980. The figures for radio and newspapers in 1984 were 26 and 17 percent, respectively. The figures were even higher for lead items on television (33 percent) and front page news stories (25 percent).[35] Unlike 1980, the final preelection polls predicted the actual distribution of the popular vote among the three parties with almost perfect accuracy. The trend toward the Conservatives was strong and consistent.

The media preoccupation with polls had a number of important consequences. First, the horse-race aspect of the coverage, focused on the race rather than its significance, was reinforced. One study of seven major dailies found that nearly two-thirds of all reports dealing with poll results presented the campaign as a race.[36] Second, the Liberals were put on the defensive by the sudden decline in popular support in early published polls, even though the experts had known all along that Liberal support was soft. Turner's image as a winner was tarnished and party morale suffered. As Liberal insider Keith Davey put it: "Poll after poll from all kinds of media outlets told of our plight in excruciating detail. Every time we got up off the floor the next poll would knock us back down."[37] The results were devastating, especially for a party with organizational and fund-raising problems.

In addition, and most pertinent for this chapter, the nature of the coverage itself was heavily influenced by the results. Several of the reporters interviewed for this study commented that they had lost interest in reporting the issue positions of the parties after it became clear that the Conservatives would win, and focused instead on the probable magnitude and likely consequences of a landslide. Charles Lynch, the veteran political commentator, observed that from July 27 on, the poll figures "made the biggest headlines, dominated the largest of the TV specials, and set the tone for the coverage of the final five weeks of the election." [38] Lynch went on to say that the high cost of the polls resulted in cutbacks in other forms of election coverage, even though pollsters often work for the media at cut rates in return for the publicity. He suggests that issue analysis and reporting on regional concerns suffered as a result of the shift in resources.[39] By mid-August, Lynch suggests, the pollsters had declared the election over: "The bandwagon was hitting on all cylinders, with all media horns blaring, and the election post-mortems started, three weeks before election day, with the accent on the make-up of Mulroney's cabinet, and the date of the future Liberal leadership convention." [40]

Although some commentators have argued that the appearance of being a winner might have been important in that outcome of the election, especially in Quebec, where voters were considering shedding their traditional Liberal allegiance,[41] the Carleton University School of Journalism pollsters argue that pollsters found themselves catching up with public opinion, rather than creating it. According to them, "the polls indicate that the switch to the Conservatives in Quebec happened before there was evidence of a landslide elsewhere." [42] Nevertheless, the poll reports were clearly damaging to the Liberals and my analysis of the assessment of parties and leaders in a national sample of daily newspapers demonstrates that the tone of the coverage followed the polls (see table 8.3). The table shows clearly that coverage for the Liberals and Turner became more negative as the campaign went on, while for Mulroney coverage became more positive. The trend can be accounted for in part by the coverage of the polls themselves but there was clearly a spillover effect as well, especially on the editorial pages. It has been suggested that pack journalism has a hyena effect, with the pack turning on a leader when they smell blood.

There is reason to believe that strategic voting, made possible by the publication of credible media-initiated party preference polls, played a role in the outcome of the election. At the national level it seems likely that some voters who might have voted Conservative to ensure the defeat of the Liberals switched to the NDP when a Conservative victory was assured, with a view to having an effective voice for "ordinary Canadians" in the new House. It also seems likely that some Quebec voters elected to join the bandwagon when the Conservative victory became clear, though the bulk of voters who moved to the Tories seem to have done so before the national result became

Table 8.3 Percentage of Items in Daily Newspapers Sample Coded Positive or Negative for Two Major Parties and Leaders in 1984, by Period.[a]

	Early		Middle		Late	
	FP[b]	Edit[c]	FP	Edit	FP	Edit
Liberal, positive	2.0	3.2	6.6	5.8	8.6	2.1
Liberal, negative	19.5	32.6	24.5	37.4	27.2	40.6
Net	−17.5	−29.4	−17.9	−31.6	−18.6	−38.8
Conservative, positive	5.5	4.5	20.3	7.7	22.2	14.6
Conservative, negative	5.0	9.7	5.7	15.7	7.4	13.4
Net	+0.5	−4.2	+14.6	−8.0	+14.8	+1.2
Turner, positive	3.0	4.5	7.1	6.4	11.7	2.9
Turner, negative	17.8	28.1	23.6	34.2	16.0	36.8
Net	−14.8	−23.6	−16.5	−27.8	−4.3	−33.9
Mulroney, positive	4.0	4.9	17.8	9.3	12.3	14.6
Mulroney, negative	8.0	17.5	8.9	18.5	9.3	18.8
Net	−4.0	−12.6	+8.7	−9.2	+3.0	−4.2
N	201	309	212	313	162	239

[a] The periods were defined as follows: early=first three weeks of campaign; middle=second three weeks; late=final two weeks.
[b] Front page.
[c] Editorial page (all items).
Source: Newspaper coverage project. See appendix.

evident. Certainly the two parties tried to promote such strategic voting.[43] The case of Turner's personal candidacy in Vancouver Quadra is also relevant. Six surveys of voters in the constituency were published during the campaign by the two Vancouver dailies. At no time during the campaign did Turner lead the Conservative incumbent, according to the polls. He trailed by at least ten points in all polls published in August, and the final survey, published only days before the vote, showed him trailing by eighteen percentage points, with only 14 percent undecided. Yet he won by a margin of seven percentage points on September 4. Knowing that the national election was won, a number of previously Conservative voters appear to have felt sympathy for Turner or decided that it would be good for the riding or the country to have a party leader representing Vancouver Quadra.[44] The knowledge derived from the published polls made such strategic voting possible.

Focus of the Coverage

The competence and performance of the party leaders continued in 1984 to be a major focus of campaign coverage. This aspect of the campaign was

Table 8.4 Persons Mentioned in Front-page Campaign Stories
in National Sample of Daily Newspapers, 1980 and 1984.[a]

	1980		1984	
	Primary[b]	All[c]	Primary	All
Party leaders	73.5%	81.8%	61.0%	89.7%
Other federal M.P.s	9.1	37.6	10.6	48.9
Local candidates	5.3	21.7	7.6	26.2
Party strategists	1.7	11.0	2.5	19.7
Interest group spokespersons	0.3	2.7	0.9	8.3
N	660		739	

[a] The two samples are not identical as a result of newspaper closings but they do include the major daily newspapers in each region of the country.
[b] Primary or first mention.
[c] Total mentions. Totals exceed 100 percent because most reports mention more than one category of persons.
Source: Newspaper coverage project (see appendix).

the focus of 26 percent of all network television campaign reports and daily newspaper front-page stories, as well as 31 percent of newspaper editorials and columns in 1984. The figure for network radio was 21 percent.[45] The pattern becomes clearer when one examines the personalities mentioned in front-page election stories. As table 8.4 shows, the party leaders were mentioned far more frequently than any other political actors, despite the fact that other leading party figures were campaigning actively.[46] While a somewhat wider net was cast in 1984 than in 1980, the leaders remained at center stage. Statements by party leaders accounted for about half of all front-page stories in 1984. In most cases other actors were quoted in reaction to the statements of party leaders. Local candidates and interest group spokespersons were virtually absent from high-profile coverage (see table 8.5). Even on the inside pages of newspapers, leaders were mentioned at least as often as all other candidates combined. On the editorial pages the focus was overwhelmingly on the national parties and their leaders.[47] The dominance of party leaders meant that the contest to set the campaign agenda focused on them, with others having difficulty being heard.

The importance of leader assessments in the vote decisions of Canadians cannot be denied, of course. In 1984, for example, nearly 50 percent of those who voted for a different party in 1984 than in 1980 cited leadership as having the greatest impact on their decisions. The figure for 1972 to 1974 switchers was only 20 percent and has grown with each election since. Leadership was a particularly important factor among those who voted Liberal in 1980 and Conservative in 1984. Voters cited both a negative response to Turner and a positive response to Mulroney, but the former seems to have been more

Table 8.5 Primary Event Covered in Front-page Election Stories,
Daily Newspapers, 1980 and 1984.

	Percentage of election news stories	
Statement or action by	1980	1984
Liberal leader	24.5	28.1
Conservative leader	18.3	14.3
NDP leader	6.9	8.8
Polls	8.6	11.6
Other federal M.P.s	5.0	7.9
Local candidates	5.4	4.3
Interest groups	0.1	1.9
Other	31.2	23.1
Total	100.0	100.0
N	756	673

Source: Newspaper coverage project; see appendix.

influential.[48] It is impossible to discern the extent to which the media have conditioned voters to their leader focus or responded to a growing concern about leadership in the electorate. Certainly, images of party and leader have become intertwined in both media coverage and public perception.[49]

Tone of the Coverage

The importance of party and leader image in the vote decision of many Canadians means that the tone of campaign coverage could influence many votes. The extent to which the coverage of the leaders and their parties tends to be positive or negative could be of major importance to the outcome. The 1984 figures are the only ones in the past four elections that show sufficient differences in both direction and magnitude to suggest the possibility of a significant impact on public preferences. The 1984 National Election Study found the media presentation of the leaders reproduced among its respondents, with a generally positive attitude toward Mulroney and a generally negative attitude toward Turner.[50]

As is evident in tables 8.6 and 8.7, the general pattern of coverage of parties and leaders has been negative over the past three elections (with the exception of Broadbent and the NDP, usually attributed to the fact that the third party is unlikely to form the government). In 1984, however, the treatment of Turner and the Liberals was negative to an unprecedented extent, while Mulroney and the Conservatives were portrayed in a generally positive manner.

Table 8.6 Percentage of Items on TV News[a] Coded Positive or Negative for Major Parties and Leaders in 1979, 1980, and 1984.

	1979			1980			1984		
	Pos.	Neg.	Net	Pos.	Neg.	Net	Pos.	Neg.	Net
Parties[b]									
Liberal	6	15	−9	4	14	−9	3	20	−17
Conservative	6	11	−5	6	13	−7	8	5	+3
NDP	5	3	+2	2	3	−1	4	1	+3
N		1,232			806			705	

	Pos.	Neg.	Net	N	Pos.	Neg.	Net	N	Pos.	Neg.	Net	N
Leaders[c]												
Trudeau/Turner	24	63	−39	179	30	61	−31	107	11	80	−69	74
Clark/Mulroney	16	74	−58	140	35	56	−21	78	49	43	+6	76
Broadbent	39	27	+12	49	30	56	−26	27	74	7	+67	27

[a] 1979 and 1980 samples: CBC (English), CBC (French), CTV and Global; 1984 sample: the above plus TVA, a Quebec French-language network.
[b] Percentages based on total sample.
[c] Percentages based on references to each leader.
Sources: Calculated from tables 3.8 and 3.9 in Soderlund, *Media and Elections in Canada*; and tables 4 and 5 in Romanow, "Television News."

This unusual differentiation may well have had an impact. The pattern was evident for television and newspapers in tables 8.6 and 8.7. Similar patterns were observed for radio.[51] It is noteworthy that the editorial writers took a rather negative attitude toward all of the parties and leaders. As has been the case in most recent elections, editorial endorsements were lukewarm at best.

The patterns noted here have been confirmed in other studies. One study using unreported criteria found that more than half of the stories dealing with Turner on CBC's "The National" contained assessments, and that 90 percent of these were unfavorable. The authors found that Mulroney items were roughly in balance. In the *Toronto Globe and Mail*, they found a negative balance for both leaders, with Mulroney assessments 57 percent unfavorable and 43 percent favorable and Turner at 84 percent negative and 16 percent positive.[52] The numbers differ but the results of my research and that of the Windsor group are similar. Frizzell and Westell in their study of seven dailies concluded that readers of all but the carefully neutral *Halifax Chronicle-Herald* "would probably have finished the campaign with significantly more unfavorable impressions of Turner than of Mulroney" and an even more negative picture of the Liberal party.[53]

In an interesting analysis of the words and phrases used to describe the

Table 8.7 Percentage of Items on Daily Newspaper Front Pages and Editorial Pages Coded Positive or Negative for Major Parties and Leaders, 1980–84.

| | Front Page | | | | | | Editorial Page[a] | | | | | |
| | 1980 | | | 1984 | | | 1980 | | | 1984 | | |
	Pos.	Neg.	Net	Pos.	Neg.	Net	Pos.	Neg.	Net	Pos.	Neg.	Net
Parties												
Liberal	4	13	−9	7	29	−22	7	52	−45	6	50	−44
Conser-												
vative	4	12	−8	25	9	+16	22	30	−8	16	23	−7
NDP	3	3	0	8	8	0	13	31	−28	13	20	−7
N		673			988			1,207			988	
Leaders												
Trudeau/												
Turner	11	24	−13	10	28	−18	11	24	−13	8	51	−43
Clark/												
Mulroney	10	21	−11	15	20	+5	10	20	−10	17	33	−15
Broadbent	14	6	+8	8	2	+6	14	6	+9	18	19	−1
N		778			660			673			988	

[a] Includes all items printed on editorial page.
Source: Newspaper coverage project.

leaders, Wagenberg and his colleagues illustrate very clearly the tone of the coverage.[54] In quantitative terms Turner was the subject of many more negative than positive "descriptors." He had a negative balance of 67 percent on television, 44 percent on radio, and 70 percent in the press. In contrast, Mulroney had a positive balance of 5 percent on the crucial medium, television, though his net figures for radio (29 percent) and the press (17 percent) were negative. Broadbent had a positive balance in all three media. The most common descriptive words and phrases are revealing. For Turner, they revolved around competence (mistake-prone, fumbling), personal style (insecure, nervous), and ties to the past. The most common positive reference referred to his honesty. Mulroney's positive image was one of competence and confidence, a winner. The bulk of the negative references were related to his credibility: untrustworthy, tricky, dishonest, misleads voters. Broadbent was seen as popular but unrealistic.

Unlike the previous two campaigns, where the parties set the negative tone, the unfavorable assessments of Turner's leadership did not derive primarily from the attacks of his opponents. Although Mulroney did remind voters regularly of Turner's record, especially on patronage (and Turner did make a last-minute attack on Mulroney's personal credibility), neither Mulroney's speeches nor the Conservative spots were major factors in setting the tone of the campaign. Rather, the negative assessments of Turner appear to have derived from his obvious discomfort on television, his sometimes shaky performances in the two network debates, and the issues around which the election revolved. As one study points out, at least eight of the ten issues most frequently mentioned in the television coverage made Turner and the Liberals look bad.[55] The attention patterns were similar in the other media and the Liberal campaign was frequently on the defensive. A large group of patronage appointments that Turner made as part of an agreement with the retiring prime minister were the subject of almost universal public and editorial condemnation. The bottom-patting issues—Turner's "friendly gestures of support directed to the posteriors of female candidates"[56]—remained big news in the English media for nearly half of the campaign, largely because Turner failed to apologize and put the matter behind him. The incident, which might well have been glossed over by the less adversarial press Turner was used to, may have destroyed his opportunity to take advantage of a distrust for Mulroney expressed by many women. In addition, the disintegration of his campaign organization and his decision to bring in Senator Keith Davey, a longtime Trudeau campaign organizer, to put things back together produced much news and comment that challenged his claim to be a significant change from the Liberal past. He did indeed look like "yesterday's man," and his capacity to appeal to an electorate that wanted change was undermined.

The Issues

Previous studies demonstrate that the Liberals have generally been able to control the issue agenda in recent elections. Even in 1979, when the Liberals lost, the campaign revolved around Liberal issues, but many voters had already decided to vote for change.[57] In 1972, when Trudeau let the Conservatives set the agenda, the Liberals barely clung to office and, in 1984, when the election was fought on Conservative issues, the Liberals absorbed a major defeat. It is arguable, therefore, that Mulroney's ability to fight the election on his own turf was at least as important as his edge over Turner in leader image in bringing about the 1984 Conservative landslide.[58]

As I have argued elsewhere, the fluctuations in emphasis on major issues shown in table 8.8 reflect quite precisely the issues stressed by the major parties in each of the four elections.[59] It appears that a shared agenda emerges as a result of the interaction of the party campaigns, based largely on private polling and media news decisions. The media rarely challenge the party agendas but they do appear to have a major influence on which issues "catch on" with the public; issues that are ignored by the media have little chance of gaining public attention and are soon dropped by the parties. Table 8.4 indicates that the parties and the media are generally successful in setting

Table 8.8 Most Important Issues, 1979–84.[a]

Issue	1979 Newspaper	TV	Survey	1980 Newspaper	TV	Survey	1984 Newspaper	TV	Survey
Economy	62	43	48	25	28	48	28	19	86
inflation	8	14	13	6	—[b]	4	2	—	20
unemploy- ment	15	11	10	6	—	4	7	19	43
Confedera- tion	44	42	28	12	9	13	9	8	7
Resources	21	9	9	24	18	32	2	—	4
Social	13	—	5	7	—	2	18	9	13
Other	80	—	27	43	—	32	—	—	33
foreign rel.	3	—	2	22	38	3	8	—	3
leaders	32	32	14	12	36	15	11	26	9
N	1,756	1,232	2,668	984	806	1,786	575	705	2,858

[a] Based on frequency of mention on television news, daily newspaper front pages, and survey results. Note that these data have been compiled from several sources and are based on different coding systems. Comparisons must be made with care. Rank orders within columns can probably be compared with confidence. The newspaper data are based on analysis of the front pages of a national sample of dailies. Samples vary slightly from year to year.
[b] The dash indicates that the issue was not among the top ten and therefore was not reported in the original source.
Sources: Newspaper data: Clarke, *Absent Mandate*, table 4-3, for 1979. The 1980 and 1984 data are from the newspaper coverage project. Television data: calculated from tables 3.1 and 3.2 in Soderlund, *Media and Elections in Canada*; table 3 in Romanow, "Television News." Public opinion data: Kay, "Character of Electoral Change," table 10.

the public agenda.[60] Of course, some issues interest the media without exciting widespread public response, as with foreign relations in 1980. In other cases, such as unemployment, the public has often seemed more concerned than the media. In 1984 inflation had dropped off the media agenda but was still of concern to many voters. The most obvious differences between 1980 and 1984 were the decline in concern for resource and foreign relations issues and increased attention to social issues. Not shown in table 8.8 is a decline in attention to leadership as an issue (as opposed to leaders' performances) and the emergence of concern for ethics in government (patronage and related issues). This concern was featured in 21 percent of front-page stories and 30 percent of editorials in my study.

For the growing number of issue-oriented voters[61] the lack of attention to party policies in the media in 1984 must have been a disappointment. Several analyses found that only about one-quarter of the coverage of the campaign dealt with substantive policy issues. Even the *Toronto Globe and Mail* devoted only 29 percent of its campaign coverage to such issues, according to one study.[62] In their study of seven dailies Frizzell and Westell found that only 26 percent of campaign items dealt with policy, while 39 percent were about the campaign process: campaign activities and organization, candidate selection, and so on.[63] They note "a heavy concentration on the process of politics, perhaps to the exclusion of longer and better coverage of issues: the Liberal party organization became a major story that preoccupied many journalists and consumed great amounts of space."[64] In 1984 the attention to patronage and bottom-patting seemed to many observers the acme of diversion from real issues. They gained continued media attention not only because they fit easily within standard news values, but also because they came to symbolize a strongly felt need—among journalists and the voters—for a change in the style of government. The efforts of some public affairs programs and major newspapers to examine issues in terms other than their effects on the horse race and to provide opportunities for interest groups to force consideration of issues of concern to them are noted below.

In an interesting analysis of the relationship between the topic of news items and their assessment of parties, Wagenberg and his colleagues found that the Liberals were assessed far more negatively than the Conservatives in stories dealing with polls, the television debates, patronage, leader competence, and federal-provincial relations. The Conservatives were treated less favorably than the Liberals only on tax reform and interest rates. The authors conclude that coverage of substantive economic and social issues, those with longer-term implications, was relatively evenhanded but that "it was on the horserace issues that media coverage of the two major political parties worked to the great advantage of the Progressive Conservatives."[65] In 1984 these issues, along with patronage, which was mentioned in about 15 percent of all news items, got the most attention, especially in the English media.

It is interesting to note, however, that these horse-race issues were not mentioned by very many voters as important to their voting choice. Even the patronage issue was discounted by the great majority of voters, despite the attention given it by the media. Survey respondents appear to define issues very broadly and often supporters of all parties identify the same central issues. It appears that, as Frizzell and Westell put it, "it is not specific issues which determine votes, but perhaps a constellation of issues which set a mood, or a general disposition, towards a government or party."[66] In the 1984 campaign style seemed more important than substance and media preoccupation with style issues appears to have helped to create the Conservative landslide.

The 1984 campaign coverage continued the trend toward the decline in regional and language differences in the campaign coverage. The differences that emerged along these lines in 1984 were essentially regional variations on a national agenda, usually reflecting identifiable regional concerns. For example, Quebec media gave more attention than the national average to language and federalism issues, while the media in Atlantic Canada showed higher than average concern with unemployment. Only the most Quebec-oriented of the private networks deviated in any significant way from the national agenda in 1984.[67] Thus, Canadian voters received an essentially similar portrait of the campaign, regardless of residence or medium used. The homogenization of coverage reflects the agenda-setting influence of the national media, especially the television networks and the Canadian Press news service, the focus on the leaders' tours, and some elements of pack journalism. In addition, there was the tendency for the focus of the campaign to be on the swing seats in southern Ontario. On the CBC's national news in 1984, for example, nearly two-thirds of all election reports originated in Ontario. For newspapers, the key sources were Ottawa, Toronto, and Montreal, with Vancouver getting more attention than usual because a party leader (Turner) was running there.

There is something of a paradox in this trend. While the parties were doing more regional targeting of their appeals the media still had a national campaign focus. In addition it is an anomaly, in a federal system with strong regional differences and a parliamentary system in which representation is territorial, that national campaigns have come to dominate the electoral process, with local and regional issues relegated to the background.

Two developments in coverage of the 1984 campaign deserve special mention because they contributed significantly to the quality of public debate. The most notable of these was the National Action Committee (NAC) debate on women's issues. This was the only one of the three debates in which the party leaders were questioned in such a way as to expand the campaign agenda. The increase in coverage of social issues in 1984 shown in table 8.8 is entirely attributable to increased coverage of women's issues. The leaders agreed to face a panel committed to a specific set of interests, a first, because they all had something to gain. The NDP always benefits from such exposure, the Liberals were desperate, and the Conservatives were concerned about a "gender gap" in public response to Mulroney.

The second development was the advent of the CBC's nightly public affairs program, "The Journal."[68] The 1984 campaign was its first and it made a significant contribution to expanding the range of actors and issues. Among other features, the program ran a series of debates called "the front benches" in which members of Parliament from each of the three parties—usually the minister and opposition critics for the topic—were confronted by spokespersons for relevant interest groups. These discussions, which were about sixteen minutes in length, covered social policy, foreign policy, women's issues, tax policy, energy, arts and culture, unemployment, the economy, and the proposal for a nuclear freeze. Most of them were accompanied by a background report on the subject. Interest group spokespersons, independent experts, and M.P.s were given air time, and a relatively large audience (1.5 to 2 million) was exposed to issues beyond the campaign agenda of the leaders' tours.

The Debates

The two televised leaders' debates organized by the major networks may well have been turning points in the 1984 campaign. In addition, the women's issues debate was regarded as an important innovation. The debates drew very large audiences but were also important because they dominated the news for the next few days and remained key talking points for the remainder of the campaign. There were two network debates, one in each official language, and the privately organized women's issues debate, covered by the networks as a news event. More than two-thirds of adult Canadians watched at least one of the three 1984 debates.[69]

The 1979 debate, although in English only, established the principles for such programs: (1) the leaders must relate directly to one another; (2) the content must be of real substance, not just campaign rhetoric; (3) the pace must be fast enough to hold audience attention for two hours; and (4) production quality must be high. The networks proposed that a nonpartisan moderator (the principal of McGill University) and a panel of journalists (the chief political correspondent from each network) be used to keep things focused and moving. The parties agreed to a round-robin format, with opening and closing statements by each of the three leaders. Each thirty-minute segment pitted two of the three leaders against one another, discussing questions raised by the journalists. The networks retained control of the programs and covered them like sporting events, complete with reaction shots, shifting camera angles and, after the two hours, instant analysis. The 1984 debates were also carried on all major networks and followed the same format.

Aside from heightening interest in the election the 1979 encounters had little impact. Neither the vote nor the campaign agenda was greatly affected.[70] The 1984 debates—especially the network debates, which were held early in the campaign—had a much more dramatic effect. Polls taken immediately after the French debate showed a swing of 10 to 12 percent from the Liberals to the Conservatives in Quebec. Similar findings for Ontario appeared after the English debate.[71] The 1984 National Election Study found in its postelection survey that Mulroney had clearly defeated Turner but that Broadbent had done nearly as well. Of those who watched any of the debates, 78 percent thought Mulroney had outperformed Turner and there were indications that this judgment was related to switching from a 1980 Liberal vote to a 1984 Conservative one.[72] While these judgments may have been based on the substance of the debate, the media assessments were based primarily on style, as they had been in 1979. Indeed, CBC's flagship public affairs program, "The Journal," had two pollsters and a communications consultant in for its instant analysis, which focused almost entirely on style and horse race considerations.[73] The major focus was on Turner's "Big Mistake," raising the patronage issue as a challenge to Mulroney, even though it was Turner's seventeen appointments that had created the issue. Mulroney forced Turner onto the defensive and clearly scored. As one commentator put it, "The entire exchange lasted only a couple of minutes, but they were two of the most electrifying minutes in the history of televised political debates."[74] As in 1979 the debates did not expand the campaign agenda significantly. After the French debate Mulroney's advisers bragged that they had anticipated every one of the fifteen questions asked by the journalists.[75]

While the polls support the notion that the debates had an immediate effect on party standings, it is also clear that the feeling that Mulroney had won (or Turner lost) was strongly reinforced by the subsequent media assessments. After the French debate the leading Montreal dailies all declared Mulroney the winner in large headlines. This judgment was reported and seconded in the English press, although early reports declared the exchange a draw. Mulroney won the English debate on July 25 on almost all the media scorecards, though the judgment was based almost entirely on the patronage exchange. Turner was judged by many to have won the women's issues debate, but few voters remained undecided by that stage of the campaign.

The debates appear to have crystallized feelings that were forming regarding the two leaders. Turner's prime ministerial image had already begun to crumble but expectations were still higher for him. Moreover, he suffered from comparisons with Trudeau, and Mulroney's more colloquial French and better feel for Quebec sensitivities made a notable difference in the first debate. The English debate appears to have accelerated an already existing trend away from the Liberals, part of the inevitable postconvention decline. The French debate may, however, have been a major factor in loosening the Liberal hold on Quebec. During July the Liberals lost 24 percent and the Conservatives gained 21 percent in Quebec, an astounding swing.[76]

The conditions under which leaders are likely to agree to debate are such that a high level of media attention—and potential for influence on the vote—are guaranteed. It is axiomatic that debates take place only when all leaders perceive that they have something to gain by participating (or something substantial to lose by refusing). The tight contest in 1979 and the volatility of voter preferences in 1984 were factors. The 1984 campaign appeared to be close until after the initial debates and party polls showed that both parties had many weakly committed supporters. Turner's advisers believed that the risk of refusal to participate was greater than the risk of a narrow loss, their worst-case scenario. This might not have been their assessment had Turner given himself more time to establish a prime ministerial image before calling the election. By the time of the NAC debate the Liberals had little to lose and the Conservatives were concerned about a gender gap that had emerged in party support. The third party, of course, stands to gain in any debate. The timing of the 1984 debates—early in the campaign when Turner strategists felt (wrongly) that they would do the least damage—probably accounts in part for their apparently greater influence on the vote than in 1979. The 1979 debate took place after most voters had made up their minds.

Concluding Comments

Although the Liberals may have had only a slight chance to win the 1984 election in any case, given the longer-term trends in party preference, the fact that they lost the national media campaign by almost every measure no doubt ensured their defeat. As noted above, they lost the contest to control the agenda, they lost the battle of leader image, and the party organization was portrayed, accurately, as in disarray. As Frizzell and Westell put it, "the party shot itself, with some help from journalists who were extraordinarily interested in its problems." [77] The Liberals' inept performance might have had less impact in another era, with a less aggressive form of campaign coverage. It is plausible to argue that the media-sponsored polls and the hyena journalism they triggered helped to turn a defeat into a rout. Many observers were outraged by the opinionated quality of the coverage and by what the then publisher of the *Toronto Sun* called the "cheap shot" journalism directed at John Turner.[78] Bob Hepburn, Ottawa bureau chief for the *Toronto Star*, commented that reporters were tougher on Turner: "With Turner, we always went after him as a group. We smelled blood, and we attacked." [79] Mulroney was attacked only after the voters had made up their minds.

Many of the coverage decisions appear to have been made for symbolic reasons. The much-discussed bottom-patting incident is an interesting case. Print journalists suggest that it would have had little impact had it not been captured on film. It is reported that CTV had it for several days but hesitated to use it. It is not clear whether or not the decision to air it came in reaction to pressure from reporters [80] or to the fact that Turner did it again. What is clear is that it came to symbolize Turner's style problems, as perceived by reporters. As Peter Desbarats put it: "Like the photograph of Stanfield's fumble in 1974, this image reverberated across the country because it corresponded to an image of Turner already held by many Canadians." [81] It was this perception as well as Turner's failure to apologize that kept the story alive in the English media. Similarly, the photo published by the *Toronto Globe and Mail* late in the campaign, of Turner with two forks apparently growing from his head like horns was symbolic of the Liberal leader's status as the "goat" of the campaign. While it was unlikely to have had much of an effect on the vote, the decision to run it engendered considerable outrage. Coverage of the English debate also had a symbolic and distorting aspect. Virtually all of the coverage focused on the two-minute exchange between Mulroney and Turner on patronage, despite the fact that a wide range of much more important issues had been discussed.[82] The exchange symbolized for many reporters the arrogance of the Liberal party and Turner's failure to live up to the expectations the media had created for him as "leader-in-exile."

The increased emphasis on style and process in the coverage can be explained in part by the new openness of the party back rooms and in part by the nature of the campaign. It was believed by many reporters that the election would be decided on the basis of which leader could convince the voters that he would bring about a change in the style of governing: less arrogance, less confrontation, less patronage. The major parties were not far apart on many issues, according to this view, and the contrast of styles was therefore the story of the campaign.

From the voters' point of view, campaign coverage such as that observed in 1984 limits the grounds for choice. It encourages voters to assess leaders by using "show-business criteria," as Comber and Mayne put it.[83] Voters are left to consider style, sincerity (something Mulroney practiced projecting with his media advisers), and the image of competence. Capacity to sell oneself on television could become the primary criterion for selecting party leaders. This is an overly cynical view, however. The voting studies show that voters also consider the general policy direction of the parties and more specific regional issues. Nevertheless, a style of campaign reporting that repeatedly denigrates the parties and their leaders has obvious consequences for their capacity to govern once in office.

Despite the unsatisfactory nature of the campaign as a public debate on the future of the country, there were a number of noteworthy innovations. Among these were (1) the first parallel set of debates in both of Canada's official languages (a requirement that future party leaders will find it hard to duck); (2) the first national leaders' debate sponsored by an advocacy group; and (3) the wide-ranging issue discussions on "The Journal." These all increased the information available to voters, as did the polls. The polls permitted strategic voting but would have been of greater educational benefit had more effort been made to get beyond party preferences. Although the debates encourage the leader focus and may encourage oversimplification of complex issues, they can add much to voter information. The women's issues debate was most useful in this regard, though it raises questions about the propriety of debates organized around particular interests.

In the 1984 campaign the media were clearly participants. The polls, the debates, and the personal journalism were all media creations. The campaign and its coverage clearly had an important influence on the outcome. The inappropriateness of the Liberal campaign for a modern, media-oriented contest was in stark contrast to the slickness of the Conservative organization. The outcome, in terms of public debate and voting patterns, was clearly a result of the interaction of the campaigns with emerging journalistic practices. Both party and media require reexamination as we try to come to grips with operating a parliamentary democracy in the boob tube age.

Appendix

The past four Canadian federal elections provide a sound basis for detailed study of the party-media relationships, in large part because of the data available. For each there is a major national election survey and numerous more specialized surveys and comprehensive content analyses of news coverage of national newscasts on television and radio, and of the major daily newspapers. For content data, I have drawn on the work of the Windsor group (Walter C. Soderlund, Walter I. Romanow, E. Donald Briggs, Ronald H. Wagenberg), as reported in their recent book, *Mass Media and Elections in Canada*, and a number of papers, some work done as part of the National Election Studies, reported in Clarke et al., *Absent Mandate*, and my own work. In addition, I have used transcripts of interviews conducted by William Gilsdorf of Concordia University and myself with key journalists and party strategists for the 1979 and 1980 campaigns. Some additional work has been done for the 1984 campaign.

Data without specific citations are drawn from my own data sets. The 1980 and 1984 daily newspaper content analyses are part of a larger study of those election campaigns. Funded by the Social Science and Humanities Research Council of Canada and York University, the coding was done at York under my supervision. The variables reported here all had reliability coefficients of at least .80. Most were higher.

The following newspapers were in both samples:

West: *Victoria Daily Colonist* (*Times-Colonist* in 1984), *Vancouver Sun*, *Calgary Herald*, *Edmonton Journal*, *Regina Leader-Post*, *Winnipeg Free Press*

Ontario: *Toronto Globe and Mail*, *Toronto Star*, *Ottawa Citizen*, *Windsor Star*

Quebec: *La Presse* (Montreal), *Le Devoir* (Montreal), *Le Soleil* (Quebec City), *Montreal Gazette*

East: *Saint John Telegraph Journal*, *Halifax Chronicle-Herald*, *Charlottetown Guardian*, *St. John's Evening-Telegram*

1980 only: *La Tribune* (Sherbrooke)

1984 only: *Le Droit* (Ottawa), *Toronto Sun*, *Kingston Whig-Standard*

Notes

1. This paper is based on a review of the literature as well as data gathered for my project, Newspaper Coverage of the 1980 and 1984 Federal Election Campaigns, described in the

appendix. I am grateful for the financial assistance of the Social Science and Humanities Research Council of Canada and York University's Faculty of Arts Research Fund. I am also indebted to my research assistants, especially Lorraine Luski, Bruce Smardon, Victoria Greco, William Lim, Monica Neitzert, Barry Waite, and Cathy Livingston, as well as the students who did much of the coding for 1984. This paper is designed to provide as much continuity as possible with my studies of the three previous campaigns and to facilitate comparison with other studies. Some of the ideas have been explored in another context in F. J. Fletcher, "Mass Media and Parliamentary Elections in Canada," *Legislative Studies Quarterly*, 12, no. 3 (August 1987), pp. 341–72.

2. John Meisel, "The Boob-tube Election: Three Aspects of the 1984 Landslide," in John C. Courtney, ed., *The Canadian House of Commons: Essays in Honour of Norman Ward* (Calgary: University of Calgary Press, 1985), pp. 173–94.

3. The Canadian Centre for Investigative Journalism, for example, held a seminar on the coverage of the campaign in October 1984, and a number of publications have appeared on the subject. See, for example, the discussion in Alan Frizzell and Anthony Westell, *The Canadian General Election of 1984: Politicians, Parties, Press and Polls* (Ottawa: Carleton University Press, 1985), ch. 3.

4. Barry J. Kay, Steven D. Brown, James E. Curtis, Ronald D. Lambert, and John M. Wilson, "The Character of Electoral Change: A Preliminary Report from the 1984 National Election Study," paper presented at the annual meeting of the Canadian Political Science Association, Montreal, 1985, p. 4.

5. Ibid., pp. 19–20, 54, and 58–59, n.15.

6. For a discussion of the leadership selection process, see George Perlin, ed., *Party Democracy in Canada: The Role of National Party Conventions* (Scarborough, Ont.: Prentice-Hall, 1987). For a discussion of the role of the media, see my chapter, "The Mass Media in the Convention Process," ibid.

7. Frizzell and Westell, *The Canadian Election*, pp. 38–39.

8. F. Leslie Seidle, "The Election Expenses Act: The House of Commons and the Parties," in Courtney, *The Canadian House of Commons*, pp. 126–29.

9. *Statutory Report of the Chief Electoral Officer of Canada* (Ottawa: Supply and Services Canada, 1984), p. 24.

10. Royal Commission on Newspapers, *Report* (Ottawa: Supply and Services Canada, 1981), pp. 163–67.

11. Ron Graham, *One-Eyed Kings: Promise and Illusion in Canadian Politics* (Toronto: Collins, 1986), pp. 285–86. See also Frizzell and Westell, *The Canadian Election*, p. 103.

12. As Senator Keith Davey, the longtime Liberal strategist put it in his recently published memoirs: "Arguably, the 1979 campaign was about 'Anybody but Pierre Elliott Trudeau. We'll even take Joe Clark!' The 1980 campaign was all about: 'Anybody but Joe Clark. We'll even take Pierre Trudeau!' " *The Rainmaker: A Passion for Politics* (Toronto: Stoddard, 1986), p. 365.

13. L. Ian MacDonald, *Mulroney: The Making of a Prime Minister* (Toronto: McClelland and Stewart, 1984), p. 278.

14. Frizzell and Westell, *The Canadian Election*, p. 37.

15. MacDonald, *Mulroney*, pp. 310–11.

16. Senator Davey insists that a sophisticated campaign was ready to go but was not used. *The Rainmaker*, p. 330.

17. R. H. Wagenberg, W. C. Soderlund, W. I. Romanow, and E. D. Briggs, "Media Coverage of the 1984 Canadian Election," paper presented at the annual meeting of the Canadian Political Science Association, Winnipeg, June 1986, p. 8.

18. Frizzell and Westell, *The Canadian Election*, pp. 17 and 27.

19. Ibid., pp. 44–53.
20. Frizzell and Westell, *The Canadian Election*, p. 57.
21. These figures were provided by the CBC.
22. The results of a study by the Windsor group, using a sample of eighteen daily newspapers, were very similar to my own (in percent): front page: Liberal 44, Conservative 36, NDP 30 (*N* = 921); editorial page: Liberal 50, Conservative 33, NDP 17 (*N* = 432); features: Liberal 44, Conservative 37, NDP 18 (*N* = 601). Calculated from Wagenberg, "Media Coverage," p. 14.
23. The figures, calculated from CBC logs, were: Liberal, 25 percent; Conservatives and NDP, 21 percent each; other and nonparty items, 33 percent. Total time devoted to the campaign was 582 minutes.
24. Charles Lynch, *Race for the Rose: Election 1984* (Toronto: Methuen, 1984), p. 165.
25. Mary Anne Comber and Robert S. Mayne, *The Newsmongers: How the Media Distort the Political News* (Toronto: McClelland and Stewart, 1986), p. 92.
26. Peter Desbarats, " 'New Journalism' in Flower," The *Financial Post*, September 29, 1984, p. 9.
27. For differing views on these points, see ibid., and Comber and Mayne, *The Newsmongers*, pp. 31 and 103ff.
28. Comber and Mayne, *The Newsmongers*, pp. 118–19.
29. Ibid., p. 128.
30. Ibid., pp. 58–61.
31. Wagenberg, "Media Coverage," p. 6.
32. Davey, *The Rainmaker*, p. 324.
33. Ibid., p. 347.
34. MacDonald, *Mulroney*, p. 285.
35. Wagenberg, "Media Coverage," p. 14, table 2. Using a more stringent measure, my coders found that 12 percent of front-page election reports dealt with poll results in 1984, an increase of 3 percent over 1980.
36. Frizzell and Westell, *The Canadian Election*, p. 82.
37. Davey, *The Rainmaker*, p. 353.
38. Lynch, *Race for the Rose*, p. 148.
39. Ibid., pp. 155–56.
40. Ibid., p. 158.
41. MacDonald, *Mulroney*, p. 281.
42. Frizzell and Westell, *The Canadian Election*, p. 86.
43. Ibid., pp. 105–6. The authors note a swing to the NDP from the Conservatives in the final week of the campaign and suggest that strategic voting may have been a factor.
44. For a discussion of the Vancouver Quadra case, see Gary A. Mauser, "Political Campaigning: The View from Marketing, " paper presented at the annual meeting of the American Political Science Association, New Orleans, August 1985, pp. 14–15.
45. The television and radio data are from Wagenberg, "Media Coverage," table 1, p. 13. The newspaper data are from my Newspaper Coverage of the 1980 and 1984 Federal Election Campaigns, described in the appendix. Wagenberg and his colleagues, using a narrower definition of leader focus, found that 15 percent of newspaper front-page stories dealt with that topic. Ibid.
46. Frizzell and Westell, *The Canadian Election*, found in their analysis of seven major dailies that the percentage of stories focusing on party leaders ranged from 19 in the *Winnipeg Free Press* to 38 in the *Toronto Star*. Calculated from table 6, p. 60.
47. In 1984, in my sample of daily newspapers, party leaders were mentioned in 70 percent of election stories on inside pages, whereas local candidates were mentioned in 38 percent

and other politicians in 35 percent. For editorial pages the figures were: party leaders, 62 percent; local candidates, 5 percent; other politicians, 7 percent.

48. The voting data are from Clarke, *Absent Mandate*, pp. 142–45 and 170–72; and Kay, "Character of Electoral Change," pp. 29–30 and 55.

49. Frizzell and Westell, *The Canadian Election*, p. 97.

50. Kay, "Character of Electoral Change," p. 32.

51. Wagenberg and his colleagues found that the Liberals had an excess of unfavorable to favorable coverage of 10 percent on radio, 15 percent on television and 28 percent in the press. The Conservative balance was slightly favorable on television (3 percent), even on radio, and slightly unfavorable in the dailies (6 percent). The NDP had a slightly favorable balance in all media. Wagenberg, "Media Coverage," table 7, p. 19.

52. Comber and Mayne, *The Newsmongers*, pp. 131–32.

53. Frizzell and Westell, *The Canadian Election*, p. 70.

54. The data in this paragraph are drawn from Wagenberg, "Media Coverage," table 8, p. 20, and appendixes A, B, and C.

55. Walter I. Romanow, Walter C. Soderlund, E. Donald Briggs, and Ronald H. Wagenberg, "The 1984 Canadian Federal Election: A Study of Television News Coverage," paper presented at the annual meeting of the Canadian Communication Association, Montreal, 1985, pp. 14–15.

56. Romanow, "Television News," pp. 15–16.

57. See F. J. Fletcher, "Playing the Game: The Mass Media and the 1979 Campaign," in Howard R. Penniman, ed., *Canada at the Polls, 1979 and 1980* (Washington, D.C.: American Enterprise Institute, 1981), pp. 313–16.

58. Nearly half of all Canadian voters in recent elections have cited issues as the primary basis for their voting choices. See Harold D. Clarke, Jane Jenson, Lawrence LeDuc, and Jon H. Pammett, *Absent Mandate: The Politics of Discontent in Canada* (Toronto: Gage, 1984), 89ff.; and Kay, "Character of Electoral Change," p. 29.

59. Fletcher, "Mass Media and Parliamentary Elections."

60. The National Election Studies found that "few voters had private issue agendas. Rather, most responded to the public issue agendas as these were formulated by the major actors in the various election campaigns, i.e., the parties and politicians, and the mass media." See Clarke, *Absent Mandate*, p. 137.

61. Clarke, *Absent Mandate*, p. 93.

62. Comber and Mayne, *The Newsmongers*, p. 103.

63. Frizzell and Westell, *The Canadian Election*, pp. 62–64.

64. Ibid., p. 71.

65. "The Mass Media," pp. 5–6 and table 6, p. 18.

66. Frizzell and Westell, *The Canadian Election*, p. 97.

67. The Spearman rank order correlations of the frequency of mention of broad issue categories for television network newscasts ranged from .61 to .79 and in general were higher than in 1979 and 1980, with the exception of a Quebec-based network added to the sample in 1984. Walter C. Soderlund, Walter I. Romanow, E. Donald Briggs, and Ronald H. Wagenberg, *Media and Elections in Canada* (Toronto: Holt, Rinehart and Winston of Canada, 1984), pp. 60–63; and Romanow, "Television," p. 14.

68. The data on "The Journal" were provided by the CBC.

69. Kay, "Character of Electoral Change," p. 23. CBC figures show that about 5.4 million watched at least part of the English debate, with about 2 million for the French debate and nearly 5 million for the bilingual debate on women's issues.

70. See Lawrence R. LeDuc and Richard Price, "Great Debates: The Televised Leadership Debates of 1979," *Canadian Journal of Political Science*, 18, no. 1 (March 1985), pp. 135–

53. The substance of the debate is summarized in ibid., p. 139. Summaries of the 1984 debate may be found in many sources, including Meisel, "Boob-tube Election," pp. 172–76 and Snider, *Changing of the Guard*, pp. 121–27 and 165–68.

71. These polls are cited in MacDonald, *Mulroney*, pp. 287–94. According to party strategists, party polls showed similar results.

72. Kay, "Character of Electoral Change," p. 23.

73. For examples of such assessments, see Fletcher, "Playing the Game," p. 311; Snider, *Changing of the Guard*, pp. 121–27; MacDonald, *Mulroney*, pp. 287–94.

74. MacDonald, *Mulroney*, p. 289.

75. Ibid., p. 290.

76. Frizzell and Westell, *The Canadian Election*, pp. 104–6.

77. Ibid., p. 171.

78. Lynch, *Race for the Rose*, p. 176. Given the sensational and opinionated nature of *Toronto Sun* coverage, this statement is noteworthy. Comber and Mayne state that their book, *The Newsmongers*, was triggered by their outrage at the coverage of the 1984 campaign.

79. Quoted in Frizzell and Westell, *The Canadian Election*, pp. 55–56.

80. See Comber and Mayne, *The Newsmongers*, pp. 45–49.

81. Desbarats, "New Journalism."

82. Meisel, "Boob-tube," pp. 174–76; see also Comber and Mayne, *The Newsmongers*, pp. 72–73 and 116–17.

83. Comber and Mayne, *The Newsmongers*, p. 40.

9 Reinventing the Brokerage Wheel: The Tory Success in 1984

JOHN C. COURTNEY

Introduction

————— Canadians have long been accustomed to federal elections unmarked by any significant shift in popular support among the various parties during the eight-week campaign. In that respect, as in others, the 1984 election proved to be a notable exception. From early July, when the Liberals under their new leader, John Turner, called the election, to voting day on September 4, an electoral metamorphosis took place in Canada. The nine-point Gallup poll lead initially held by the Liberals over the Progressive Conservatives vanished within weeks of the election being called. By mid-campaign the principal parties' respective positions had reversed, and on election day the largest vote spread in Canadian history between the winning and second-place parties broke overwhelmingly in the Tories' favor (see table 9.1). The growing arrogance of the Liberals in power, as reported by an increasingly critical media and judged by an uncertain and volatile electorate, together with a skilled and sophisticated electoral organization assembled by the Conservatives in opposition, combined to produce the most one-sided election results since the Diefenbaker sweep of 1958.

For the most part the mood of the country was markedly different in September 1984 from what it had been in February 1980 when the Liberals under Pierre Trudeau defeated the nine-month-old Conservative government of Joe Clark. Only in western Canada, where the 1984 electoral support for the three major parties was much as it had been in 1980, did the regional seat distribution by party remain largely unchanged. There was nothing new in the west's behavior. For several elections that region had given only grudging and, at that, gradually decreasing support to the Liberals, preferring instead (except for solidly Blue Alberta) to split its votes and seats more or less evenly between the Conservatives and the NDP. If anything, there was a subtle irony

Table 9.1 Gallup Poll and General Election Results,
March 29–September 4, 1984, by percentage.

	Liberal	Progressive Conservative	New Democratic party	Other	Undecided or refused
Gallup Poll					
March 29–31	46	40	13	2	(26)
May 3–5	46	40	11	3	(23)
May 24–26	46	42	11	1	(32)
June 21–23	49	38	11	1	(28)
July 5–8	48	39	11	2	(38)
August 9–11	32	46	18	4	(11)
August 30	28	50	19	3	(10)
Election					
September 4	28	50	19	3	

Source: Canadian Institute of Public Opinion, Gallup Polls, March to September, 1984; and Chief Electoral Officer, *Report, 1984* (table 5).

in the fact that in 1984 the west provided no more than the frosting for the Conservative cake. After years of having shunned successive Liberal governments at elections and, accordingly, of having paid the price (as westerners liked to remind themselves) of being without an adequate "voice" in Ottawa's decisionmaking, the west learned from television commentators on election night that Brian Mulroney could have formed a majority Conservative government without any of the Tory seats west of the Ontario-Manitoba border (see tables 9.2 and 9.3).

It was central and eastern Canada that gave the Tories their victory. The number of seats won by the Conservatives virtually doubled in Atlantic Canada (from thirteen in 1980 to twenty-five in 1984) and increased by twenty-nine in Ontario (from thirty-eight to sixty-seven). For its part, Quebec defied its history in at least one respect, while remaining true to it in another. The overwhelming support given to the Conservatives (one-half of Quebec's votes and over three-quarters of its seats) had been matched by the Conservatives only once in the previous 100 years—in 1958 with the brief success of the Diefenbaker-Duplessis alliance. In the most recent election (1980) the Liberals had won all but one of the province's seventy-five seats. But Pierre Trudeau's retirement from federal politics was to alter his party's fortunes dramatically in his home province in 1984. The Liberals found it virtually impossible to defend their Quebec bastion. Their leader had stepped down and, for the first time in their history, the Conservatives were led by a man regarded by both French and English Québecers as "one of their own." By mid-campaign

Table 9.2 1980 Election Results (percentage of popular vote and number of seats).

	PC		Liberal		NDP		Others	
	Popular vote	Seats	Popular vote	Seats	Popular vote	Seats	Popular vote	Seats
Newfoundland	36	2	47	5	17	—	—	—
Prince Edward Island	46	2	47	2	7	—	—	—
Nova Scotia	39	6	40	5	21	—	—	—
New Brunswick	33	3	50	7	16	—	1	—
Quebec	13	1	68	74	9	—	10	—
Ontario	35	38	42	52	22	5	1	—
Manitoba	38	5	28	2	33	7	1	—
Saskatchewan	39	7	24	—	36	7	1	—
Alberta	65	21	22	—	10	—	3	—
British Columbia	42	16	22	—	35	12	1	—
Yukon/Northwest Territories	31	2	37	—	31	1	1	—
Total	33	103	44	147	20	32	3	—

Source: Chief Electoral Officer, *Report, 1980* (tables 5 and 6).

a previously unthinkable reversal of public opinion had taken place: more Quebec residents identified the Tories than the Liberals as the party most closely representing the interests of their province.[1] In Quebec in 1984 blood ran thicker than political colors.

The Political Climate

The political climate of the summer of 1984 was four years in the making. In the period following the election of the majority Trudeau government in 1980 several events contributed to the gradual erosion of Liberal support and the successful coalition-building of the Conservatives. Of those, three in particular deserve brief attention: the constitution, federal-provincial relations, and changes in party leadership.

The Constitution Act of 1982   Pierre Trudeau will in all likelihood best be remembered in future history textbooks as the prime minister who "brought home" Canada's constitution. Patriation of the British North America Act had been a contentious issue in Canadian politics for nearly six decades. Few held out hope for any satisfactory solution to the issue without widespread, probably unanimous, federal-provincial approval and, possibly, major transfers of powers between the two levels of government. The federal initiative

Table 9.3 1984 Election Results (percentage of popular vote and number of seats).

	PC		Liberal		NDP		Others	
	Popular vote	Seats	Popular vote	Seats	Popular vote	Seats	Popular vote	Seats
Newfoundland	58	4	36	3	6	—	—	—
Prince Edward Island	52	3	41	1	7	—	—	—
Nova Scotia	51	9	34	2	15	—	—	—
New Brunswick	54	9	32	1	14	—	—	—
Quebec	50	58	35	17	9	—	6	—
Ontario	48	67	30	14	21	13	2	1
Manitoba	43	9	22	1	27	4	8	—
Saskatchewan	42	9	18	—	38	5	2	—
Alberta	69	21	13	—	14	—	4	—
British Columbia	47	19	17	1	35	8	2	—
Yukon/Northwest Territories	47	3	25	—	28	—	—	—
Total	50	211	28	40	19	30	3	1

Source: Chief Electoral Officer, *Report, 1984* (tables 6 and 7).

announced by the prime minister in October 1980 to patriate the Canadian constitution contemplated none of these features. The action would be unilateral on Ottawa's part; there would be no significant intergovernmental transfers of powers; and the centerpiece of the "new" constitution would be a Canadian Charter of Rights and Freedoms long advocated by Trudeau. The proposal prompted a bitter and tortuous debate between the Liberal government and the Conservative opposition, and between Ottawa and eight of the ten provinces. (New Brunswick and Ontario supported the federal proposal.) Following court challenges and renewed negotiations with the provinces, the eventual upshot was approval late in 1981 by all governments, save Quebec's, of a patriation package modified in some respects from the original federal proposal.[2]

The legacy of the dispute itself and the dynamics of the new constitutional arrangements were both apparent during the 1984 campaign. The failure in 1981 to find a constitutional compromise acceptable to Quebec left that province politically vulnerable and isolated during the run-up to the 1984 election. Trudeau, prime minister until less than a month before the election was called, showed no inclination to attempt to find some constitutional accommodation with his political archrival, Parti Québécois leader Premier Réne Lévesque. By contrast, Mulroney's frequently repeated pledge in 1983–84 to explore the possibility of reaching a constitutional accord with Quebec struck a responsive note with politicians, intellectuals, and voters in that province. In a move calculated to fill the void left by Trudeau's constitutional intransigence and the prime minister's departure from federal politics, Mulroney presented himself as a staunch federalist capable of adjusting to the distinctive realities of Quebec's place in a renewed federalism. This was all part of the Tories' coalition-building strategy in their traditionally weakest province—to capitalize on the political fallout from the constitutional dispute in the short run and to fuse a new federal majority party from Quebec in the long run. One perceptive assessment of the Progressive Conservatives' electoral victory and the strategies that produced it noted that among Mulroney's closest advisers,

> there is unanimity on this point: the future success of the Conservative Party depends more on Quebec than anything else.
> The 1984 election saw a strange alliance of Quebec interests lining up behind the Conservatives: moderate Pequistes, former Union Nationalistes, old Creditistes and disgruntled Liberals joined the handful of traditional Tory supporters in giving Mr. Mulroney just over 50 per cent of the vote in the province.
> To hold onto this unusual grouping, the Conservatives will need to apply a mixture of policy and patronage.
> Quebec nationalists seemed impressed by Mr. Mulroney's approach to policy. He struck a chord in the French-language TV debate where he argued for provincial powers—asserting the right of the Caisse de depot et placement, the administrator of the provincial pension funds, to buy a major share of an inter-provincial transportation company.
> His appointment of Bernard Roy, his chief Quebec organizer and best friend, as his principal secretary and his expected use of another friend, Lucien Bouchard (good friend also of Pierre-Marc Johnson, Quebec's Minister of Justice and heir-apparent to Premier Réne Lévesque) are attempts to make sure Tory policy always reflects this constituency.[3]

At the time of the 1980–81 constitutional dispute national organizations representing natives, visible minorities, women, and the handicapped became active participants in the debate over the terms of the Canadian Charter of Rights and Freedoms. Trudeau encouraged such participation by noting frequently that power needed to be transferred from the politicians, where in his view it had rested too long, to "the people." There was a widespread expectation at the time that individuals and courts would gain powers at the expense of federal and provincial governments. But the effect of the concerted lobbying in 1980–81 by specialized groups interested in having guarantees included in the new charter that would be relevant to their own concerns was not so much to support the Trudeau notion that individuals would participate in policymaking as it was to give legitimacy and authority to the groups themselves for their future political activities.

In no case was this truer than with the National Action Committee on the Status of Women (NACSW). Organized women's groups had emerged triumphantly from the constitutional debate, having succeeded in getting a sexual equality section included in the charter. By 1984 the position of the NACSW in the political system was sufficiently strong to enable it to organize a nationally televised debate among the three party leaders on "women's issues." This example suggests that Canadian politics may well have been altered with the growth of strong special interest groups, each capable of making particular electoral demands on the political system. How this will be resolved in the future is uncertain. Doubtless the 1984 experience will make it no easier to withstand appeals from society's increasingly specialized and vocal groups. It could, as well, bring about important changes in the political system, although that remains to be seen. As John Meisel has noted, if issues

> pressed by women's interest groups are to be treated thus, then why not capital punishment, urged by chiefs of police, or the claims of pro-lifers, or groups championing a more relaxed approach to abortions? And what of labour, business, environmentalists, free traders and the arts lobbies? The combination of televised debates and single-issue politics could seriously undermine the capacity of politicians to fashion accommodation and consensus over time. The long-established pattern of responding to various needs over the whole period of a party's period in office could give way to agenda-setting by powerful single-interest groups commanding access to the electronic media. This could substantially alter the prevailing conventions and practices of parliamentary government.[4]

Federal-Provincial Relations As part of Trudeau's drive to reassert federal supremacy in intergovernmental relations, Ottawa adopted a deliberately bullish attitude in 1980–84 in its dealings with the provinces. Unilateral action on the constitution by Ottawa was more than an idle threat, as was recognized by the provincial premiers when the federal constitutional game plan was leaked immediately before a critical first ministers' conference in September 1980. Its participants knew that the conference was destined to end in failure because Ottawa was determined to move on its own.[5] The same federal approach characterized the National Energy Program (NEP). First introduced in the Liberal budget in the fall of 1980, the NEP unilaterally set prices for crude oil and natural gas following the earlier breakdown of oil pricing and revenue sharing negotiations with the province of Alberta. The ensuing controversy was arguably the most acrimonious of the historically long list of disputes between Alberta and Ottawa.[6] Similarly, the Trudeau government's move to strengthen national social policies (particularly medicare) while at the same time shifting the financial burden to provincial governments met with widespread objections from the provinces.[7]

Table 9.4 National Trends in Party Support, February 1980–
September 1984, by percentage.

	Liberal	Progressive Conservative	New Democratic party	Other
February 1980 (election)	44	33	20	3
April 1980	46	30	21	3
September 1980	50	32	14	3
November 1980	45	35	18	2
February 1981	42	37	19	2
June 1981	37	39	22	2
September 1981	33	41	23	3
February 1982	33	38	27	3
April 1982	31	42	25	2
June 1982	26	44	26	3
November 1982	33	48	18	1
February 1983	32	47	19	1
June 1983	32	54	14	1
September 1983	30	53	16	1
March 1984	38	50	11	1
April 1984	41	46	11	1
June 1984	49	39	11	1
August 1984	32	49	18	1
September 1984 (election)	28	50	19	1

Source: Toronto Globe and Mail, CROP Polls (*Toronto Globe and Mail*, April 29, 1985, p. 8).

The effects of such conflicts proved to be politically devastating for the Liberals. The growing public resentment of the prime minister's confrontational attitude and his government's haughty dismissal of provincial complaints made it increasingly doubtful as the months passed that a successful recovery could be made in time for the expected 1984 election. Polls such as those conducted periodically by the *Toronto Globe and Mail* confirmed what was widely recognized as the key political change to have taken place from 1981 to 1984—the Conservatives consistently enjoyed commanding leads over the Liberals, and the NDP vote gradually slipped in the Tories' direction (see table 9.4). Such poll results, coupled with the fact that the Liberals did not hold office in one province at the time of the 1984 election and therefore lacked valuable organizational links (the Progressive Conservatives formed the government in seven provinces, and the NDP, Parti Québécois, and Social Credit in one each), suggested that the Liberals almost certainly would fail to retain power in 1984. Only a change in leaders seemed to hold out much hope of reversing the trend.

Party Leadership   In at least one respect Brian Mulroney's successful challenge to Joe Clark's leadership of the Progressive Conservatives in June 1983
and John Turner's election as Liberal leader one year later were in keeping with
earlier selections at national leadership conventions. In the past the candidate
with little or no experience in federal politics, or without a seat in the Commons, generally beat opponents with established parliamentary and cabinet
careers. Selecting Canadian party leaders in conventions has had the curious
effect of opening up the competition to outsiders in a manner that in other
parliamentary jurisdictions would be judged to be incompatible with their system of government. Since the adoption in 1919 of leadership conventions,
Canadian party leaders and prime ministers have included former provincial
premiers, public servants, lawyers, and businessmen who, as in Mulroney's
case, had not run for or served in any elected office before entering the contest
for the party leadership or who, as was true of Turner, had long since resigned
a seat in Parliament. The relative newcomer to politics—the fresh face of the
outsider—has been too much for a majority of leadership convention delegates
to resist.[8]

Like Clark, Mulroney's political style was conciliatory. It needed to be,
for he inherited a bitterly divided party following the June 1983 Progressive Conservative leadership convention.[9] That Mulroney carefully selected a
majority of his shadow cabinet (twenty of its thirty-five positions) from among
the Clark parliamentary supporters was the first public suggestion following
his election to the party leadership that the new leader intended to set about
healing longstanding intraparty wounds as best he could. Mulroney carefully
eschewed staking out policy positions on such controversial matters as medicare that would be different from the Liberals' if, in so doing, they would be
likely to embroil him in a politically damaging battle. His extraparliamentary
network of friends and cronies (described in legendary terms by a basically
adulatory press during Mulroney's first year as leader) was reconstructed into
an impressive political and electoral organization.[10] In consequence, the sizable Tory lead in the public opinion polls bequeathed to Mulroney by Clark
continued to grow through 1983 and early 1984. Most important for the Tories,
it was soon matched by similarly favorable support for Mulroney himself. For
the first time since 1976, Pierre Trudeau was no longer the first choice of
Canadians for prime minister.[11]

For his part, Turner inherited a party atrophied by its years in office.
It was quickly obvious, once Parliament had been dissolved and the election
called, that the state of the Liberal party's electoral preparedness was no match
for the Tories. Money was more difficult to raise and prominent candidates
were harder to recruit (especially in the west) than had previously been the case
with the Liberals. The Turner cabinet was understandably seen as a recycled
Trudeau cabinet. With the retirement of Trudeau and Marc Lalonde, and with

the defeat of Jean Chrétien in his bid for the party's leadership, the Quebec wing of the party became particularly dispirited. During the election campaign Turner often appeared stiff and uneasy on television, much given to awkward gestures and a nervous laugh. His occasional rustiness on matters of policy and substance after nine years away from frontline politics was forcefully drawn to the public's attention by an attentive media, who had seemed less willing to apply the same tests to Mulroney a year before. Finally, the patronage orgy of the departing Trudeau administration, which was used repeatedly by Mulroney to his party's advantage throughout the campaign, proved to be more than Turner could defend with honor and credibility. In all, his brief leadership of the party had had insufficient time to make its mark on the country when the election was called. During the campaign Turner seemed uncertain and inexperienced—qualities one would not in the past have ascribed to Liberal leaders.[12]

Reinventing the Brokerage Wheel

Building electoral coalitions of diverse social, economic, and regional groups has been the hallmark of Canadian political parties since confederation. The political brokers most adept at coalition-building have gained and retained office; the others have not. Marked by compromissary leadership, an aversion to ideology, and an absence of consistency in policies and programs, broker- age parties in Canada have crowded around the center of the political spectrum seeking support from essentially the same voters. For Canadians the conse- quences of brokerage politics, as noted in a work on the 1974, 1979, and 1980 elections, have been basically threefold: policy articulation by parties during election campaigns is virtually nonexistent; levels of partisan instability are high; and constant emphasis is placed on party leadership by the press, the public, and the parties.[13] There was nothing in the 1984 election to suggest that any of these features had changed.

Policy Articulation   In the heat of electoral battles the parties have avoided proposing specific policies whenever possible, and Canadian voters in the past have found that they could rarely base their decisions on a clear choice of policies between the two principal parties. This was equally the case in 1984 when, once again, voters had to rely on the parties' general substitutes for pre- cise proposals—"strengthening national unity," "making the west again a part of confederation," "creating jobs," "reducing the government deficit," "cut- ting taxes," and "restoring confidence in the economy" became the universal buzz words of the campaign. Little wonder that 68 percent of the respondents to the August CBC poll admitted that in their view there were either no differences or only minor differences in policy between Turner's Liberals and Mulroney's Conservatives.[14]

The implications of such a situation can be profound. Relying on generalities may help the parties survive an election campaign, but at the same time the practice tends to defer much of the discourse over public policy to other political institutions. The 1984 election confirmed a long-established pattern of Canadian brokerage politics. As before, the campaign produced no "mechanisms for [policy] innovation internal to the process of party competition."[15] In consequence, it is reasonable to anticipate that with the Mulroney government, as with its predecessors, policy innovation will continue to be dominated by the prime minister's office and the cabinet (both highly secretive executive institutions), the bureaucracy ("an arena that [is] constitutionally isolated and protected from electoral politics"), and federal-provincial relations ("where party labels [are] relatively unimportant").[16]

Partisan Instability The 1984 election confirmed dramatically the extent to which partisan instability has become one of the marked features of Canadian voting behavior. Beginning with John Meisel's pioneering work on Canadian elections in the 1960s, various national studies have confirmed that "levels of partisan instability were greater in Canada than in many other advanced industrial societies. Voters did not see fundamental differences among the parties, differences which might have encouraged them to develop long-term loyalties. Nor were they likely to see consistent variations in the parties' policy goals that might have led them to identify their own interests with a single party for a lifetime."[17] But judged even by past standards, the degree of partisan instability evident in the 1984 election was extraordinary.

The polls had revealed as much in the months leading up to the election. There was ample measure of the degree of uncertainty in the record 38 percent of the electorate who were undecided as to their voting intentions at the time that the election was called in early July (see table 9.1). The Conservatives, who had seen their three-year-long lead in the polls disappear with the change in Liberal leadership in June 1984, regained their previous position within weeks of the Liberal convention as Tory and NDP support grew rapidly at Liberal expense (see tables 9.1 and 9.4). The extent of the defections from the Liberal party within the first month of the campaign was apparent in the results of the CBC August poll. Fully 43 percent of the decided voters who normally supported the Liberals intended to vote for other parties, preferring the Conservatives to the NDP by a margin of roughly three to one.[18] The leading empirical study of the 1984 election has since determined that the Tories emerged as the principal beneficiary (in some cases by a factor of nine or ten to one over the NDP) of the slippage in Liberal support in every sociodemographic group. As table 9.5 makes clear, the greatest Tory gains at Liberal

Table 9.5 Where the 1980 Liberal Vote Went in 1984, by Sociodemographic Groups.

	Lib. → Lib.	Lib. → PC	Lib. → NDP	Lib. → Other	(N=)
	48%	43%	7%	2%	(917)
Region					
Atlantic	61	31	8	0	(60)
Quebec	40	55	4	1	(370)
Ontario	56	33	8	3	(353)
Prairies	51	44	4	1	(75)
B.C.	40	41	19	1	(58)
Community size					
500,000+	44	47	7	2	(448)
30–500,000	52	39	9	1	(154)
1–30,000	53	39	8	0	(142)
Rural	52	41	5	2	(172)
Sex					
Men	48	44	7	1	(427)
Women	48	42	7	2	(491)
Education					
Postsecondary	40	48	9	3	(354)
Secondary	50	43	6	1	(424)
Primary	64	32	4	0	(138)
Income					
High	45	45	6	4	(278)
Medium	48	43	9	1	(310)
Low	56	38	5	1	(183)
Subjective class					
Upper middle	41	49	11	0	(90)
Middle	48	46	4	3	(518)
Working	49	39	12	0	(273)
Religion					
Catholic	48	46	5	2	(593)
Protestant	51	38	11	0	(242)
Other	37	48	4	11	(27)
None	43	37	16	2	(49)
Language spoken					
English	49	39	9	2	(479)
French	44	50	5	1	(372)
Other	60	31	6	3	(67)
Age					
18–24	45	43	13	0	(47)
25–34	40	44	12	3	(208)

Table 9.5 Continued

	Lib. → Lib.	Lib. → PC	Lib. → NDP	Lib. → Other	(N=)
35–44	44	47	8	1	(185)
45–54	48	47	4	2	(172)
55–64	53	43	2	2	(164)
65+	65	29	6	0	(126)

Note: Percentages are rounded.
Source: Barry J. Kay, Steven D. Brown, James E. Curtis, Ronald D. Lambert, and John M. Wilson, "The Character of Electoral Change: A Preliminary Report from the 1984 National Election Study," paper presented to the annual meeting of the Canadian Political Science Association, Montreal, June 2, 1985, p. 12. (Table reproduced with permission of the authors.)

expense came from groups traditionally amongst the most solid Liberal supporters: Quebec, Catholic, French-speaking, urban, high income, and better educated voters.[19]

At the aggregate level the magnitude of the shift in electoral support was naturally accentuated by the workings of the single-member constituency plurality vote system. Nowhere was this more apparent than in the numbers of seats that changed hands and first-time M.P.s who were elected. Forty-two percent of the 282 constituencies elected a member from a different party than the one favored in 1980. This amounted to the highest turnover of seats by a party since 1935. Fully 50 percent of the M.P.s chosen in 1984 (143 of 282) and 60 percent of the Conservative caucus (125 of 211) were not members of the previous Parliament—a high figure even by normally high Canadian standards (see table 9.6). These are staggering figures when compared to the generally low turnover and replacement rates of members in Great Britain and the United States.[20]

Leader as Party   The Canadian electorate, freed as it has been of strong partisan and ideological commitments, has turned to party leadership as the principal source of its partisan cues. It is true, of course, that the emphasis on party leaders has been accentuated by the role played by the mass media, particularly television, in contemporary politics. But that alone would not explain the widespread preoccupation with leadership during an election campaign. Parties, too, have selfish reasons for exploiting the leadership phenomenon. In terms that are consistently and predictably either positive or negative (never neutral), and that depend upon the immediate goals and partisan interests to be served, Canadian parties have shaped political agendas and public attitudes for the past several elections by making their own and their opponents' leadership the central focus of their campaigns. By extension, parties in Canada have become their leaders "writ large," having taken on, as it were, "the personality of their leaders."[21]

Table 9.6 M.P.s Elected in 1984 Who Were Not
Members of the Previous Parliament.

	PC	Lib.	NDP	Indep.	Total
Ontario	33	4	7	1	45
Quebec	56	4	0	0	60
Nova Scotia	4	0	0	0	4
New Brunswick	6	1	0	0	7
Manitoba	4	0	0	0	4
British Columbia	6	1	0	0	7
Prince Edward Island	1	0	0	0	1
Saskatchewan	5	0	0	0	5
Alberta	7	0	0	0	7
Newfoundland	2	0	0	0	2
Yukon Territory	0	0	0	0	0
Northwest Territories	1	0	0	0	1
Total	125	10	7	1	143

Source: Chief Electoral Office, *Contact*, no. 54 (December 1984), p. 7.

Modern Canadian leadership conventions have emerged as one of the principal nationally televised media events capable of shaping a party's character and support base. Aware of the fact that conventions generally boost their standing in the polls and enhance their organizational capacity, both the Liberals and Conservatives have attempted to time and orchestrate their conventions to the parties' maximum electoral advantage. In 1984 the considerable volatility of the electorate during the months preceding the election was almost certainly in response to the Tory convention of June 1983 (in which Mulroney defeated Joe Clark), Pierre Trudeau's resignation, and the Liberal convention of June 1984 (in which Turner replaced Trudeau). That the Liberals chose to call the election when they did was in large measure due to their favorable standing in the polls in the heady postconvention days. But their support proved to be "soft" (in the politico's vernacular) and the lead quickly disappeared.[22]

The Liberals' electoral miscalculation stemmed from a variety of reasons. But chief among these must be the extent to which Turner (and by extension the Liberal party) was vulnerable on the issue of change when compared to Mulroney and the Tories. Mulroney claimed to represent the forces of change. The familiar though nihilistic slogan, "time for a change," fell on the ears of receptive voters who had tired of a virtually unbroken twenty-one-year spell of Liberal governments. By mid-campaign the Tories' carefully coordinated leader's speeches, campaign literature, and media advertising had had their intended impact. The CBC August poll discovered that in a comparison of the

Table 9.7 Qualities Associated with the Two Party Leaders, by percentage.

	Brian Mulroney	John Turner
Best represents your region	42%	26%
Can appeal to Canada's various regions	41	24
Is most likable	38	22
Best displays overall ability and competence	38	25
Will give you the most confidence in government	37	25
Best prepared to make difficult decisions to overcome problems the country faces	35	29
Would make the most significant changes to government	32	16
Has the best grasp of the issues	32	23
Can earn greatest respect among world leaders	32	35
Can best represent interests of women	28	20
Is most trustworthy	27	19
Is most sincere	26	19

Source: CBC Poll, table 25.

qualities associated with the leaders of the two major parties, Mulroney was ahead in all but one—capacity to earn respect among world leaders (see table 9.7). Even among Liberal loyalists interviewed in the national election study, but especially among normally Liberal supporters defecting to the Conservatives in 1984, Mulroney was chosen by a wide margin over Turner as the candidate best representing change.[23] What all this meant was that Turner, whose withdrawal from active politics nine years earlier had had the desired effect at the time of distancing him from the Trudeau administration, had nonetheless quickly become identified in the voters' eyes with the status quo ante once he had assumed his party's leadership and called the election. Without a recent record of his own to defend, Turner was placed in the politically embarrassing position of having to account for someone else's—in this case a government with distressingly few remaining pockets of strong electoral support.

The New Government

The 1984 election produced the first truly national government caucus since the Trudeau Liberal victory of 1968. In fact, the Mulroney forces accomplished something in 1984 that had eluded even the Diefenbaker Conservatives at the time of their sweep in 1958. They won a majority of the seats in every province and territory—a feat without precedent in Canadian history. On a regional basis their success echoed a feature of earlier elections in which there had been a transfer of power. At each of the eight elections bringing about a change of government from 1874 to 1957, the popular vote in all four regions of Canada had moved in the same direction—away from the old governing party and to the new one.[24] That tendency ended with the 1962-63 elections, from which time can be dated the breakdown of the national party system and the virtual disappearance of a national governing party. Minority governments became the norm (in five of the eight pre-1984 elections no party won a majority of the seats) and regionally unbalanced caucuses reflected the extent to which interregional voting patterns had diverged. The Mulroney victory of 1984 reintroduced the earlier Canadian model of a governing parliamentary party—the broadly based, cross-regional coalition similar to those constructed by Macdonald, Laurier, and Mackenzie King. It remains too early to judge whether this latest version will endure as long as those former ones. Trudeau had had a similar opportunity in 1968, but his government's subsequent policy initiatives systematically eroded Liberal support in western Canada and cost it the opportunity to forge an alliance of the classic Canadian variety.

In addition to the sizable number of first-time M.P.s elected in 1984 (60 percent), the demographic composition of the new Commons reflected a change that had taken place in candidate recruitment during the years of the last Trudeau government. From 1980 to 1984, the political parties, especially the Conservatives, had recruited larger numbers of candidates than had previously been the case from traditionally less politically active occupations. Engineers, management consultants, investment counselors, small businessmen, and others with entrepreneurial and business backgrounds won party nominations, often in keen contests with more politically experienced opponents who, in some cases at least, were sitting members. On balance, the members of this newly elected group had more formal education and less previous political experience than had been true of other recent Canadian parliaments. They were attracted to the Conservative party in large part because of their evident concern with the economic consequences of the Trudeau administration's interventionist economic policies. At the same time they showed less interest in constitutional questions than the government they defeated. Perhaps it was fitting, then, that their election came principally at the expense of the lawyers—an occupational group whose numbers in the Canadian House of Commons slipped below 20 percent for the first time with the 1984 election (see table 9.8).

All of these changes in the regional and occupational backgrounds of members elected in 1984, together with the fact that a record number of women were elected both to Parliament (9.6 percent) and to the governing caucus (9 percent), were reflected in Mulroney's cabinet when it was sworn into office on September 17. Even though in the past the lawyers' share of party nominations and elections to Parliament had dwindled steadily, members of that profession had nonetheless remained the largest single group in cabi-

Table 9.8 Canadian House of Commons after 1980 and 1984 Elections, Professional, Educational, and Political Backgrounds.

	1980 Election		1984 Election		Percentage change
	N	Percentage	N	Percentage	
Professional backgrounds					
Business	52	(18.4)	80	(28.4)	+10.0
Education	41	(14.5)	48	(17.0)	+2.5
Law	72	(25.5)	55	(19.5)	−6.0
Farming	22	(7.8)	19	(6.7)	−1.1
Other	80	(28.4)	73	(25.9)	−2.5
No information	15	(5.3)	7	(2.5)	−2.8
Educational backgrounds					
Secondary	70	(24.8)	38	(13.5)	−11.3
Postsecondary	91	(32.2)	109	(42.9)	+6.3
Postgraduate	121	(42.9)	121	(42.9)	—
No information	—		14	(5.0)	+5.0
Previous political experience					
Municipal	77	(27.3)	57	(20.2)	−7.1
Provincial	19	(6.7)	18	(6.4)	−0.3

Source: Chief Electoral Officer, *Contact*, no. 55 (March 1985), p. 8.

nets.[25] During the Trudeau period, for example, lawyers typically held one-half of the cabinet posts. That dominance ended with the Mulroney cabinet, in which other occupational groups, drawn principally from private business, outnumbered lawyers by three to one. A record number of women were named to the cabinet: six of the forty ministries, including two of the most critical ones (employment and immigration, and energy, mines, and resources) were assigned to women.

But undoubtedly the most significant feature of the Mulroney cabinet derived from its regional composition. It returned to the older, much-lamented pan-Canadian model which, because of regional representational deficiencies, had eluded Pearson in the 1960s, Trudeau for most of his fifteen years as prime minister, and Clark at the time of his short-lived administration. With the Mulroney cabinet western Canada no longer had cause for complaint about inadequate executive representation. Thirteen ministers, of whom seven were named to the strategic fifteen-member Priorities and Planning Committee of the cabinet, were Tories from western Canada. A sign of the change in government was to be found in the fact that Vancouver had more cabinet ministers than Montreal. In the words of one of the newly appointed cabinet ministers: "We have reconstructed the old Mackenzie King coalition of Quebec and the

West. Mr. Mulroney will not easily give up or squander either side of that combination." [26]

The political agenda of the Mulroney government would naturally prove to be an extension of the interests and expertise of the members of this new governing coalition. Policies less likely to provoke hostile provincial reactions (at least so long as the Tories remained in office in so many provincial capitals) would almost certainly be pursued. These would include, significantly, renewed negotiations in the resources sector, especially with respect to oil and gas pricing agreements and offshore royalties. On the economic front, moves to sell off some Crown corporations, to encourage the spirit of entrepreneurship in the business community, and to attempt to contain the federal deficit could be expected. The oft-repeated election pledge of Mulroney to improve relations with the United States would mean, among other things, changes to the National Energy Program, the end of the Foreign Investment Review Agency as Canadians had known it for most of the Trudeau era, increased defense spending, and a stronger commitment to NATO. In all, the general philosophic direction of the new Canadian government sounded like a northern echo of the Reagan presidency—all the more surprising given the Tories' history of moderate to occasionally strident anti-Americanism. But then, as the Quebec results in particular emphasized about the election, the Conservative coalition brought to power in 1984 was unlike any other in Canadian history.

Notes

1. CBC poll, taken August 4–12, released August 20 ($N = 2,200$). Thirty-nine percent of Québecois felt the Conservatives most closely represented the interests of Quebec; 37 percent believed the Liberals did. The time lag accompanying the change in Quebec was evident in the rest of the country. The same poll showed that Canadians outside Quebec linked the self-interests of that province with the Liberal party. The poll results by region were as follows:

Party most closely representing the interests of Quebec

	Percentage							
	Total	Quebec	Maritimes	Ont.	Man.	Sask.	Alta.	B.C.
Liberal	55	37	55	61	60	60	73	61
Conservative	25	39	27	20	18	18	17	16
NDP	3	3	2	3	4	2	1	4
None	4	5	2	4	3	1	5	3
Don't Know	12	15	12	11	14	15	4	15

The author wishes to acknowledge with thanks the assistance of Duncan A. McKie, head, Audience Research, Canadian Broadcasting Corporation, Toronto, in making available the CBC poll results.

2. The patriation debate and the negotiations over and settlement of the constitutional issue are covered in Roy Romanow, John Whyte, and Howard Leeson, *Canada . . . Notwithstanding: The Making of the Constitution 1976–1982* (Toronto: Methuen, 1984). See also Keith Banting and Richard Simeon, eds., *And No One Cheered: Federalism, Democracy and the Constitution Act* (Toronto: Methuen, 1983); and *Canadian Annual Review of Politics and Public Affairs, 1980, 1981* and *1982* (Toronto: University of Toronto Press, 1982 and 1984).

3. Patrick Martin, "Mulroney Aims for a Dynasty: The Ten Steps," *Toronto Globe and Mail*, November 22, 1984, p. 7.

4. John Meisel, "The Boob-Tube Election: Three Aspects of the 1984 Landslide," in John C. Courtney, ed., *The Canadian House of Commons: Essays in Honour of Norman Ward* (Calgary: University of Calgary Press, 1985).

5. Romanow et al., *Canada . . . Notwithstanding*, p. 95.

6. *Canadian Annual Review, 1980*, pp. 116–30.

7. See David C. Hawkes and Bruce G. Pollard, "The Medicare Debate in Canada: The Politics of New Federalism," *Publius*, (Summer 1984), pp. 183–98.

8. This point is explored in John C. Courtney, "Leadership Conventions and the Development of the National Political Community in Canada," in W. Peter Ward and R. Ken Carty, eds., *National Politics and Community in Canada* (Vancouver: University of British Columbia Press, 1986).

9. For a study of the 1983 convention see Patrick Martin, Allan Gregg, and George Perlin, *Contenders: The Tory Quest for Power* (Scarborough, Ont.: Prentice-Hall, 1983).

10. On Mulroney's network and his rise to power, see L. Ian MacDonald, *Mulroney: The Making of the Prime Minister* (Toronto: McClelland and Stewart, 1984).

11. Of those Canadians willing to choose the party leader "making the best prime minister" in their opinion, Mulroney was preferred by 32 percent and 36 percent in the Gallup polls of September 1983 and March 1984, respectively (to Trudeau's 23 and 30 percent) and by 40 percent (to John Turner's 28 percent) in the August 1984 CBC poll. Only briefly following his selection in June 1984 did Turner take the lead: 39 percent and 33 percent for Turner in June and July 1984, respectively, compared to Mulroney's 22 and 29 percent.

12. For a recent account of Turner's career see Jack Cahill, *John Turner: The Long Run* (Toronto: McClelland and Stewart, 1984).

13. Harold D. Clarke, Jane Jenson, Lawrence LeDuc, and Jon H. Pammett, *Absent Mandate: The Politics of Discontent in Canada* (Toronto: Gage, 1984), especially ch. 1.

14. CBC Poll, table 27.

15. Clarke et al., *Absent Mandate*, p. 12.

16. Ibid.

17. Ibid., p. 13. See also Harold D. Clarke, Jane Jenson, Lawrence LeDuc, and Jon H. Pammett, *Political Choice in Canada* (Toronto: McGraw-Hill Ryerson, 1979), especially ch. 5; Jane Jenson, "Party Loyalty in Canada: The Question of Party Identification," *Canadian Journal of Political Science*, (December 1975), pp. 543–53; and John Meisel, *Working Papers on Canadian Politics*, enl. ed. (Montreal: McGill-Queen's University Press, 1973).

18. According to the CBC August poll, the voting intention by past voting behavior for decided voters was as follows:

Party normally voted for	Party intending to vote for		
	PC	*Liberal*	NDP
PC	86%	7%	7%
Liberal	33	56	10
NDP	14	7	79

(*Source:* CBC Poll, table 6). Note also that among those defecting from the NDP, the Conservatives were preferred to the Liberals by a two to one margin.

19. Barry J. Kay, Steven D. Brown, James E. Curtis, Ronald D. Lambert, and John M. Wilson, "The Character of Electoral Change: A Preliminary Report from the 1984 National Election Study," paper presented at the 1985 annual meeting of the Canadian Political Science Association, Montreal, June 2, 1985.

20. The ratio of newly elected members to total membership figures is generally one-half to one-third in Britain and the United States to what it is in Canada. See John C. Courtney, *The Selection of National Party Leaders in Canada* (Toronto: Macmillan, 1973), tables 6-21 and 6-22; Gerhard Loewenberg and Samuel C. Patterson, *Comparing Legislatures* (Toronto: Little, Brown, 1979), pp. 110–11; and Chief Electoral Officer, *Contact*, no. 54 (December 1984), p. 7.

21. Clarke et al., *Absent Mandate*, p. 14.

22. The 1984 national election study found that specific precampaign or campaign events, including the two party conventions, influenced voters to the following extent: (Note the larger negative than positive effect of the Liberal convention on voters, which presumably might be explained in part by the defection of Quebec Liberals to the Tories following the defeat of "native son" Jean Chrétien for the Liberal leadership.)

Direction of 1984 Vote For Those Influenced by Specific Events.

	All voters				
	PC convention	Trudeau retirement	Liberal convention	July debates	Women's debate
Liberal	10%	18%	41%	21%	18%
PC	85	70	51	62	46
NDP	2	11	8	14	34
Other	3	1	0	3	3
N	263	320	168	206	150

(*Source:* Kay et al., table 6.)

23. Mulroney "represented change" more than Turner by a percentage gap between the two leaders of 36 percent among Liberal loyalists and 86 percent among defectors to the Conservative party. (Tau-C = .27, significance level of <.001). See Kay et al., table 9.

24. On this feature of Canadian politics, see J. Murray Beck, "The Democratic Process at Work in Canadian General Elections," in John C. Courtney, ed., *Voting in Canada* (Toronto: Prentice-Hall, 1967), pp. 25–31.

25. In recent years the number of lawyers in the Canadian House of Commons has generally been greater by about one-half than in Great Britain (25 percent compared to 15 percent) and less by about one-half the figure for the U.S. Congress (25 percent compared to 49 percent). See Dermot Englefield, *Parliament and Information: The Westminster Scene* (London: Library Association Publishing, 1981), table 1.2; and Loewenberg and Patterson, *Comparing Legislatures*, pp. 70–71.

26. Harvie Andre, as quoted in "The West's Perilous Day," *Alberta Report*, September 17, 1984, p. 8.

Appendix

Canadian House of Commons Election Returns, 1884

Compiled by Richard M. Scammon.

Province	Total valid vote	Liberal	PC	NDP	Other[a]
ALBERTA	1,019,539	129,945	701,344	143,588	44,662
Percentage of vote		12.7	68.8	14.1	4.4
Number of seats	21	—	21	—	—
BRITISH COLUMBIA	1,433,048	235,394	668,432	502,331	26,891
Percentage of vote		16.4	46.6	35.1	1.9
Number of seats	28	1	19	8	—
MANITOBA	513,834	112,123	221,947	139,999	39,765
Percentage of vote		21.8	43.2	27.2	7.7
Number of seats	14	1	9	4	—
NEW BRUNSWICK	377,350	120,326	202,144	53,332	1,548
Percentage of vote		31.9	53.6	14.1	0.4
Number of seats	10	1	9	—	—
NEWFOUNDLAND	241,159	87,778	138,867	13,993	521
Percentage of vote		36.4	57.6	5.8	0.2
Number of seats	7	3	4	—	—
NOVA SCOTIA	460,592	154,954	233,713	70,190	1,735
Percentage of vote		33.6	50.7	15.2	0.4
Number of seats	11	2	9	—	—
ONTARIO	4,435,411	1,323,835	2,113,187	921,504	76,885
Percentage of vote		29.8	47.6	20.8	1.7
Number of seats	95	14	67	13	1
PRINCE EDWARD ISLAND	73,414	30,075	38,160	4,737	442
Percentage of vote		41.0	52.0	6.5	0.6
Number of seats	4	1	3	—	—
QUEBEC	3,440,360	1,219,124	1,728,196	301,928	191,112
Percentage of vote		35.4	50.2	8.8	5.6
Number of seats	75	17	58	—	—

Province	Total valid vote	Liberal	PC	NDP	Other[a]
SASKATCHEWAN	522,800	95,143	218,000	200,918	8,739
Percentage of vote		18.2	41.7	38.4	1.7
Number of seats	14	—	9	5	—
YUKON–NORTHWEST					
TERRITORIES	31,214	7,789	14,707	7,395	1,323
Percentage of vote		25.0	47.1	23.7	4.2
Number of seats	3	—	3	—	—
TOTAL	12,549,010	3,516,529	6,278,910	2,359,947	393,624
Percentage of vote		28.0	50.0	18.8	3.1
Number of seats	282	40	211	30	1
METROPOLITAN AREAS					
Metropolitan Montreal	1,076,392	421,135	454,082	124,856	76,319
Percentage of vote		39.1	42.2	11.6	7.1
Number of seats	24	13	11	—	—
Metropolitan Toronto	1,034,051	361,837	446,730	207,390	18,094
Percentage of vote		35.0	43.2	20.1	1.7
Number of seats	23	6	14	3	—

[a] Includes Rhinoceros party, 99,178; Nationalist Party of Quebec, 86,305; Confederation of Regions Western party, 65,655; No party listed, 39,425; Green party, 26,921; Libertarian party, 23,514; Independent party, 21,508; Social Credit party, 16,659; Communist party, 7,609; Party for Commonwealth, 6,849.

Source: Canada, Ministry of Supply and Services, Thirty-third General Election 1984: Report of the Chief Electoral Officer, Ottawa, 1984.

Index

Contributors

R. KENNETH CARTY is a member of the Department of Political Science in the University of British Columbia. His works include *Party and Parish Pump: Electoral Politics in Ireland* and articles and essays on Irish politics and Canadian parties and politics. He has recently edited *National Politics and Community in Canada*.

STEPHEN CLARKSON is professor in the Department of Political Economy at the University of Toronto. He is the author of *The Soviet Theory of Development: India and the Third World in Marxist-Leninist Scholarship* (1978), and he has contributed chapters to the earlier volumes on Canadian elections in this series.

JOHN C. COURTNEY is professor of political science at the University of Saskatchewan. His works include *The Selection of National Party Leaders in Canada* and articles on Canadian political parties, political leadership, electoral redistributions, and electoral systems. He is the editor of the recently published *The Canadian House of Commons: Essays in Honour of Norman Ward*.

FREDERICK J. FLETCHER is associate professor of political science at York University, North York, Ontario. He is the author of *The Newspaper and Public Affairs*, a research study for the Royal Commission on Newspapers, and numerous articles on the media and elections in Canada.

LAWRENCE LEDUC is professor of political science at the University of Toronto. He is coauthor of *Political Choice in Canada* and *Absent Mandate: The Politics of Discontent in Canada*, and he has written other articles and papers dealing with elections and voting in Canada.

JOHN MEISEL is the Sir Edward Peacock Professor of Political Science at Queen's University, Kingston. He has written widely on Canadian politics, particularly on parties, elections, ethnic politics, and cultural policy. He has contributed to both previous volumes of *Canada at the Polls*. From 1980 to 1983 he served as chairman of the Canadian Radio-Television and Telecommunications Commission.

TERENCE MORLEY is an associate professor of political science at the University of Victoria, Victoria, British Columbia. He is the author of *Secular Socialists: The CCF/NDP in Ontario, A Biography* (Montreal and Kingston: McGill-Queen's University Press, 1984) and a co-author of *The Reins of Power: Governing British Columbia* (Vancouver: Douglas and McIntyre, 1983).

KHAYYAM ZEV PALTIEL is professor of political science at Carleton University in Ottawa. He is the author of *Political Party Financing in Canada* and has contributed chapters to *Democracy at the Polls: A Comparative Study of Competitive National Elections* and the At the Polls studies of

Canadian elections. His writings include numerous studies of interest groups and of Israeli and Canadian politics.

GEORGE C. PERLIN is professor of political studies at Queen's University. He is the author of *The Tory Syndrome: Leadership Politics in the Progressive Conservative Party* (1980), coauthor of *Contenders: The ToryQuest for Power* (1983), and editor and coauthor of *Party Democracy in Canada: The Politics of National Party Conventions* (1987)

RICHARD M.SCAMMON, coauthor of *This U.S.A.* and *The Real Majority*, is director of the Elections Research Center in Washington, D.C. He has edited the biennial series America Votes since 1956, and he has supplied national election data for all volumes in the At the Polls series.

Library of Congress Cataloging-in-Publication Data

Canada at the polls, 1984 : a study of the federal general elections / Howard Penniman, editor.
p.   cm. — (At the polls)
Includes index.
ISBN 0-8223-0805-3.   ISBN 0-8223-0821-5 (pbk)
1. Canada.   Parliament—Elections, 1984.   2. Political parties—
Canada.   3. Canada—Politics and government—1980-   I. Penniman,
Howard Rae, 1916–   .   II. Series.
JL193.C344 1988
324.971´0645—dc 19   87-27252